A WALK THROUGH YESTERDAY

Our family.
Back row from left to right: William,
Jeanie, Alexander.
Front row from left to right: Da, Lillie
Ann, Mother with author at eight
months. 1897.

A WALK THROUGH YESTERDAY

Memoirs of Jessie L. Beattie

Dictated to Jean T. Thomson

McCLELLAND AND STEWART

ISBN: 0-7710-1163-6

The Canadian Publishers
McClelland and Stewart Limited
25 Hollinger Road, Toronto

All photographs are from
the author's own collection.

Printed and bound in Canada

Grateful thanks are due to the many
who volunteered to act as eyes for me in
the preparation and writing of this book.

To those who walked with me

I WOULD KNOW ALL

I would know all of life —
Cool slumber, and fierce fire;
The holy place of purified desire,
The road worn dusty by unsandalled feet
In freedom sweet;
I would know all as winds know all that pass
Above the tree-tops, and below the grass;
The quiet pool a while, if it must be —
And then, though shivering before the gale,
Please, God, the open sea!

Written by the author, April, 1920

BOOKS BY THIS AUTHOR

Blown Leaves
Shifting Sails
Hill-Top
Three Measures
John Christie Holland
White Wings Around the World
Along the Road
Black Moses
The Split in the Sky
Hasten the Day
Strength for the Bridge
A Season Past
The Log-Line
Winter Night and Other Poems
A Rope in the Hand
A Walk Through Yesterday

CONTENTS

PART ONE

THE QUIET POOL

We hear the silence while we wait the wave,
Knowing the need of courage to support us hence.

The author

I

The Old House

I remember, I remember
The house where I was born,
The little window where the sun
Came peeping in at morn.

Thomas Hood

Our house, like many pioneer homes in Ontario, was built of logs covered by clapboard. It stood with a hill behind it, itself on a rise, looking southward. Before it stretched grassy meadows and fertile tilled fields. Undulating pasture land lay to the east and the west.

The house took a beating from the weather. Severe storms blew up from the north and the boards that had once been painted brown turned grey under the whip of the wind, the battering of snow, and the pounding of rain. A veranda along two sides was its only protection. There were trees, but set too far from it to break the force of attack. Balm of Gileads, slim and graceful, a giant elm at the bottom of the yard, low flowering shrubs of pink bush and lilac along the south wall, a skimpy hedge of cedars between the house and the road.

Our property – one hundred acres – began at the foot of the hill behind the house and was cut in half by the road. On the east side, the land dipped away sharply, running at low level for two field lengths. On the west stood the house, the barns and sheds, and the orchard. Behind these lay the swamp and the only bush left after stumping was finished. Forward went straight treeless fields

11

attending the road on both sides for almost a quarter of a mile. They ended when it inclined down a rocky slope. In the marshy valley, even the road bed was spongy, and water-loving trees and tall grasses crowded close to the wheelways. A trout stream crossed under a rickety wooden bridge. But on the other side the land rollicked upward again and the road ran with it over a knobby ridge, disappearing from our view at the skyline.

The swamp was part moss-grown treeless loam and part slashing. In the latter, scrub cedar and bush willows, red elder and wild plum were hung with a tangle of vines – wild grape, brambleberry, ivy, climbing black-caps, cucumber, and the woody nightshade. The place was a haven for the birds. Guarding it was our neighbour's maple bush, quiet in summer, but about the middle of March noisy with the tapping of trees and the crackling of fire when the gathered sap was boiling. The sweet smell of sugaring-off was carried on the west wind. We caught it as we stood looking into the slashing for the first signs of spring. For there, in patches open to the sun, wild flowers appeared earliest and in abundance – bloodroot, hepatica, spring beauty, dog-toothed violet; then trilliums white and dark red, and the much-admired rare pitcher plant, all rising from a bed of leaf mould produced from years of undisturbed riches. And in late March, the swamp willows were warmed by a yellow tinge and the elder stems flushed with rosy light, proving without a doubt that spring was on its way.

Much time is spent out-of-doors by country people, but in the long cold months the need is for rooms, cheerful and warm. Despite its exposed location, the old house had these, for the walls were thick and the furnishings comfortable. There were glowing coal fires, and on the window-sills, facing south, geraniums bloomed. The windows were small-paned but well-situated. They caught the first rays of morning and the last of sunset. After nightfall in The Room, as we called our living-room, a lamp was placed where its light would direct the traveller. Until bedtime, the shades were never drawn.

Between The Room and the small parlour, tucked behind the staircase, was a tiny bedroom – a room I shared with my parents until I was five. Its one window was narrow but it looked into the boughs of the Balm of Gileads. They were beautiful trees, their bark washed to bronze lustre by rain, or traced in white by whirling snow, their slender twigs lifted expectantly in April to the blue sky or gently under the weight of glossy leaves in summer.

My mother often regretted that our house stood so close to the road. The lane began at the end of the yard and led toward the barns. The yard was unfenced, there was no gate, no barking dog to warn of the stranger's approach. Our collie preferred to spend his time in the fields with our men, but even when at home with us he welcomed all who came with a happy wag of his tail.

Those were the days which closely preceded the prevalence of the motor car; horse-drawn vehicles, cyclists, and riders on horseback still dominated traffic in the country. Travel for the farmer was usually a matter of necessity. Of course there were pleasure trips, important occasions indeed, but rare. The farm was our world, and what lay beyond the bend we vaguely realized as through a glass darkly, and not face to face.

Many who came along the road were unhurried, willing to pause for a while and to tell us what they knew of life in far-away places. Far away to us, though often within the boundaries of our own country. Beggar and philanthropist, the sinned against and the sinning, those seeking and those sought for, the simple and the shrewd, those in search of adventure and those desiring rest. Few passed us by. No one was refused food and drink and a night's sleep. As well, there were hired help who became temporary members of our family: good and bad, interesting and dull, timid and bold. A small girl came to pay us a visit and remained to womanhood; a motherless boy found a home.

All who came and went, whether transients or temporary residents, enriched our lives. Many a comedy was enacted, many a tragedy occurred; few days passed without some event of dramatic interest.

But there came a time when it was necessary for us to leave the familiar scenes and the home of our childhood and to enter that world beyond the bend. Fond memories went with us.

Now, during a period of enforced rest, we travel with the white clouds that scud across the blue of city skies, in search of a winding road that leads to a weather-beaten house on a windy hill.

Here I was born.

Alexander Fleming at 100 years. My
maternal grandfather.

II

My Inheritance

Strong be the root
From which the flower takes form . . .

The author

He was seventy-five when he told me. That was the year he came to live with us in the old house.

It was January – a winter night, clear and cold. My grandfather Fleming and I sat close to the coal heater while the fire glowed and sparkled behind the mica.

The silence was broken only by the strong ticking of a century-old floor clock with hand-painted face. The clock had come with Grandpa from the pioneer home in Puslinch Township. It was hand-made. One could detect the mark of the carpenter's tool behind the polish of its surface.

We were alone. All other members of our household had gone to a community rally at the village schoolhouse, in honour of a departing preacher. From early evening the jingle of sleigh bells had indicated the gathering of country people over snowy roads to unite in paying tribute to a friendly little man who had preached of hell-fire and damnation. Nevertheless, his treatment of all men, whatever their behaviour, had revealed mercy. Unfortunately, he had failed to consider this to be a quality of the Almighty. Grandpa Fleming was scornful of organized religion although a profound believer in Divine Providence.

The preacher had come to call respectfully from time to time

15

and Grandpa had enjoyed his visits, but I fidgeted knowing that a challenge of wits would take place sooner or later. The Reverend Johnson had shown apprehension also as he observed Grandpa's blue eyes taking on an added brightness while the latter sat cross-legged, the right foot elevated from the floor beginning to move with pendulum regularity. This was significant of preparation for a polite questioning to be based upon a scriptural reference and the asking for an explanation defying the intellect of many a theologian.

Tonight Grandpa's thoughts were not engaged in probing the mysteries of theology. He sat in his favourite rocking-chair but he did not rock. He leaned forward looking into the fiery bed of coals and sighed audibly. I sat near, in my own rocking-chair, watching him. He was tall. His skin had a youthful ruddiness and his white hair was as thick as a boy's. His beard too had a healthy fullness although pointed. My eyes rested finally on his expressive hands which told unquestionably of hard manual effort, the evidence of pioneering in a virgin land. The forests had been uncut, the land untilled when Grandpa came to Canada. A story was forming, I knew. Grandpa held a pipe in his left hand and a match ready to strike in the other. He might or might not put the pipe stem to his lips. Often, when overcome by memories, he would fill his pipe, carefully press down the contents and strike match after match, forgetting its purpose until the flame came close to his fingers; then he would quickly press the burned match stem into the pipe bowl and begin the process all over again. Many matches would be lit, many burned without a sign of smoke rising. He relived past years and endeavoured to translate in story the incidents of interest to whoever might be listening.

That night I was listening, and uninterrupted, Grandpa talked on and on. This often happened when we were alone, but tonight it would be a sad story for I observed the escaping of a tear once or twice which he brushed roughly away as if ashamed. Yes, the story would be a sad one.

" 'Twas on a night like this," Grandpa began. "The thermo-meter had dropped below zero and for two days there was a biting wind. It still came in gusts but the cabin of logs was well-built and warm. The children had gone to their beds in the ben. We had put a bed in the butt for your grandmother two weeks before. The room was cheery with an open fire. We knew the end was near and

16

I was with her every hour I could spare from my duties in the stables and what care I was able to give the children. Johnnie was eight, Cissy your mother was six, Jeanie was three, and Lily was but a few months. There was no hope and the few hours still to come were precious to both of us.

"There was a small table beside the bed. I had cut it from a walnut tree to surprise her on her last birthday. A candle sat on the table. By its flickering you could tell that air was moving in the room from the windy condition of the weather outside.

"My heart was sair as I looked at the frail bit of womanhood that was my wife. My Jeanie was as dainty and delicate as a lily. Her dark hair was spread out on either side of her fair young face. Her eyes looked too big and her hands, white and still, were clasped across her breast.

"'It's coming, Sandy,' she said to me, 'and when it comes don't grieve for me. I'll ask for my spirit to stay by you. I've been a sair burden to you but you'll have the bonnie wee ones as part of me.' I looked at the babe asleep in the cradle right beside us and a shiver passed over me."

Grandfather paused briefly.

"It was the consumption that had struck your Grandma. She was the third of her family to be taken with it," he said. "I lifted the candle and held it closer so I could better see her dear face. Our love had never faltered but now we were being put to the test.

"'Jeanie," I said to her, 'what am I to do wi' all thae bairns?'

"She unclasped her hands and laid one cold and trembling against my cheek.

"'You'll just hae to do the best ye can, Sandy,' she said to me."

Grandpa paused again.

"It was only a few days after that when she left us," he said. "I was broken-hearted. I did what I could for the wee ones but they needed a mother. Housekeepers, housekeepers. One spoiled their insides with too much food, another half starved them. I was at my wit's end. Three years of it and I had to make up my mind. There was a strong fine young woman living with her grandparents two farms away – Janet McNaughton. My thoughts kept turning to her. I had seen her once at a barn-raising at a neighbour's farm. She was healthy looking and kind. Her manners were polite and modest. She was not looking about her for attention but she had mine. I went home to think it over. A week later I visited the relatives she lived with and made my intentions known. They gave their consent and it was arranged that I should meet and talk with her the following evening. Mind you, my lassie, I was not a cheat. I would tell the truth whatever came of it.

"'My love is in the grave,' I said to her, 'but I am looking for a mother for my children.'" Again Grandpa wiped away a tear. "I couldn't have made a better choice," he said. "The Almighty had His hand in it, nae doot."

Janet McNaughton was no longer living when I was born but Grandpa's opinion of her had been confirmed many times by my own mother.

"She was kindness itself to all of us," Mother often said.

Janet had died at fifty-two from a malignant tumour.

For a long time there was only the ticking of the clock. I was a child. What could I say? But in my heart there was a surge of emotion which brought tears to my own eyes.

And then it was that Grandpa came out of the past to comment.

"Often that last night with Jeanie comes back to me," he said, "and I see myself, helpless, sitting by the bed with the flickering candle in my hand, and the dark room with her white face, and her hair like a dark frame on the pillow. I was young and sair tried. Had I been able to see it, my own face would have been a sad sight."

He turned to me. "Think of it," he said. "It would have made a wonderful picter!"

It was in the year 1834, on the sailing ship *Alfred of Alloway*, that three of my four great-grandparents came from Scotland to Canada with their children. There were eight Scottish families on board. The voyage across the Atlantic took nine weeks and three days, during which time, storm-tossed, the passengers suffered from severe seasickness.

"We were scarce of water," said Grandpa. "The food was mostly fat pork and black bread with one bowl of oatmeal porridge in the morning. Then an epidemic of bowel disease, they called it dysentery, began to affect one after another. The older folk realized the danger we were in and feared we would never reach Canada. I was a boy of eight then coming to a strange land with two younger brothers and a widowed mother. We would live with my mother's parents, Peter and Margaret Gregor, and their family of seven; where, we did not know.

"I was too young to remember how it came to be that my grandfather bought a strip of bush land in Puslinch Township while we took cover in a half-finished log house that someone had started and grown weary of building, I suppose. A house of our own, also of logs, was built. Two other families who came with us followed our example and bought bush land near us. Their children were ages with us except for one boy of fourteen. I suppose it was natural that when we were old enough, we intermarried within the two families, the Cockburns and the Beatties.

"In twenty years one could say that the people who came to this land in that sailing ship were a' mixed through ither. Jeanie Cockburn was to become my wife and your grandmother. The boy of fourteen, William Beattie, took a wife from the Walker family – Isabella. They were Lowlanders, fine common folk. Not uppity like some. Your father was their firstborn so that's how you got the Beattie name. We all clung together in our good times and our misfortunes almost as one family for we needed each other in those first hard years in a new land."

Although I was interested in my grandfather's stories it was past my bedtime and they had been so often repeated that, as I listened, his voice became a lullaby. I was close to sleeping when the door opened and the family entered bringing a rush of invigorating air into the room.

"You should be in bed, Jessie," Mother said, coming to me and taking me by the hand. She did not wait to do more than throw aside a heavy cape before I was undressed and snugly tucked into my trundle bed which stood in my parents' room, a bed which was occupied by each one of us children in turn.

I can do no better in tracing my inheritance than to refer to continuing stories from the lips of my maternal grandfather.

The rocky hill country of Puslinch Township with its lush bogs and swampy hollows where edible wild berries grew, blueberries and elder, was the natural choice of people from the Highlands of Scotland. The Flemings and the Gregors were of Highland stock and there were others. Companions on shipboard, it was natural that those who might have chosen the lowlands followed their friends into the rolling high country. When the younger generation came to marriageable age they purchased acreage near the homes of their forebears. Thus it was that the Flemings, the Gregors, the Walkers and the Beatties, families of my forefathers, settled in the same community.

Yet there was some divergence, as the venturous began to emigrate from the initial settlement. My father's parents bought a large tract of land in North Dumfries, clearing forest and tilling virgin soil which was rich in productivity. There were to be ten children in that family, all of whom grew to healthy maturity. But William and Isabella, their parents, died before I was born. I knew them only in story.

"Your father's folk were sturdy farming people," Grandpa said. "In Scotland they had been successful shepherds with land and flocks of sheep of their own. But they soon showed their interest in education. It was something for a pioneer in those days to afford the sending of maybe one son to college. The Beatties had eight sons. Three of them went to the university in Toronto, two of them became doctors and the other a minister. They rented one room and carried their food, in the main, from their father's farm. They showed what could be done in the face of little to spend. They were an inspiration to the young folk of other families." Here Grandpa lowered his voice. "It was my lot," he said, "to lose Jeanie's only son with a like disease to hers. Johnnie was a noble lad with a keen brain. He fought a good fight but the disease got him at twenty-six. I was feared for the others, but the Almighty be thanked, they escaped."

After Grandpa Fleming's marriage to Janet McNaughton, two children were born, Alexander and Mary.

"I had been saddened at Johnnie's death," Grandpa confessed, "for more than one reason. There would be no one to carry the name of which I had been trained to be proud, but this was taken care of by the hand of Providence, it is my belief, when another son was born."

In spite of his critical questioning of scriptural recordings there was no doubt in our minds that Grandpa's theism was very strong.

Grandpa often lamented his own lack of education. To him it was a magic key to success in living. There were no schools to attend when as a little boy he shared with the family of Peter Gregor a house in the bush lands of Puslinch, but the dream of acquiring knowledge haunted him from his very childhood. All hands were needed in the working of the soil to productivity, but when at seventeen he broke away from the Gregor household to assert his independence he became a millhand at a local grist mill near Guelph, Ontario, for wages of three dollars a month. The work ended with the autumn and his first application for employment elsewhere was at a country schoolhouse where he entered as a student of the First Book and did not miss one school day until the mill demanded his attention the following spring.

"Book learning was my first love in those days," Grandpa said, "and for three winters I sat with the wee ones in the schoolroom. I was not ashamed of my age. I held my head high for I had ambitions and what I did to realize them was my own business. Very few of the young ones made sport of me. I worked as a farm hand night and morning for my board and I was so happy that the farmer chided me for always whistling. By the time I was ready to marry, I had reached what we called the Fourth Book and in those days, that meant Algebra and Geometry as well as Reading and Writing."

After marriage Grandpa bent all his efforts upon earning a living, but books to him remained treasures and those which he acquired through the years were carefully preserved and guarded until his death. Today they are still treasured by descendants of the Fleming family.

Grandpa's father, John Fleming, who died before the family left Scotland, was a graduate of the College of Edinburgh in veterinary surgery. Grandpa told of the book-lined office, "a wee bit of a place" built onto the side of the farm home, Black Hall, a short distance from Edinburgh. His own love of books and learning may have stemmed from this early contact with a library containing an encyclopaedia covering all manner of subjects. This set of books his mother, Lillias Gregor, brought with her to Canada. The coming and going of people with sick or maimed animals brought to his father for attention surely stirred compassion in my grandfather's heart, and an interest in the welfare of beasts and birds which was revealed later in his own life. When Grandpa came to visit us we knew of his coming by the swift turning of wheels on the roadway. The open-faced buggy was drawn by two French mares bred from stock which he raised on his own farm.

"There were birds and beasts that prowled and stole as well as fine specimens in the bush lands at that time," Grandpa said, "but

21

I could not bring myself to destroy what had life in it unless to save other lives."

It was so that Grandpa lived out his belief that the Almighty had His hand in all things born into the world. And his influence as a story-teller upon the mind of a child I believe to be an integral part of my inheritance.

III

The Beginning of Life

No matter what my birth may be,
    No matter where my lot is cast,
I am the heir in equity
    Of all the precious Past.

from "The Heritage"
by A. F. Brown

Medical science has expressed the view or more strongly the certainty that a child unborn even when approaching full development cannot hear nor feel. This belief I contest. But can it be that repetition in story through the early years of childhood of certain facts pertaining to my own pre-natal experiences has deceived me into believing that I, in fact, did hear and did feel before I was born?

Questioning this I give herewith the account of events which I believe were known to me when they took place.

It was in the summer of 1896. My parents had followed the four miles of roadway from the small village of Blair on the Grand River to the town of Galt, Ontario. The democrat in which they rode was heavy-wheeled. Nell, our bay mare, was slow and clumsy footed. The journey was made in mid-afternoon when the foliage of the woodlands which bordered the road on the right was fragrant with the touch of sunshine and a recent rain. A leaf fragrance like that of flowers yet in some way more delicate.

The destination was the office of our country doctor. On the

23

My paternal grandparents: Isabella
Walker, William Beattie. (Reproduced
from pastels.)

left flowed the shining blue Grand River through the lush grass of the flats. It was lost sight of when the town itself swallowed it up between concrete banks and carried it under three bridges, one at the north end of the town, one at the south end and one at the centre leading from the west side into the main street on the east side. The doctor's office was at the first corner after the second turn to the left from the main street.

On that day I was aware only of irregularity of movement as the democrat wheels slipped in and out of the unpaved road-bed and stopped suddenly. I was used to the motion of my mother's body and I have no recollection of any further feeling until I experienced the pressure of someone's hands upon my mother's abdomen. The pressure was firm and strange to me.

The doctor's voice was positive and gruffly kind.

"A tumour," he said to my mother. "How old are you?"

At his words my mother gave a little gasp which had an unpleasant effect upon me.

"Forty-two," she answered.

"Good," said the doctor heartily. "We won't operate. These often develop quickly as women approach the change, and as quickly disappear. Don't worry, you'll be fine, but if Frank is coming into town in a week or two, tell him I said to bring you along. I want to keep an eye on you."

"Oh thank you, Doctor," my mother murmured. And again there was that irregularity in her breathing which disturbed me. I know now that this must have been a sigh of relief.

Soon the democrat wheels were carrying us home again. Nell seemed to be trotting faster and before long the journey was over.

But it was repeated again two weeks later. Sensations had increased for me in that time and I was more aware when the wheels of the democrat slipped into a rut in the road or lifted over a stone. Again all motion stopped. The office of the doctor had been reached.

Once more I felt the strong pressure of hands and heard that gruff voice speaking different words than before. Then he left us and a door opened and closed.

"He went out to the waiting-room," my mother told me in later years, "to speak to Da."

I did not hear him speak but soon he was with us again, talking seriously and gently to my mother.

"You must be careful," he said, "very careful from now on."

25

The ride home did not disturb me as it had before. We moved more slowly and I believe that Nell was induced to pick the smoothest part of the roadway.

My parents talked very little and their voices were low. Did they think that I might hear? But a few words were clearly spoken.

"Oh Frank," my mother said, "I can't believe it. Do you think there may be some mistake?"

There was a pause; then my father said gently: "I don't think so. It's a nice surprise isn't it?"

I am sure that my mother pressed closer to my father after he said that, and now I am sure that he spared one hand to take hers.

"Oh Frank," she repeated. "Then, I'm glad, too, but I still can't believe it – it's eleven years!"

I was wanted but not by all.

There had been six children in the family. Two of them had been lost by dread diseases of that time for which a cure had not been found. "Little Isabella," always so referred to, had died at three years with "diphtheric croup," Frankie at eighteen months with "cholera infantum." There remained two sons, Will and Al, twenty-one and nineteen respectively, two daughters, Jeanie Cockburn and Lillie Ann, fifteen and eleven. How the news of an addition was received I know only from the lips of Will shortly before his death at eighty-seven years. We were close friends and our relationship through the years had been unwaveringly pleasant.

"When I heard that Mother was pregnant after Lill was eleven years old, I was furious," he said. "I was then thinking about marriage myself and had no patience with the idea of a baby disturbing the peacefulness of our family. There would be twenty-one years between us. I said nothing of how I felt to Mother and I do not believe she guessed my indignation. But inwardly I was resentful."

Sometimes I think that I must have written the lines attributed to John Keats, "Season of mists and mellow fruitfulness," for it was the second of October, 1896, and such a day, Mother said, when I was born.

"I had been to town with the team and a load of potatoes," my brother Will continued. "I loved my horses and by me they were never unduly hurried nor neglected. I cannot remember using a whip. But in mid-afternoon of the day you were born, as I drove

26

through the village on my way home, the blacksmith who was shoeing a mare caught sight of me. He came out and hailed me to stop. He was Scottish.

"'Wullie,' he called, and there was pleasure in his voice, 'do ye ken that ye hae a little sister?'

"I didn't answer him. Instead I took the end of the lines and struck my team over the hips. The wagon went rolling up the hill. I drove into the lane, unharnessed, watered and fed my horses, taking a long time to do so. I left the stable and walked straight-backed and rather sulkily to the house.

"We had a bedroom on the ground floor and steps led from this room and from the living-room to the main stairway.

"As I went to mount the stairs to my room," Will continued, "the bedroom door was open and I could see Mother lying in the bed. There was a cradle standing beside the bed. Mother called to me.

"'Will,' she said, 'come and see what I have here.' Her eyes were happy and her lips were smiling. I went, in spite of an inner anger.

"You were lying in the cradle," Will said. "You did not look like a new-born baby."

"'Nine pounds eight ounces,' Mother told me proudly. 'The doctor said he never saw such a fat baby and such a thin mother.'

"I looked at my mother. This was no time for personal opinions to be aired. Before I knew it, I was smiling too."

My eldest brother Will replaced his disgust with a genuine interest in my welfare. It was he who taught me to read and to write before I attended school. Soon I was accepted by my family as an act of Providence.

There was a brief period following my birth when I believe that my mother may have been affected by fear of another conception. During this time, I was aware of an altered relationship between my parents. Could this have been the effect of my mother's state of mind? In recollection, it appears to be a natural explanation for her cooling attentions to my father and a withdrawal into herself which was apparent even to a small child. She had borne seven children and she was now forty-six years of age. It was before the time of contraceptives and other types of unnatural restraints. My father was an emotional man and I had inherited his nature; my mother, although affectionate, was more reserved in her expressions. Sometimes I felt a displeasure between them, about what I had no idea, but loving them equally I ran from one to the other attempting to compensate by gestures of childish devotion.

It was the thirteenth of December and snow was falling when Da made one of his hurried trips to town without explanation, which indicated an important reason not to be revealed aforetime. The road was filling in with drifts when he set out after the noon meal. The sun was slipping behind the pinnacle and a lovely glow flushed the fields and woodlands when he returned. I sat on a stool by the north-east window of the kitchen and an indescribable gladness associated with my father's presence affected me as old Nell and the red cutter came cheerily around the curve of the road.

"Da's home, Da's home," I remember saying. I got down from the stool and pirouetted from the kitchen to The Room while I waited for the door to open. It took time to unharness the mare, to provide her with supper and to reach the house. But he came, at last, his black coat sprinkled with snowflakes, his face very rosy from exposure and a particular kind of happy anticipation in his eyes.

"You're back," Mother said quietly while I ran to be sprinkled by the patterned flakes as he bent down to receive my enthusiastic welcome. Then he crossed the room, my hand in his, while his other hand reached into the pocket of his greatcoat and brought out a small box wrapped in pretty flowered paper.

Mother looked up from the sock she was knitting as he laid the parcel on her knee.

"Happy birthday," he said, and waited. Mother looked at the box. I watched impatiently until she laid down her knitting and began to unwrap it. There was something about the way in which she said "Oh my goodness, Frank" that did not express the pleasurable excitement which I was feeling.

Inside the box on a cushion of soft white lay a coil of alternating plain gold and filigree, centred by a sparkling ruby. The piece of jewellery combined perfect taste and dainty elegance. I was entranced.

He put an arm around her shoulders and bent to kiss her.

"You shouldn't have," she said. Although she added "It's beautiful, beautiful," there was something lacking in her appreciation, something indefinable which made the gesture of my father's particular remembrance of her tinged with sadness for me. I turned from devotion to the elegant gift and looked anxiously from one to the other.

My father said "I'm glad you like it," then, with a half sigh, he went to remove his coat and cap to shake them free of melting snowflakes and to hang them over double hooks on the wall especially placed where an oil-cloth mat would catch the drip. Why is it that I have never forgotten his sigh as he did so? Why was it that the brooch remained on its velvet cushion, never to be worn by my mother?

Soon after that, the normal tenor of their relationship, never again to be altered, returned to the life of my parents in the old house. Like a cloud swept away from the face of the sun, the evidence of incomplete communication between them entirely disappeared. My mother suffered for several years from severe headaches and intestinal disturbances. I remember hearing my Aunt Mary, on one of her rare visits, whispering audibly.

"It's the change, Sister, you're later than most, but you'll soon be right as rain again."

Aunt Mary's prediction came true and there lay ahead of my parents many years of happy, untroubled companionship.

It was several months later. Spring was opening the buds on the Balm of Gilead trees standing slim and graceful outside the narrow west window of my parents' room, which I shared. Early sunshine was touching their still bare smooth bark, when I opened my eyes. Behind and above them, the sky was clear blue but it was not quite day. I could count and the room clock struck five.

My father stood in the half-light, fully dressed. He always rose with the sun and I had never seen him unclothed, nor my mother, although I shared their room. For a time, my mother slept restlessly. When I got up in the night it was Da who stood by me as I sat nodding on my small potty, but his nightshirt was long and only his bony ankles and feet were visible, like the claws of some great bird, grey on the floor in the dim light.

"Piddle now, piddle," he would say gently, and then I would be tucked back into my trundle bed and he would return to Mother.

That morning he had dressed without a sound, as was his habit. Perhaps the chirp of a robin had wakened me. His hand was

29

on the door leading through the little parlour to The Room. But he turned and went back to lean over my mother to kiss her forehead. His voice was low, but I heard it.

"Thank you," he said.

Then he went out to the work which was always waiting, but I lay very wide awake, thinking. The house was still and morning only half there. Yet I pondered and the thinking kept me from sleep as the sun raised itself higher with golden lights.

What was it that my father had thanked my mother for?

It was still summertime when I heard Jean say to Mother, "Jessie's getting old enough to sleep upstairs"; and a dainty, single walnut bed was bought for me. In a matter of weeks, I was moved aloft to share a big room with my two sisters. I was a young woman before I understood.

The view from the upstairs window was very different; I missed the Balm of Gileads. I missed the trundle bed. I missed the dream which had frequently come to frighten all of us who slept in it. My sister Lill was the one exception. She had been transferred from the old cradle to share Jean's bedroom in the north-west corner of the second floor. Lill had not dreamt of marching soldiers with steel helmets and pointed spears below the level of the floor in a sort of viaduct. The sight of them had been an awesome one. Their appearance occurred only briefly and rarely, but often enough to bring cries of terror from a waking child. After my removal from the trundle bed, it was taken away to be stored in the loft of the carriage shed. All through my childhood, I suffered fear when I caught sight of it.

I was comfortable in my new quarters, but I missed the familiar snoring of my father and the gentle hand of my mother reaching out to make sure I was covered when the nights were cool. It was some time before loneliness left me, before I accepted my sisters as companions of the darkness which seemed darker than that of the little room where I had begun to perceive too much. No longer was the outline of the highboy known as "mother's bureau" to be found in the corner of the room. Occasionally I had been allowed to peer into its secret drawer where, in its velvet-lined small box, still reposed the brooch which was never worn. No longer could I watch the sickle of the moon slipping down westward behind the branches of Gileads before I slept. My parents' quiet voices had been like a lullaby, for often they retired

30

early enough for me to be found awake. Farm life was demanding, and after middle-age their bodies were tired. An oval mirror in a carved walnut frame hung on the wall opposite the window and sometimes I was able to find the reflection of a star or of a moonbeam in the clouded glass. The dresser upstairs was low set. Its swivelled mirror was tilted backward and did not reflect images that my eyes could see. It took time to gain a feeling of kinship with my new environment, but Jean's motherly concern and Lill's cheerful welcome replaced the parental solicitude from which I was being weaned.

IV

A Touch of Fate

Our destiny exercises its influence over us even when, as
yet, we have not learned its nature.

Friedrich W. Nietzsche

The kitchen of the old house had been added on the north-east and
through its two windows the morning sun flooded the room. My
first recollection of our kitchen was the sight of a large table spread
for breakfast with bowls of steaming porridge. Our family was
extended to include several hired men who varied in number from
six to a dozen according to the season of the year.

On the east side of the road stood three large greenhouses and
where the land dipped down there were several acres of rich dark
loam.

My brother Will had been inspired with the idea that the use
of such land could be more profitable for gardening than for
farming. In recalling the natures of my two brothers sometimes I
feel that their interests were divided by the division of the road. For
it was Will who sketched plans for the greenhouses and who made
a study of market gardening. But Al had a distaste for such an
occupation. His interest was in stretching fields and greening
woods and in the raising of thoroughbred livestock. My father
encouraged the interests of both his sons. But I was only five when
Will left us to study in the nearest town. He would visit us every
week-end and keep in close touch with the development of my
father's business as a gardener which was still new to him.

Although I was only a small child I recall distinctly the end of the first year of market gardening. Will, at home for the week-end, spread books of records on a table in The Room while with glowing eyes he explained to my parents that their new venture had brought one thousand dollars of profit in one year. Al had shown little concern and even as a child I felt scorn at his attitude as he quietly left The Room while Will was expostulating. In the raising of thoroughbred livestock he could not show such a profit. But my parents revealed pride in what had been accomplished under my elder brother's direction.

That was the first Christmas when the gifts to the adults of the family and to me showed a marked improvement in our financial status. From somewhere funds had provided a fur coat for my father and in turn he had purchased one for my mother. My brothers and sisters received handsome gold watches and I an inscribed locket on a lovely chain. How could I forget that Christmas? How could I fail to compare it with the one only a year before?

There had been a heavy snowfall and the roads were piled high on either side where men had dug through the drifts to make it possible for travel. That Christmas I did not hang up my stocking and I did not have a Christmas tree. The morning broke bleak and sunless. On the table in the kitchen beside my plate was a saucer of cheap candies and a little brass-framed mirror. Among the candies was a piece of silver. I do not remember its denomination. For others there seemed to be nothing. I shall explain the reason.

The week before, my brother Al had been stricken with a severe attack of pain. So severe that the neighbours had helped my father to dig out the roadway that he might drive into town to fetch the doctor. They returned together about mid-afternoon. The doctor's visit was brief. My brother had ceased moaning; the doctor had been helpful, I thought, as I followed him to the door where my father and he spoke in low voices.

"I'll send an ambulance at once," I heard him say.

"Must this be?" from my father.

"It must." The doctor's voice was sharp. He put a kindly hand on my curls in a gesture to comfort everyone.

"We know how to do it now," he said. "He'll come home fit as a fiddle."

It had been dusk when the ambulance came, drawn by two

sweating horses over the heavy snow. Two men came in and went upstairs to my brother's room. Another unfolded a cot outside the door on the veranda. The two men made a chair of their hands and brought my brother down the narrow stair. They laid him on the cot and covered him warmly. Then they carried him out the narrow pathway to the road where the horses stamped and snorted as they waited. I can feel the panic still in my mother's touch as she caught up a heavy shawl and wrapped it about us. Unmindful of the snow underfoot she carried me to that strange-looking vehicle with its big gaping doorway. She slipped me from her grasp onto the floor inside. My brother raised his head and put out his arms. There were tears on his cheeks as he kissed me.

"Good-bye, baby," he said.

And crying, I stumbled back to my mother. We stood aside while the queer covered sleigh moved down the hill. Then she carried me back to the warm kitchen where the rest of the family were waiting.

It seems to me in remembering that no one spoke a single word until my father who had waited outside the door came in. The ambulance was now around the bend. He took off his coat and cap and hung them on a hook on the kitchen wall. He slipped off his heavy boots. Then he came to my mother. He put an arm about her and took my hand for I was pressing close to them now.

"He'll be all right," he said. "Inflammation of the bowels – they call it appendicitis now. They can operate. There are seven others with the same trouble in the hospital. The doctor says they can all be saved, now that they know what to do."

There was no moon that night and only a few stars. From dusk until I fell asleep the wind moaned and although I had every faith in my father I knew a child's apprehension of that which was beyond me to understand.

That night Lill slept in my bed while Jean held me close where Lill had been. Somehow I knew by this act that I was not alone in my fears.

Really there was no Christmas for us that year, for we all loved one another and if one was in travail we were all in travail.

It was hard on a child. I did not eat the few candies in my saucer and I found it difficult to swallow the oatmeal porridge of which I was usually fond.

But my brother after three long anxious weeks came home to

us, although pale and still ailing. He had survived the operation, he and one other. That was the year 1900.

That might have been called the winter of sorrows for our neighbourhood. In early March when the drifts along the road were even higher than in December, illness struck a second time.

Beyond our farm to the south-west, over the bridge and up toward a row of knobby hills, the McNallys had a large acreage with well-constructed buildings. Freddie was about my age and was often my playmate when his parents left him at our farm on their way to town. Freddie was a handsome boy and a good companion for a somewhat delicate child, which I had become.

Our lawn was large and beautifully kept, ringed around with flower beds. There was always room in the greenhouses for the raising of plants to beautify the grey old farm house. We romped on the green grass and played with our collie who was gently treated and therefore gentle. The hours passed quickly. Sometimes Jean surprised us with home-made ice cream and fat ginger cookies for which Mother was famous. Sometimes we went with her to gather berries in strawberry or raspberry time, fresh from the field and sweeter for that fact, especially when treated with Jersey cream and accompanied by slices of fresh bread and butter.

One October day, my birthday, when Freddie came to visit he brought me a golden swan with a place between its wings for flowers. I treasured it especially when light from the pink-globed lamp which stood in the small parlour touched it to glittering beauty as it stood on a little walnut bracket in sight but out of reach.

The old-fashioned malady "la grippe" came in a severe form that year and with the falling of the first snow it began to take its toll. The snow was deep and the winter well set in when it reached the McNally farm and caught a delicate child who had not the strength to endure it.

The sun was bright and the temperature well below zero the morning that my mother built the fire to a steady heat in the kitchen and my father brought a trimmed log to place in a low-set iron stove in the small parlour. It was not usual for Mother to encourage me to play in the parlour especially in winter although it was a west room with afternoon sunshine and a view of the ruddy winter sunsets beyond a pine clad hill.

It had another window facing south which gave one a view of

35

the road. That day I watched in curious surprise as my mother lit the pink-globed lamp and pulled the shade on the south side of the room. Then she closed the door into the large living-room and began to read to me about the world we cannot see where a kind God cares for little children who must go there before they grow to men and women. The story was written in poetry. My mother had a singing voice and the musical sound withheld from me the pitiful nature of the story theme.

But there was something different about my mother's voice that afternoon, a restrained solemnity and a tenderness which made me think of how I had seen sheltering leaves prevent the wind from harming a budding rose. Yes, there was something different about my mother's voice and about the way in which she held me to her. She was not a talkative woman but on that occasion she seemed to be searching for things to say that would interest me.

Then my sister Jean opened the door and smiled right into Mother's eyes. Seeing this was like knowing of a secret without knowing what the secret was.

"I've made some cocoa," Jean said, smiling to me also. "Come and have a piece of scone and honey."

Then Mother told me as Jean turned out the light in the pink lamp and released the window-shade.

"God took Freddie to Heaven today," Mother said. "He will be very happy there and not sick anymore."

A little bewildered, a little stunned, feeling as if someone was being unfair to me and to Freddie, I pulled away from my mother who had risen and taken my hand. Before I followed her to where Jean was waiting, I stood for a moment and looked at the golden swan. I was near to tears without really understanding why.

I knew now why my mother had drawn the window-shade. Out there somewhere along the road a horse-drawn enormous box with carved posts was taking Freddie away forever. I had seen it passing from street to street in the town one summer day when I was taken there by my father. He had sighed and murmured.

"Ah, that is the way of the world."

"What way, Da?" I had asked him.

"To live and to die," he had replied.

I remembered.

Why had I heard no sound as the ugly box on runners slipped

over the snow? I was to learn later that such a conveyance had no chiming bells.

April was warming up into May. I sat on the wood box in our kitchen and beheld a sight which awed while it fascinated me.

Close to the sink sat my brother Al straddling a chair while Jean gently fed him a small tube which with great difficulty he slowly swallowed. When the small-sized portion of the tube was inserted, Jean attached one of a triple size with a funnel on the upper end. This she elevated to the extent of its length. Now she began to pour a liquid very slowly from a pitcher into the funnel.

My brother sat very still with eyes closed, perhaps to hide himself from the operation. Now and then there was a slight gurgling sound.

Al had returned from the hospital early in February after a successful appendix operation – successful according to the doctor. But from this time Al had suffered from what I heard my parents call "stomach trouble." It was assumed that this trouble was a natural sequel, and the treatment required was being administered by my sister after careful instructions from our doctor. Until this condition subsided, Al was required to have his stomach "washed out" every other day.

I do not know what liquid or mixture of medication, if any, was contained in the pitcher. It was of pint size with an Egyptian-style spout and made of pewter. That I remember, and when the last drop had been poured and five minutes by the clock had passed while Al maintained heroic control, the funnel was lowered into a concealing large-mouthed stone jar and there was the sound of the fluid being expelled. My mother quickly whisked the stone jar away and replaced it with one of a similar kind. Again the funnel was elevated, the small pitcher was refilled, this time from cool tap water which an hydraulic ram pumped from a crystal-clear spring to our house. The irrigation was repeated, then Jean's gentle hands slowly removed the unbearable apparatus and the ordeal was at an end.

Pale and unsteady, my brother would proceed into The Room and lie on the couch where Mother stood waiting, whatever the weather, with her woollen shawl. As a family we learned to interpret love in the touch of that shawl. It reached from shoulder to hem of my mother's figure. It was of the finest Scottish wool woven in the pattern of her clan, the Flemings. Whenever sickness or sorrow overcame a member of our family it required the touch of that shawl as a covering to bring about healing. A conversation between my brothers during that summer comes back to me.

Will had left us a year before to try his luck in the industrial world. He had the intention when a very young man of studying for the ministry and my father had spared his help from the venture in gardening that he might attend the Institute for secondary education. Tassie Hall was one of the first schools to be opened for an extension of learning after public school in our part of Ontario. Will had done well as a student but he was discouraged from entering his chosen profession by the school Principal.

"You were born to be an inventor, not a preacher," the well-meaning Principal told him, "and inventors aren't welcome in the pulpit. Also," he continued to advise my brother, "your voice is too quiet to encourage converts."

"That's a queer kind of advice to give a young man," my father remarked to my mother, "but maybe there is more truth in it than we want to believe."

There was truth in it. Will revealed this fact after he left the classroom for a machine shop where within a year he became a foreman and a part-time instructor. The money was of secondary importance to Will although the wages were good. What encouraged him was the possibility of promotion, until one day he might become, who could say, a manager? Even the president of a company?

His dreams of achievement he confided to Al one summer evening when they sat together on a bench under the veranda. I can remember the nature of their conversation which was heard by me as I sat on the upper step of the veranda entrance with a bantam in one arm and my doll in the other.

"You've got to face the truth," Will said. "You're not strong enough for heavy farm work and you hate the garden. You have a liking for argument and you are convincing. Why don't you go in for an education like I wanted to do, but don't choose without doing a lot of thinking. Lawyers have a chance to express their opinions and they are trained to win arguments. You've always liked a battle of wits and if I may say so you enjoy being a little tough on the other fellow."

"Shut up in an office all day long?" Al prophesied.

Will laughed. "That's looking ahead a long way. All right then, come to town with me a..d I'll get you a job in the machine shop. You always liked to tinker with tools. There's money in it too and you have to have money for an education. I never told Da but when he started grumbling about the cost of schooling for me, I began to think that what he had to spend on me wouldn't last very long. That gave me another reason for leaving school."

In the autumn, Al left us and accepted work offered to him. It was a sad leave-taking, for even I could detect that Al's heart was not in it. After my father had driven him away with his satchel of clothing down the road toward town, my mother sat down in the kitchen and buried her face in her apron. Mother was not in the habit of showing her emotions and when I heard her crying I cried too, scarcely knowing why. Jean set the kettle forward on the range and made a cup of tea. I saw her hand go to her eyes several times but when she spoke to Mother, her voice was steady.

"It isn't far," she said, "and if he doesn't like it he can always come home."

Lill had been watching the departing vehicle until it turned the bend in the road and passed out of sight. Then she came in to join us. She had been crying too, I could see by the red rims around her large blue eyes. She sat down with a thud on a chair by the table ready for her share of tea and she said in a strong cheerful voice, "Good for Al, he had guts to take this plunge the way he's been feeling. But he'll make it, you watch, he's got backbone if he hasn't a good stomach."

Mother took down her apron. She took a handkerchief from her bosom and dried her eyes. She remembered that she had more than one responsibility.

"You shouldn't speak such rough words, Lill. But what you mean is very true. The boy has courage and he is ambitious too, but his heart wasn't in the going, you know it as well as I do. If he comes back, don't be surprised and don't show him if you feel disappointed. He's gone through terrible things for over a year without giving up. He won't give up *now* unless it's the best thing for him. That is the way I look at it and I hope your Da will too."

As I grew older and viewed the succeeding incidents which formed the pattern of my brother's life I knew that my mother, who was also his, had a better understanding of his nature than any of us.

The brothers came home together each Saturday and returned to town on Sunday evening. They walked home but Da drove them back in the buggy. Al was very thin and sitting three in the one-seated vehicle was no hardship.

I remember that there was a distinct absence of discussion about work while the boys were at home, also I remember that Al and Jean did not attend church with the rest of the family on Sunday mornings and that a coil of moist rubber lay visible in a basin of water beneath the sink until it was quickly whisked out of sight by Jean before anyone including myself had time to comment on it. But when the New Year celebrations brought my brothers home again for a few days, I noticed with mixed concern and pleasure that Al ate heartily and that the rubber tube was no longer in evidence. With relief I had seen it coiled neatly and stored in a cardboard box and then placed on the upper shelf of a seldom used clothes cupboard. The sight which had fascinated me while it caused me to shudder would not be seen again.

January moved into February, February to March and March into April. The shop workers occasionally missed coming home on Saturdays because of the inclement weather. When the winter began to wane at the end of March, they arrived jubilant. Will rejoiced for Al and Al for himself. Al had been commended by his foreman and given a promotion. His face was fuller, his eyes bright and sometimes he smiled. I was old enough to note a difference and as a gesture of approval I did something which was unusual for me. I approached my father and my brother Will freely, always sure of a welcome, but with Al I was always less at ease. I cannot remember that he ever spoke to me harshly or was ever unkind to me but he did not seem to notice me and rarely addressed me directly. On that week-end I went to him and leaned against his knee. It was not as bony, I thought, as it had been before he went to town and I smiled up at him approvingly. To my amazement he put a gentle hand on my curls and smiled back at me.

"You're growing like a weed, Jessie," was all he said, but I felt a rush of happiness that I have not often felt and that I've always remembered.

It was not failure at work nor lack of determination to achieve nor distaste and rebellion against authority which brought Al back to the farm. It was the spring. When the ploughman began to turn the moist brown earth into furrows, when the larks and the

"Al had found his happiness and he was
never to leave the land again until the
earth itself called him away."

The old swamp became a prosperous
celery farm.

bobolink could be seen and heard searching for places to nest over the meadows, when blood-root and wild violet and marsh marigold lifted their blooms to the moist blue of late April skies and when lambs bleated at lambing time and the whole world in town and in country showed signs of rebirth, there was a something in the air – a smell of the land and of things growing, a memory of the excitement of sharing in the miracle of revival. For Al it was the summons to his great love, the land, and without apology he abruptly gave notice of leave-taking and came home. His team of dappled greys neighed their pleasure as he guided them, reins twisted around the handle of the plough as he drove straight furrows from east to west in the field to be sown with fall wheat.

"I'm glad he came back," Da said. "He'd never be happy cooped up indoors, and he'll lighten the load for me too. I never said it, but hired help alone makes a difference. Sometimes – well – you know."

He and Mother were standing together at the open door facing southward. Al was almost two fields' width away but his confident voice directing the horses and his alternating whistles were carried on the wind. I saw Da brush his cheek with a quick hand and I'm sure Mother saw him, too.

"I know," she said, "I know, Da. This is best for everybody."

Mother's words proved true. Al had found his happiness and he was never to leave the land again until the earth itself called him away.

V

My Family

Differences of nature
make for a satisfied whole.

Jarcie Lee

My mother was a busy woman with little time for relaxation. Our household was an ever overflowing one. As well as our hired men and Grandpa Fleming who had come to live with us, my parents had accepted the custody of Max, a nine-year-old cousin whose mother had died suddenly, leaving a family of eight. Uncle John was my father's brother and Max his second-to-youngest son. I was only two when he became a member of our family, a shy, bewildered boy wrenched from brothers and sisters with whom he had enjoyed a happy life. Now they were all placed with relatives and when I recall the fair-haired newcomer sitting on the edge of a chair in our kitchen, his blue blouse stiffly starched and his shoes very shiny as if just from the cobbler's hand, I feel the same clutching at my heart that I felt that day in childhood while I sat opposite him on another chair as we considered each other. He did not smile nor did I. Looking back I feel that although we were only children both of us realized that this was not a time for smiling.

Perhaps it was then that my sister Jean took over the duties of a second mother with me. Jean was tall and dark with a Spanish-type beauty which I later learned was an inheritance. An ancestor of my father had married an officer of the famous Spanish Armada which was wrecked on Scottish shores. Jean was quiet and thoughtful. When visitors came, she disappeared into the kitchen

43

I am five.

to busy herself with duties there, or, said Mother, "If I couldn't find her I knew where she would be – in the attic."

Our attic was a place of storage for treasures. Most valued by Jean were hundreds of books and piles of magazines: the *Illustrated London News*, the *British Weekly*, the *Girls' Own Annual*, and other publications from the Old Land.

"Jean," Mother said, "was never happier than when alone with a book."

When at five years I began to read, it was Jean who from her slim wages which my father paid each child when they became of age, brought to me my first story books. Later when my appetite for reading began to outstrip the available supply, when I showed a willingness to read anything and everything that could be read, Jean took the place of censor. Until I was thirteen every book read by me first passed through her hands for examination and many which determined my choice of literature were placed in my hands at her own expense.

The choice at that time was limited, however. There were no public libraries within reach and many books judged harmless from the untidy shelves in the bookcase of our village Sunday School had been chosen without thought of literary merit. I was not deprived of these by Jean for the demand by me for books far exceeded the supply. I read every word of Finley's sentimentalism in twenty-eight volumes of Elsie Dinsmore, and E. P. Roe's revivalist dramas. Such reading was soon to be replaced at public school where a library suited to the needs of growing young minds was started by an enterprising male teacher.

Two incidents in my early childhood reveal the solace which my elder sister provided for a super-sensitive conscientiousness.

The religious element was strong in the home. My father was an elder of the Presbyterian kirk in town, my mother had sung in her home church choir before marriage. Family worship was a daily experience. In the morning my father read briefly, with respect but without piety, from the Scriptures while men of various denominations and nationalities listened without showing disapproval, if it was felt. Then each of us knelt at our respective chairs while my father prayed for the welfare of all men in simple direct language which even as a small child I memorized without effort or consciousness.

I was seven when I grew sickly and it was then that Mother's brief comment about Freddie came back to haunt me. Affected by an ailment which defied diagnosis, I was unable for weeks at a time to play as other children did. In fine weather a cot was placed for me on the long veranda. From there I could see a far stretch of sky southward, and the piling and unpiling of cloud formations entertained me. At Sunday School I had heard the dramatic stories of Elijah and the golden chariot, of Jacob and his ladder and of the man with flowing hair, robed in white, who walked upon the waters of Galilee. Sometimes Elijah drove his mighty horses over my clouds too and sometimes Jesus walked, not upon the waters, but lightly, with finely moulded curving feet, from cloud tip to cloud tip. The mind of an imaginative child was stimulated rather than dulled by ill health. Then conscience began to frown. My eyes turned from watching the Christ making His way along the pearly billows which lined the south horizon to the gambolling of cows in the meadow below and an association of words began to distress me. I got off my cot and ran to Jean who was making raspberry pies in the kitchen. I ran right into her arms.

"I'm thinking bad things," I sobbed. "Bad, bad things and I can't stop."

Jean took me into the big cool Room and laid me gently on the couch. She was smiling and her dark eyes were lovely with an affection which comforted me even before she said, "What's wrong, dear?"

Somehow I made her understand that when I wanted to think and say the word Jesus, I thought and said cow, and vice versa. The earthy nature of an animal seemed to be a blasphemy. Jean smiled and stroked my hair. I don't remember her words but whatever they were I never thought again of the natural and unnatural as in shameful relation to each other. But Jean had become my Mother Confessor and she was to remain so for the rest of her long life.

"Children, obey your parents" was the text by means of which my mother and father controlled and disciplined our family. From earliest childhood the words directed to me and before me were magic words in influencing my life.

"If you tell us what you have done," they said, "we won't punish you."

It was easier to deny oneself than to debase oneself in the eyes of those who had trusted; and what would be the results if found out? We didn't know, we were afraid to imagine, and living in

46

secret unconfessed shame was a state we seldom endured for long. Sometimes this sense of being under strict never-to-be-disregarded orders carried me into situations the dreadful challenge of which only a sensitive child knows.

We lived a long half-mile from the small village where other children lived and several fields away from those on neighbouring farms. Before school age I can remember only three being brought by their parents to visit with me, Freddie – now gone – and Lydia and Grace Wismer, who were cousins and lived on adjacent farms. They were older than I, and attended school. We played "house" mostly; they were the "grown-ups," mother and father – by imagination the change of sex was easy – and I was their child. With toy dishes and a toy stove, a tiny washtub and board, it was a pleasant enough pastime but rather dull for me. Being a child provided no food for the imagination, no transition. Once Lydia's brother Willie came along. Willie was all boy, freckled-faced and red-headed, with scorning blue eyes. Willie had not come by desire and he boldly stated that he hated girls. Our large well-kept lawn became a rodeo with Willie as a rider on the back of our collie, while they chased us before them round and round. Our ankles smarted from strokes of a willow gad which the rider used whenever he caught up with us, until Lydia dragged him from his perch and sat on him while Grace, several years older, pried the whip from his grasp.

Grace was eleven and felt her seniority. She held me close to her for I showed alarm at the wrestling match on the lawn, while Teve, rid of his burden, galloped up and down merrily barking. Jean came to the door as Grace knelt rubbing gently my nipping ankles.

"Come in and have some cookies and a drink of lemonade," Jean said. Lydia and Willie were soon on their feet. Only Teve remained outside, panting on the porch mat.

We were going over the hill road to school a few years later. Willie was ten now. It was a mid-winter day, cold and clear. We three met at the cross-road and walked on together gathering several other children as we went along.

A board fence served as a snow-break on the left side over the tip of the hill.

Jean had knitted me a double wool bonnet of red yarn. As we reached the top of the hill, Willie darted toward me and his skinny hard hands undid the ribbon ties and flung the bonnet over the fence, then he ran like a deer down the other side of the hill to the village school.

It was only a few minutes before the protective Grace had mounted the fence and rescued the bonnet.

"Mean brat," she whispered as she tied it on. "If Lydia tells Aunt Suzanna, he'll get a licking."

I did not know why Willie disliked me. Later I learned that his father and my father, whose land met at a line fence between our farms, had a common interest in a drain from a low swamp, a drain which became a miniature brook with white sand and slippery frogs and an occasional minnow as it trickled its way to a culvert in the road at the bottom of our hill. On the other side it spread in little pools and brooklets through the valley of a pasture purple with long-stemmed violets in spring.

Willie's father and mine had had a difference over the care of the drain. A surveyor was called in and my father had won in the dispute.

Willie did not forget. He became a minister of the Gospel and an eloquent speaker. I went to hear Willie preach his first sermon. His text was well chosen.

"Be merciful," Willie began, "and ye shall receive mercy."

Birthday parties were not a regular occurrence in our family. When I was a child there were gifts, yes, but only one party for me which I can remember. That was the year Grace Wismer was twelve. Although I was considerably younger I was invited to attend. The distance between our homes could be spanned by climbing a high hill in a pasture field which brought one to the road fence separating the land from the lane gateway. The other was by following the road and turning a corner, making almost a perfect triangle, then following the right arm of the road where wild cherry and beech gave shade. By this means one also reached the lane gate of the Wismer farm. I had not yet walked on the road alone, since school days were still to come, and it was Jean who led me to the V-shaped tip of the triangle, around it and on to a location where she stood watching until I reached the lane. I was then on my own, almost afraid but also proud, for the lane was a long one.

I could see Grace watching for me at the house-yard gate.

Before parting, Jean had said, "Have a good time and come home at five o'clock."

That was a wonderful afternoon. About a dozen children had been invited and I was the youngest, young enough to be made much of by the school girls and tolerated by the boys, even Willie, who did nothing more than teasingly pull my long curls whenever the opportunity presented itself. Grace's mother was a round-faced, plump German woman of the Mennonite faith. Grace had inherited her kindliness, and Willie was sternly reprimanded by both of them. I felt secure. I had never been away before without my parents or one of my sisters and it was an exciting experience, almost like being in another world. There were no Balm of Gileads here and the house was of more modern style than our home but the lawn was small and there were few flowers. The great attraction for me was an immense mulberry tree inhabited by a dozen birds and showering down thousands of purple berries onto the green grass.

"Take all you want," Mrs. Wismer said. "We never pick them and the birds have more than they can eat."

I don't remember what games we played except games of tag, London Bridge is Falling Down, and Pump Pump Pull-a-way. Grace held my hand and kept me beside her during the tug-of-war. I loved her for her solicitude but I was secretly annoyed by it at the same time. It seemed to place me apart from the others. I was so rarely one of a group of children and I so much wanted to be one of them.

The afternoon seemed very long, happy though it was, and remembering Jean's admonition I asked Mrs. Wismer shyly what was the time.

"It's just five o'clock," she said.

My spirits sank. A table was spread with food which was surely fit for a queen. It was centred by an enormous cake with pink candles the like of which I had never seen. Enough chairs for all were in readiness.

"I have to go home," I said, "I have to go home at five o'clock."

Mrs. Wismer's large blue eyes widened. Her expression was one of firm assurance.

"Without your supper?" she asked me. "Not without your supper, Jessie. Why, that would be terrible. Look at the cake! You must have some of everything and a piece of the cake before you go."

"Jean said five o'clock," I repeated. "I have to go home."

Never will I forget that moment of decision upon the part of Grace's mother and decision upon my part as well. A vision of the laden table would accompany me, all my life through it would accompany me, but I had been given orders.

"I must go home," I repeated again.

Mrs. Wismer took me by the hand.

"You are going to sit up at this table with the others," she said, "and you are going to eat some of the good things before you go. I will take the blame. Tell Jean I said you must stay. Why it would be ridiculous any other way!"

She lifted me and placed me on one of the chairs. My eyes were tearful and troubled. She saw this, I know, for at once she said:

"You don't need to wait for the others. You begin to eat right away and then it will be only a little bit after five o'clock when you've finished. Grace will take you to the corner then but you must have your supper before you go."

She made a selection of sandwiches and put these upon my plate. She filled the shining glass mug on the right with delicious-smelling lemonade. Deliberately she cut a slice of the cake although the candles were still unlit. On the slice she placed a mound of pink ice-cream.

But although I ate my portion each bite seemed to choke me. The cake and the ice-cream overwhelmed my firm resolve. But I was never to eat pink ice-cream again without remembering.

Grace took me to the lane gate and watched as I ran as fast as I could to the bend and around it. I did not look back to wave my hand. I was crying in earnest now and sobs were choking me. It was summer and Jean heard me through the open window.

All the fear and uncertainty flowed away as I watched her running down the hill with arms out to welcome me.

Somehow between sobs I blurted out my story. Somehow by her understanding words my sins were washed away and as she carried me, not crying now but with tear stains on my face, into the shelter of the old house I knew the sweet taste of obedience, a sweeter taste to my childish heart than all the birthday cakes in the world.

50

Unlike Jean, my sister Lill was fair. Her eyes were large and blue, her wealth of hair auburn with a tinge of gold. She had full laughing lips and a slightly tilted narrow-bridged nose. Lill was slender as a willow and lithe as a cat. She was sixteen when I was five and her maturing body showed a gentle rounding. Her wits were as active as her young body and if any incident or statement contained a hint of humour Lill caught and enlarged upon it.

Our house was attractive with evidences of Jean's artistic touch – white curtains at the bedroom windows stencilled in a running pattern of green shamrocks, ecru in The Room and the parlour with a row of stately tulips. On the wall a beaded ornament for holding matches, a velvet panel upon which pansies had been painted in oils. The soft wood floors were coloured by Jean in a golden brown and then shellacked. It was she who wove and hooked the decorative rag rugs in The Room. Jean was the dressmaker of the family, and all of my clothing until I was high-school age was fashioned by her long artistic fingers.

Lill went to Jean too for advice about what to wear and when to wear it. But her activities were very different. To ride, to skate, and snowshoe, to go hunting for groundhogs in the spring with my brother or fishing in the trout stream. These were the pleasures loved by Lill.

Yet from childhood her voice had been marked as exceptional in quality and range. We hadn't a musical instrument at that time, but the Tilts who lived in our village had a piano and Louise was Lill's bosom friend. Often she went home with Louie for an overnight exchange of secrets or a week-end holiday. From this instrument Lill drew an outline of the keys.

On a long piece of thin board cut to correct size by my father she drew a piano keyboard. This was placed upon a flower table which Mother kept in our guest room upstairs. Each key was marked as on her friend's instrument. When Lill visited Louie she played songs that she loved on the real keys. At home she sat for hours transferring the melodies by memory in singing as she touched imaginary ivories.

She was eighteen when Da managed to afford one music lesson a week for Lill in the town of Galt. To reach there at the time specified for her lesson she had to walk four miles.

"I sang myself there and back again," Lill said in later years.

In bad weather and in winter my brother Alex drove her there and home again, waiting uncomplainingly while she studied, for he loved music too and felt himself to be even more deprived than she. She dreamed of becoming an operatic singer but our father explained to her that the state of his finances would never permit this dream to be fulfilled. At times she showed signs of rebellion and resentment, but reasoning sensibly she began to plan a more practical career which she believed would make the funds available.

In recalling my early childhood I remember Lill as a happy young woman who came and went on this and that escapade but never seemed to be permanently stationed in our home as a contributing member of the family.

True, she did her share of household duties and the toss of her head and her merry song added much to the cheery atmosphere. Then came the day of wonder when Da bought for us a Bell organ, "the best money could buy," he said. After that, one evening each week the small parlour was thrown open for the use of our men, some of whom had come from cultured backgrounds and knew and enjoyed good music. My father joined them as watchdog while Lill played now on a real instrument with an outlet at last for her great love, and in her full sweet soprano voice led the singing.

Will was the inventor in our family and before he was twenty-one he had carved and designed a violin of model structure. Also he made the bow. But Will was not musical except in thought. He could neither sing nor play and for some reason he showed no desire to dance. Perhaps this was because we lived in a Mennonite community where dancing parties were rare. Will was as dignified in youth as in maturity and chose his companions carefully. It was my brother Alex who played Will's violin and revealed a love of rhythm and melody from the time he accompanied Lill at a concert in our church in town. Lill sang the ballad "Darling child I must leave you now." Lill was eight and Al sixteen. The sobriety of their rendition was often referred to by my mother.

"They were so sad, like the song," she said, "that everybody was crying."

Music was to become an important form of pleasure in the old farm house. The presence of the handsomely carved organ in the little parlour transformed it into a sort of temple for me. The organ stood in the corner of the room between the south window and the one facing the west. I could not yet reach the pedals but my favourite occupation during that first winter and spring was to compose poetry and with it a melody suitable to its nature as I sat for hours in memorable happiness on the organ stool, picking out keys which I believed would form tunes suited to my efforts in poesy. Wonderful hours. The sun streamed in upon me from the south window or sent dying shafts of ruddy glow from the west through the Balm of Gilead trees. The influence of the changing seasons affected the nature of my compositions; all was mine to enjoy in the privacy of that small room. From without in spring and summer, birds added their carolling in approval of my childish symphonies.

Even my name was changed. My sister Jean had taken a three months' Homemakers Course at Macdonald Institute in Guelph, Ontario. One of her classmates was an elegant-looking young woman who presented her photograph to Jean upon parting. For that year at least, after adoration engulfed me, I became Myrtle Millson. She was indeed a beauty whose perfection I could never attain but could imagine. It was as Myrtle Millson that I composed my first verse of poetry.

Poetry and music? Seemingly they both went on as companions through my childhood. As soon as I was able to press the pedals of the organ I entered the magic experience of fitting music to the words which in verse were constantly presenting themselves to me.

Beauty – how I loved it, in tree and field and sky, in sunrise and sunset, in the curving flow of the Grand River through the flats near our home, in the sound of words read to me before I myself could read. The beauty of melody I sought for as surely as did the singing birds.

It was Jean who first realized that I had a gift of poesy and that music was part of it.

"Jessie should have music lessons, too," she said.

She was standing at the open door of the little parlour and I was on the organ stool. I would be going to school in the fall. I would be seven in October.

I do not recall what was the nature of my attempt at composition as Jean listened. But Mother came to stand beside her.

"We can't afford too much," said Mother. "And how could we get her there and back?"

"Minnie Edgar might teach her," Jean said, "and Al could

53

drive that way when he takes Lill to Galt. Minnie would keep her until they came home again, I'm sure.''

Minnie Edgar lived in the town of Preston which was only two miles away. Many people went to Galt by way of Preston. I had seen Minnie, who attended my father's church. She had a round, kind face and wore pretty dresses. Often she came to speak to us in the church vestibule after the service.

Then Jean added information which discouraged my rising hopes.

"But Minnie only teaches piano," Jean said. "I forgot about that.''

I went on with my music-making, a little indifferent to the subject under discussion for I was quite happy manufacturing my own melodies and manipulating the stops of the organ, the soft or loud, as suited the mood of my composition.

I went to school that autumn and one afternoon, as I was walking home accompanied by Grace and Lydia, the miller's wife called me to her. She was standing in the doorway of their house which was built close to the road on a gentle rise of land east of the mill.

Sophia Hilborn was considered to be the prettiest woman in our village and as my mother sometimes said, with a note of disapproval in her voice, "Sophia must be close to thirty but she laughs like a young girl.''

Once at a quilting which Mother had attended, Sophia had got down on the floor and shown the other ladies how to play leap-frog. This performance was too much for my mother's dignity but for all that, Sophia came and went at our house almost as an extra daughter of the family. Before the birth of her second child, within a month of her confinement, she had arrived one evening before dusk. Mother had ushered her quickly into the parlour and I had been sent to hear Jean read a story in the kitchen, then to bed.

The next morning there had been a quiet-toned conversation between Mother and Jean, which Jean had ended by remarking audibly, "But Mother, she was wearing a long cape.''

After that I looked with some curiosity upon any woman wearing a cape, without really knowing why until I became aware of Sophia's reason.

When she called me to her I went willingly for she was

generous with cookies and even my mother's fat raisin gingers could not compare with Sophia's. That day she waited until I was in her spotless house – so spotless that one was almost afraid to step on the floor – then she said, "Sit down, Jessie. And how are you getting along with your music?"

I looked at her with some amazement.

"I don't take music lessons," I said, "but Lill does and she sings very pretty."

"I've heard that," Sophia replied, "but you would like to have music lessons, wouldn't you?"

I nodded, a little puzzled.

"Minnie Edgar was talking to me about you," she went on. "Jean told her that you like music too but since you haven't a piano Minnie can't teach you. That's what Jean thinks, but let me show you something."

She took my hand and led me into the most elegant room I had ever seen. It fairly glistened with cleanliness and order. The windows must surely have been cleaned that very day, thought I, the furniture was polished and the rug, bright green, presented a gorgeous scattering of deep pink roses. I did not venture to step inside until Sophia preceded me and fearlessly placed herself in one of the handsome rocking-chairs. She took me on her lap. She pointed to an object which outshone every other. It was a rosewood piano with such shining keys that I felt certain they had never been played upon. To me, my organ was far more precious; but Sophia was speaking.

"Nobody plays that piano," she said. "I don't know how to play and neither does Joe, but we liked the look of it and so we bought it. Now Jessie, if you want to take music lessons, Minnie will teach you and you may practise on my piano. You can come in for half an hour or so every school day and then on Saturday, when Lill goes to Galt, you can stop off at Minnie's. It's all settled. Aren't you excited?"

I was so excited and incredulous that I did not even ask Sophia how she had learned about this. However, that evening Jean told me that Sophia had come up to visit the day before and in the course of conversation my problem had been mentioned.

Thus began an exercise in endurance which I shall never

55

forget. It was autumn and the strawberry apple tree on the Hilborn property was throwing down fruit by the score.

"Take all you want," the miller told us, "for there are more than we can use." The air was nippy with frost before I drove with Al and Lill to Preston for my first music lesson. The temperature had fallen into the thirties by Monday when I stopped at Sophia's to sit for the first time before her piano.

"It's a bit chilly in here," Sophia said as I took my place.

"There isn't any heat in this room, you know. I often tell Joe it's a good thing we don't use it much, but I'll leave the door open into the kitchen."

There was a brisk fire burning in the kitchen range and I all but prayed for the heat to come my way but it seemed to avoid the entrance as people probably did because of the room's perfection in other ways.

Day after day I went reluctantly to Sophia's door. Day after day, following an hour when I was chilled to the bone and my fingers were sticks of ice, I hurried home with tears of genuine pain in my eyes. There I knew a hot mug of steaming cocoa would be waiting. For twenty weeks I did not murmur but with a great sense of relief I learned that Minnie Edgar was leaving for California at the end of February. Twenty lessons in piano. It was enough for my requirements. I never had more, but it was my good fortune to memorize without attempting to do so and by this means I continued to travel through a land of melody.

VI

I Go to School

School days, school days,
Dear old Golden Rule days.

From an old song

When I was seven I began to attend the village school and it was Jean who crocheted for me a pink corded bag lined with red in which I carried my first slate and my First Reader. Jean walked with me to the bend in the road where I was joined by other children. I remember looking before me at the long stretch of hill over which I must pass before the schoolhouse came in sight. Miles and miles of roadway it seemed, yet from our gateway to the village schoolhouse it was scarcely half a mile. But time and distance are measured by experience. After that first day I seemed scarcely to leave our house before I came in sight of the picket fence which enclosed the school yard and saw the dark-haired man with his curving black moustache pulling the rope which rang the bell. He had taught the children of our community for twenty years. His own son had been a pupil there, but before my time.

The first day I stepped into the long drab hallway I stopped beside him. I had seen him before. When I was a very small child he had come with his rubber-tired open buggy to take me riding. He had wanted a daughter as well as a son but he was not to have one. On a summer day we drove smartly across the wooden bridge of the river and circled into the nearest town, where he stopped at a cobbler's shop. He lifted me out of the buggy and led me into the

The Village School, 1903. Tillie and I
frowning at the sun in the front row.

shop. When we came out I had been fitted with a pair of elegant kid boots in a soft brown with many buttons.

As I stood watching him pulling the rope, as I listened to the ring of the school bell that first day, he looked at my shoes and smiled. I smiled back at him. I had grown too big for the brown beauties. I wore a pair of black patent with a tassel at the top.

"Pretty shoes," he remarked, and I nodded. "What is your name?" he asked me.

"My name is Jessie Louise," I replied, showing astonishment, for he had called me by name many a time. His dark eyes were stern and disapproving.

"You said 'My name is Jessie Louise,'" he mocked me. "My name is not Jessie Louise."

I felt embarrassment although I knew that in some way he was making merry. Then he laughed.

"Of course you're Jessie Louise," he agreed. "You know my name?"

"Mr. Aaron Hilborn," I said, almost in a whisper.

He dropped the bell rope and took my hand.

"That is correct," he said. "Come in, Jessie Louise. I am glad to have you for a pupil."

That is the memory of my first day at school.

Laverne Hilborn was eight when I was born. He shared with his parents the wish for a girl child in the family. On October 2nd, 1896, after gathering together the contents of two china banks, he sat upon his father's veranda steps which faced the roadway, watching for the doctor to return from our farm that he might buy for himself a baby sister. On October 2nd, 1897, a boy of nine toiled up the long hill from the village and down the other side, turned the bend in the road and came to our door. In his hands he carried a parcel containing a blue and white cup and saucer, my first birthday gift, which I have treasured to this day.

Ours was a typical one-roomed village school of the two-door variety, one door for the boys and one door for the girls. The doors entered a hall which spanned the front of the building with rows of hooks for coats, caps and bonnets. In the middle, dangling against the wall, was the heavy rope of the bell. And to left and right along each end were shelves for dinner pails and lunch boxes. Two doors from the hall led into the main room which was laid out in typical country style with rows of seats flanked on either side by large iron stoves. A woodshed at the back held the chunky logs and the pile of kindling needed for the fires in cold weather. The teacher's desk stood on a platform, dead centre.

Blackboards covered the back and the front of the room, and four small-paned windows looked out on either side. The building was old even when I was a child and the trap-door in the floor with an iron ring reminded one that a small-windowed room occupied the space beneath it where in earlier days a hot-tempered master had been known to withhold the strap but to consign the culprit to fifteen minutes or half an hour in the miniature dungeon. Only boys were so treated, and only older boys who dared challenge the orders of their master to maintain complete silence during lesson times. In the left corner at the front of the room was a firmly built triangular shelf for the water pail and dipper. A boy was appointed each week to keep the pail filled with fresh water from a neighbour's pump.

The odour of wood was ever-apparent, faintly from the boards in the floor during all seasons, strongly from the piles of cut logs beside the stoves and those burning within the stoves in cold weather. Despite the teacher's order to replace the slate rags at least twice a week, the smell of wet cloth mixed with chalky dust was ever present.

Most of the seats were made for two to a desk. On my first day at school I was placed beside a small boy who, the teacher explained, was in the First Book and would show me what to do. I did not notice that I was the only girl child who shared a desk with one of the opposite sex. I wondered with annoyance why the small boy beside me encircled his book with his left arm and turned his back to me. I was smaller than he and in a desperate effort to obey the teacher's orders I got on my knees in an attempt to see over his hunched shoulder. I was offended when he tossed in an angry gesture my long curls, which had fallen inside of the curve. A wave of hysteria passed over the classroom and I remember the teacher watching me with twinkling eyes and a hand covering the big moustache to hide his own laughter. It was years later before I realized that I was used as a joker on my first day at school.

But the work to be copied from the board was pitifully simple to me – a V which was emphasized by two dots for eyes and a small dash for a mouth. Then two ears were added and one word written beside the picture – "fox." Next to that the drawing of a two-wheeled wagon, then a dash and the word "gig." I faithfully copied my first lesson on my slate but was deeply disappointed. Why should I come to school to learn simple words which I already knew? Then came a reading lesson, and after a page and a half read without a falter, the teacher came down the aisle and moved me into an empty desk behind the one which I had occupied. He took the book from me and replaced it with a thicker one with coloured illustrations and smooth shiny paper. Then he smiled into my eyes, pulled one of my curls, and said, "You are in the Second Book, Jessie Louise."

I walked home proudly.

After that day of testing, school became a pleasure.

Recollections of school days include the passing each spring-time of a gipsy caravan along the road. Always it stopped at the blacksmith's shop where the four horses which pulled the conveyance were carefully shod, before climbing the school hill. The van had tiny windows with lace curtains. The doors at the back were always open in good weather and inside as it passed up the hill we could see dark-haired and dark-skinned women with shiny gold loops in their ears, holding babies or small children while other children dangled their feet from the back of the van. The men, usually only two in number, occupied a driving seat at the front of the van. To my eyes they were exciting and handsome. The horses strained as the van rolled up the hill and away. Somewhere nearby, preferably beside a flowing stream, the gipsies would camp for a day or two while their men and perhaps a particularly pretty young woman would canvass the farm homes for customers to buy tin wares or to have old ones repaired.

"Lucky," my father would say, "if nobody misses a horse or cow or a few chickens when they have gone on."

This "going on" usually took place in the middle of the night and quietly, after an evening of singing, dancing and flute-playing around a camp-fire.

"The gipsies are back again," we would announce to our families when we came home from school, and our eyes would search the landscape for some sight of them, happy if we spied them near enough for watching and hearing. All mothers in the community kept their children under careful watch until the gipsies left the district, for it was a common belief that the mothers of dark

61

children sought to add a fair one to the family. That this had ever been done I have no proof. It may have been only a legend but it was one which carried an element of possibility.

Then there was the day in spring when a man driving a two-wheeled cart would move slowly along the road leading a magnificent horse of great stature. We gathered by the school fence to watch in some awe as the creature snorted his disapproval of being led through the country for inspection. When I asked my mother where the man was taking the great animal she said, "To visit the country people – to show them what kind of horses we have in Canada. Maybe somebody will order a little colt, hoping that it will grow up to be a fine-looking animal too."

A number of years passed before I discovered by deduction the true story of the visiting stranger.

It seems odd that our schoolhouse, a place to house and educate lively and growing children, should have been built directly opposite a grassy hill through which had been cut a roadway to the village cemetery. The roadway had a heavy growth on either side of dwarf poplars, chokecherries, tall flowering grasses, golden-rod and wild aster. I became friendly with an alert, fearless child one year younger. "Tillie" or Ruth, as her family called her, was a favourite with everyone. She had clear and large almond-shaped grey eyes. Her dark hair hung in two braids. The time came when I longed for braids too instead of curls and when I complained that the ribbons which Tillie wore were twice as wide as my ribbons. "Tillie's folks can afford wide ribbons," my mother said and that was the end of it. I felt ashamed, as if I had launched a complaint against the parents whom I loved so much. Tillie's father wore a coonskin coat and cap, rarely seen in those days, and walked with a cane. My father's fur coat was black dogskin and his cap the same. I had not reflected upon this difference before but as I did so now, I suffered a double regret; narrow ribbons were all that our family could afford. I do not remember ever being envious of Tillie again. I would not have exchanged my parents for Tillie's and I accepted my lot as part of belonging to my family.

I had been taught that the resting place of the dead was a holy place. One did not step carelessly upon the area of a grave but carefully in the narrow paths between. Now and then in spring, Tillie and I were granted permission at the noon hour by the teacher of the school to visit the little cemetery. What was the lure of the place I do not know, but we walked up the wheelway from the road with a sort of awe accompanied by an uncontrollable desire to visit this place. It was enclosed by a fence and an iron gate. We lifted the latch of the gate almost noiselessly and, once inside, we lowered our voices to a whisper. We had heard the story that a first settler of the area in a covered wagon had paused in the vicinity of what was now our village in 1803. He sought aid for a dangerously ill child. Taking one of his horses, he rode to the nearest town to find a doctor. But the only doctor living there had been called out to a home several miles away where a mother was expecting a first-born. Sadly the man returned without aid. The next morning he climbed the hill from the village to select a resting place for his child who had died during the night. Only the parents attended the burial and the father dug up a small elm sapling growing along the roadside and planted it to mark his child's resting place. It was now an enormous tree with great spreading branches where birds sang. There was no stone to indicate the grave spot but Tillie and I had heard the story. We moved in silence until we stood beneath its branches.

"They put her here somewhere," Tillie said.

"I know," I whispered back. "It's sad isn't it?"

"Yes, it's sad," Tillie said. "It's like a story."

"It is a story," I said, "a poetry story."

When we went back to school the children were still playing in the yard. The contrast between life and death seemed very marked to me and when that afternoon I finished my arithmetic before the time was up, I wrote these lines at the end of my multiplication table:

There was a father kind and brave

Who dug his little daughter's grave.

The planting of the tree over the small grave was the first burial in the village cemetery.

There were two other graves in the cemetery which we never failed to visit. They were in our family plot, lonely little graves with none added since the second one was placed there. The stretch of undisturbed green sod waited to rest the remaining members of our family. The plot was fenced with a chain running through cement posts. The two white marble gravestones were identical in shape and design. Isabella and Frankie, whom I have mentioned before. Sometimes Tillie and I gathered wild flowers from the lane outside the gates and laid them reverently against the white stones. There was no water supply available at the cemetery then and we knew that the blossoms would survive only a brief time, but somehow gratified by the privilege of placing them there we went down the hill at the sound of the school bell with a feeling of accomplishment.

Toward the end of that year I became afflicted by severe attacks of pain which often sent me running over the hill to home, sobbing as I went. There were long weeks, even months, of absence while I tried to keep up with my lessons by following a plan laid out by the co-operative teachers who, one by one, learned to accept my disability as somehow incurable.

Yet I look back upon public school days as happy days. Usually I did not miss the events which marked each year – Arbor Day, Lockout Day and the Christmas Concert.

Arbor Day was held in May, a time of house-cleaning inside the school, putting to rights the grounds outside and the planting of a tree in the yard. Then came the free time for which we all laboured happily – a walk in the woods with teacher, who tried to instil in our young minds the miracle of re-creation when flower, shrub and tree came to life again, when birds and small animals could be found in field and woodlands, every living thing giving us a reason for questioning and teacher an opportunity for subtle teaching. It seems to me now in recalling Arbor Day that it was never overtaken by summer storm. I cannot remember a single year when we were unable to visit woodland haunts because of falling rain. A few drops perhaps out of a summer sky where clouds billowed and sped before the wind and the sun shone. Wild flowers were plentiful in those days and we were not reprimanded for taking some from beside a sheltering stump or in a moist hollow to carry away with us. In memory I think especially of the quantity and variety of the shy hepatica in blue, pink and white and the trailing arbutus, with great stretches of almost solid colour in white and red where trilliums grew in abundance. I do not recall that we picked many flowers, preferring to leave them in their native soil to gladden other eyes, yet we were not forbidden. There was excitement when we found a clump of jack-in-the-pulpits or the lady's-slipper, so elegant and rare. I am sure that no school child of that time will ever think without appreciation of the beauties of nature.

Lockout Day was a yearly event also. One which permitted the pupils to become the overlords. At the crack of dawn the older boys were up, creeping through the semi-darkness from their homes to the schoolhouse, armed with hammers and chisels by means of which to take command of whatever locks required tampering with to allow them entry, and to re-lock the building securely from within. Only when the teacher arrived early enough, if it were cool weather to see that the fires were lit, did he discover that this was Lockout Day. From dawn until nine o'clock all the other pupils arrived to assist in the takeover. They were admitted quickly by the watchers of the doors, which were then re-locked. The teacher, if a good sport, would pretend anger and shaking his fists and shouting would demand admittance. Look-outs were placed at every window and by the keyholes of the doors to mark every movement outside the building. After much shouting by the competitors for command, the teacher would relinquish his just control and make his way down to the village store. Only when he returned with the storekeeper, both of them carrying large bags of sweets, would his demand for admittance be met. There would be much dilly-dallying before the final victory in order to give the effect of a genuine contest. Then doors would be unlocked from the inside and shouting and laughing the children would accompany the teacher and his assistant into the classroom. In total disregard of the danger of contamination, the bags of sweets would be undone and a game of scramble would ensue as the men tossed the candies in all directions while the pupils sought to claim them.

The final act of mutual comradeship was the announcement of a school holiday for all. On this triumphant note the conflict ended and the pupils departed to their respective homes with bulging pockets. Meanwhile the teacher, after careful checking of the building, would go home to enjoy his holiday too.

I do not know when Lockout Day was initiated nor when it ended but it was part of our public school program for many years. I think it contributed to good fellowship between the man who taught and the boys and girls who sought to learn. The rapport was thus improved.

Another yearly event which delighted the heart of every child in the school was the Christmas Concert. This concert was planned to include a part for each pupil; from the opening of the dark curtains hung from wall to wall between the platform and the seating area to the tapping of a small desk bell calling everyone to order, a boy or girl performed each act. The type of concert offered for the pleasure of the community varied according to the nature of the teacher-in-charge. Sometimes the adults from the small Union Sunday School in the village joined forces with the schoolchildren to provide a program of interest to young and old. Well do I remember my own excitement as I watched for the first time a genuine drama, although short, presented on an extended platform which the trustees of the building had temporarily enlarged. "Lady Teazle and Sir Peter" was ably performed by aspiring young dramatists in our village. The remainder of the concert was forgotten by me after this final number. The dignity and charm of the language used by the participants moved something within me to such inspiration that, for days following, portions of the speeches repeated themselves in my ears.

My own part in the program was to share with eight girls in a fairy-like pantomime performed to music provided by Tillie's sister, who was becoming an accomplished pianist. The passing of years has not removed from my memory the haunting bars by means of which, dressed in white with tinsel crowns and bearing hoops wrapped with tinsel, we enacted a fairy dance without a falter. Even the smallest boy, aged five, rendered his little recitation:

I am just a boy
My age is five
But I will grow into a man
For I am alive.

There was no difficulty in securing an audience. The difficulty lay in finding space for all who came. Over the snowy hills on foot, laughing merrily, or in sled and cutter along the snowy roadways, the country people gathered not only from our community but from others nearby. Above stretched the arched blue dome of winter sky often scattered with twinkling stars, or tossing down snowflakes which might, by the time the concert was over, require the use of shovels carried by the drivers to open the filling wheelways of the road. Was there anyone unhappy? In memory this seems an impossibility. For many it was a yearly reunion since

66

people living several miles away met only on such occasions. Whether our contribution to the program was rendered well or poorly, the teacher did not criticize. We returned to school on the next school day sure of welcome and of praise. Such were the leaders of public school children in those days.

VII

Certain Influences

The little things of life
Make deep impressions.

The author

It was the month of June. Following the return of Al to the farm, my father began a complete renovation of the farm buildings. Will brought home from the Mechanics' Institute Library in Galt a book of drawings showing the latest developments in the erection of barns and stables.

"You're a crazy man, Frank Beattie," one of our neighbours told Da in my hearing. The concrete foundation was being laid for the main structure which included stabling for horses and cattle and space for the storage of feed grain and roots, with an extension running at right angles with a loft above it. This extension was for the housing of the purebred Berkshires which were to be raised. What a fascinating structure it was before it was occupied – a perfect playhouse on three levels for Tillie and me. The pens had an elevated section walled-in with barred steps leading from the main pens where feeding was done by means of concrete troughs with sliding doors. The men could pour whatever the food might be into the troughs from the entries.

Before the animals were placed in their new quarters, fresh sweet-smelling straw formed a bed on the second level of each pen. The loft above would be used for storage mows, with trap doors above the pens to allow for replacement of bedding when needed.

The main structure of the barn was still only a skeleton of rafters ready for the "raising." Barn-raising was a great event in the life of any country family. The main structure in skeleton was laid out in pre-arranged order before the raising. For the latter, men came gladly to assist the carpenters. They came from farms north, south, east and west, eager to do their share in helping a neighbour and in improving the appearance of the countryside. Indoors the women prepared great hampers of sandwiches and home-made pastries to satisfy the hunger of the workers. The food was accompanied by mugs of steaming hot tea and coffee. Before the raising was completed there might be as many as fifty men and women assembled.

I remember our barn-raising day. My brother Will asked for a day off from his work at the shop. He arrived at mid-morning with a young lady whom I had not seen before.

"Will's girl," whispered Lill to me as I stared rather inelegantly at the newcomer. She was known to the other members of our family. My mother and my sisters greeted her politely. This politeness was emphasized, I felt, by the unusual stylishness of her appearance. She was a farmer's daughter but to my eyes she was a special sort of creation. My sisters and their friends dressed well and gave considerable thought to feminine allurements, but Naomi, or Oma as she was called, was a perfect companion for my brother Will who always displayed a particular dignity in dress and manner not common to young men from the farm. Oma was surely of the same mind as Will in the matter of personal appearance. As I looked at her I became as enamoured as I had become when I first caught sight of the elegant photograph of Myrtle Millson.

Oma was finely built, with an infinitesimal waist line. Her skirt was of heavy black material and reached to the floor with sweeping gores. Her blouse, with long sleeves and high neck, was frilled with Valenciennes lace decorating the front in row after row and finely finishing the wrist bands and the neck, making a frilly frame for the delicately featured face with its rather distant although not unfriendly expression and calm grey eyes. The hair was naturally curly, light brown and arranged in a handsome pompadour.

I shall never forget that day nor Oma. I followed her wherever she went. With her I sat on a pile of new lumber to be used for barn-facing and watched the raising take place. My attention was divided. Oma turned occasionally from watching the men balance

69

the structure into place to smile at me. I do not remember what she said to me, if anything; her smile was enough. She was from another world, a world about which as yet I knew very little except in imagination.

That was my first impression of Oma. I noticed one feature which did not concur with her general daintiness of person. Her hands were not small, although well formed and well kept. They were practical hands, made for more than the frilling of lace and the tying of ribbon bows. They gave added character to otherwise rather delicate features. She wore polished black shoes laced well above the ankles. She was a woman of dual characteristics – charm and strength.

Oma became my sister-in-law that autumn when the asters were in full bloom. There was great excitement in our family and a general pleasure in Will's choice, for, as her capable hands indicated, she was a woman of practical abilities, despite the contradictory delicacy of her general appearance.

The wedding took place in the bride's home, a Mennonite home where religion was the deciding factor in all things. My recollection of that day is vague.

I was a little bewildered by the assembly of people with only two children that I recall – myself and one other. I was impressed by the flitting here and there of slender young women in white muslin and lace, Oma's sisters, four in number, very pretty girls with pleasing manners. Then there was the elegance of the bridesmaid, my own sister Jean, who wore a dress made by herself with a floor-length skirt. The material was cream nun's veiling with a Battenberg lace yoke and collar and lace cuffs on the draped full-length sleeves. Then there was the lovely red rosebud in her hair, matching the corsage at her waist. Lill's dress was of mauve white-flowered muslin with inserted rows of embroidery. It too was full-length, and Lill had tucked a purple aster in her auburn hair. I have no recollection of what I was wearing.

I remember soft voices singing and the appearance of Oma in white embroidery and lace on the stair. I was too small to see through the guests crowding near as the music stopped and the solemn voice of the preacher silenced everyone. The marriage service was at four o'clock. As dusk crept in and a shining two-seated buggy was drawn up to the doorway of the house, Oma appeared on the stair, pausing briefly to toss her bride's bouquet

70

into the assembly of eager young women among the guests. I don't recall who caught it, nor do I remember what Oma wore as she left the house under a shower of rice and confetti on my brother's arm, but her appearance entranced me as it had done at our barn-raising. This lovely creature was now a member of our family. I could scarcely believe it.

Then something happened which stirred my curiosity. Her mother left the assembled onlookers and ran after the departing couple. I left too and ran with her. She didn't notice me. She touched Oma on the arm and spoke her name. I heard her whisper "Pray." Oma turned to answer. Her voice was gentle and solemn. "I will, Mama," she said. Then her mother took my hand and we stood watching as the couple drove away, waving happily.

That is my memory of the first wedding I attended.

Two years later the news reached us from the town where my brother had taken his bride that a son had been born.

I had acquired the dignified title of aunt.

The change in appearance of our farm buildings, and their modern design for the benefit of the latest advances in stock-raising, must surely have been an inspiration to my brother Al. He was up early and worked late with apparent pleasure. However, even in childhood I was troubled by the sobriety of his expression and his silence at meals in the company of our men and Da. Mother sat at the head of the table to help with the serving and to watch that the serving dishes were kept filled, for the men's appetites were hearty. Meanwhile, at a small table in the kitchen sat my sisters and myself when I was home from school. This separation was not intended to indicate any difference in social status. We were merely the overflow. Grandfather Fleming, Max and my father sat at the long dining-table with the men.

When not at school, Max spent his free time with Al on the farm. His love of the land was almost as absorbing as that of my brother and his skill in the training of animals was remarkable. One of our horses, Bill, had an evil disposition. Only Max could enter his stall and lead him to water. I think it was this almost complete absorption with the happenings out-of-doors which kept Max and me from developing a companionship, as well as the difference in our ages, which was seven years. By the time I attended school Max was preparing to leave there. My clearest recollections of him are associated with his leave-taking from our home at seventeen, when, granted permission by my father, he followed his favourite interest – the training of horses for the races, which was the hobby of a wealthy farm owner only two miles away. Max retained a friendly relationship with our family, however. He came and went frequently and continued to depend upon my father for advice in making decisions.

My clearest memory of Max is the sight of him on horseback passing up the road at a dangerous speed with only time to wave his hand to me as I watched, awed and somewhat frightened, from the shelter of the veranda.

But it was from Max the year after he came to live with us that I learned the difference between male and female. Max had been left to "watch me" while my mother and sisters were absent at the barns where now stood a herd of fifteen dairy cows. This was before the time of milking machines and they shared a division of the duties.

It was a cold winter night and from the window I had watched them following a trail through heavy snow from house to stable, guided by the flickering flame of a lantern in the hand of my father who led the way. When the last figure disappeared beneath the overhang at the corner of the stables I turned to go on playing with my doll, sitting on a heavy rug which Jean had hooked in a pattern of gay flowers.

The rug covered the floor beside a couch on which Max lay with a disgruntled expression on his face. No doubt he disliked his occupation.

"Tell me a story," I said, for I loved to be entertained.

"I got plenty of stories to tell," Max assured me, "but you're only a silly little girl. You play with dolls and you're kind of a baby."

I showed my indignation immediately by placing my doll in her cradle. I got up and moved closer to the couch. I sat down on the rug and folded my hands.

"I'm not a baby," I said, "and I like stories." It was at this time that my father had begun to read me *Robinson Crusoe*.

"Please tell me a story, Max," I persisted. "Tell me about Robinson Crusoe."

He grunted his lack of respect.

"Girls don't like them kind of stories," he said.

"I do," I said. "Tell me about Man Friday."

He grunted again.

"He was a man," he said, "and boys are different than girls. That's a boys' story."

"Boys aren't different than girls," I stubbornly protested. "They only wear different clothes."

Max was ten. He laughed long and loudly.

"You don't know much," he said. "They are different and they can do things that girls can't do."

"They can't," I repeated.

"I'll show you," Max said. "Just for that I'll show you."

He got off the couch and opened the door of the little parlour. From there a door opened into my parents' bedroom where I still slept in the trundle bed. Below the bed, standing on the floor was a round white vessel. Max pushed open the door and picked it up.

"I'll show you," he said.

In a matter of minutes I knew that boys were different from girls and much smarter. We returned to The Room. Max lay down on the couch with a sigh of satisfaction.

"There," he said, "there, stupid."

I had no reply. I was awed and mystified; also I had been defeated. I turned my back on Max, who had closed his eyes in pretended slumber, and busied myself rocking my doll to sleep in its cradle.

That episode was never to be forgotten by me.

My uncle John had left Canada after the premature death of his wife and after his children were placed with relatives. He became the business manager of a hotel in Grand Rapids, Michigan, and slowly but surely one child after another sought to be reunited with him by finding employment in that city. He did not live with them but they felt that he was among them. Max was twenty-one when he came to say good-bye to us.

"The call he feels is a natural one," my father said, after we watched him proceeding down the road toward town. "My hope is that John's influence will be good."

Uncle John had paid us one visit during the period of Max's stay with us. He was elegant in black broadcloth and patent leather shoes. I had always admired my uncle's beautifully kept hands. They were as I remembered them, long fingered, unmarked by hard toil, with carefully manicured nails.

"He's improved a lot in many ways," was all that my father said when his visit was at an end. Perhaps it was this visit which awakened in Max a stronger longing to be one of his own family again.

Better remembered than the presence of Max in our household was the continuing residence of my grandfather Fleming. I was aware that he considered me with some disapproval.

"She's fey, Cissy," he had observed to my mother when I came running home from the tomato field declaring that I was being followed by a worm.

"I never thought you would have one of them, but she's fey."

Grandpa watched me filling page after page with unintelligible words. Later he watched me accumulating scribblers of stories and poetry written by me. One evening as he sat smoking in his favourite rocking-chair while I bent over a book by the table – a flashy-covered notebook for which I had, to his horror, spent the sum of twenty-five cents – he asked, "And what are you up to now, lassie?"

"I'm writing a book," I said. I was ten. Grandpa got up from his rocking-chair and with pipe in hand leaned over my shoulder. His eyes were sharp; he did not wear glasses. He read aloud:

"Her lover was waiting under the shadow of an elm tree. She ran to him weeping and said that she would never go home again."

"Lochins me, lassie," Grandpa ejaculated. "You're fair daft. That's no the kind a' thing to be writin' at your age. What's gone wrong wi' you? You're old enough to be knittin' socks for your brothers and learnin' to bake bread instead of wastin' your time makin' up sic nonsense. You'll be a pair wife for some man."

All through my childhood I suffered a feeling of rejection by my grandfather. Yet I believe that what creativity in the matter of story writing I possessed, I had inherited from him.

Perhaps my mother reproached him regarding his complaints about me, for he ceased to convey them openly. Nevertheless there was in me a sense of guilt whenever I was found by him absorbed in my favourite pursuit.

Although Grandpa had been an early pioneer, his industry had made of him a man of some property by middle age. Grandpa's rather pretentious white brick house with (as he boasted) "the widest decorative cornice in Puslinch Township" was erected before he was forty-five. At that age he retired without selling his land, which he rented to my step-uncle Alex before he came to live with us. From that time on he spent his days visiting, reading and reflecting. His name became associated in a radius of many miles with authentic stories of pioneer life. His love of story-telling was as great as my own, but I wrote my stories, and from the imagination. My experiences were within a confined circle and limited. My dreams and my acquaintance with people who breathed only in fancy were unlimited. After I reached the age of seven and began to suffer from the malady which all but severed my life on several occasions, this brought with it a strong awareness that life might indeed be terminated at any time.

In my poems and stories written between the ages of seven and twelve, again and again I refer to this subject.

I lay in my bed unsleeping,
And heard the night wind's breath;
I know not why as I heard it
It spoke to me of death.

Frost peaks grew up on the window
To shut away the stars
Clear in the clear blue of heaven,
Deathless those God-lit fires.

What if on some hour nearing
The peaks of death shall rise?
The light of heaven will be stronger
Than that before mine eyes.

I lie in my bed unsleeping,
I do not think of death;
Strange that I should have mistaken –
"Life," said the night wind's breath.

(1908)

I do not recall any sense of fear associated with the thoughts of dying which frequently entered my mind. Although illnesses came suddenly and sometimes continued for a period of weeks, although pain was severe, a pattern was formed – a pattern containing the marvellous peace which followed pain. There were sometimes

75

months of reasonably good health when I all but forgot the threat that was ever present.

"She has an incredible faculty of getting well," the doctor told my parents in my hearing, and this may have stimulated the certainty which grew within me, each time I was under attack, that I would survive and live my span.

It is probable that the alternating periods of pleasure and pain which combined to provide life with uncertainty accounted for my interest in the subject of religion.

This interest was stimulated by impressive news confided to me by Tillie.

"Louie's got religion," Tillie whispered to me one day at school. "She's been converted. Isn't that exciting?"

A few weeks later, Louie became our Sunday School teacher.

VIII

Tillie and I Get Religion

We shall come rejoicing
Bringing in the sheaves . . .

Knowles Shaw

Our village nestled in a valley outlined on the north by a modest ravine below which lay the flats of the Grand River. Edging the flats at the bottom of the ravine, the Grand Trunk Railway from Berlin (now Kitchener) to Galt twisted and turned.

From the village, almost dead centre, to the other side of the river stretched a wooden bridge with great abutments of stone masonry and a protecting fence-work of iron. Even so protected, I never crossed the bridge without a mixed feeling of fear, reverence and wonder. This may have been born of the severe flooding which took place each springtime when the ice was broken up by an increased undertow. On one occasion, the bridge had been washed away and a cow carried down on a cake of ice mooed its agony of fear as it passed by the village; men would have rescued it but at this point in the flooding, rescue had been impossible. Or my feeling of awe may have been due to the absence of any other body of water with which I was familiar. Boats on the river were only used at flooding time and only to rescue the people who dared to occupy a few humble homes on the flats.

It was a cosy village. Even as a child I felt its warmth when I walked on its sandy pathways or drove through its curving street with my father. Eastward from the bridge crossing was a pink stucco terrace containing six apartments, three above and three below. The building sat close to the street and the gardens stretching behind it were small and unsodded lengths of earth. This building was usually occupied by newcomers to the community, immigrant families with little money to spare. Somehow, to my eyes, it did not really belong to the place it held but was a house of mystery, perhaps because strangers lived in it. The village had a mixture of inhabitants. There were the long-resident villagers, mostly German or British. Some had and some had not religious leanings. There were also families with strong convictions – the Mennonites. In all, about a hundred souls occupied the village proper, but to the school and to the small white church on the country side of the hill before the school was reached, many came from surrounding farms. As the years passed, the spirituality grew stronger through the influence of the little church and the trend toward worldliness weakened. Opposing factors, ever in conflict, were the church and an over-active saloon. The little white church had been built by the Mennonites who emigrated to Waterloo County from Pennsylvania. They were a sturdy people, strong of body and of mind. Their convictions were firmly entrenched and their influence on a rather widespread community was astonishingly general.

It was after they voted unanimously to donate the use of the church to all denominations for a Sunday afternoon Union Sunday School that I entered and became familiar with the fascinating features of that little place which was a tiny offshoot from the main Mennonite settlement about fifteen miles away.

Although my father was an elder of the Presbyterian church in town, he often attended the evening services of the Mennonites and when they had a special speaker, always an evangelist for a week of such services, he showed respect for a type of religious fervour which was not common among Presbyterians. Usually the leader of the services was invited to our home for an evening meal. Table-clearing was forgotten as we all sat listening to his expositions.

"They should be patronized. They are a fine people," Da used to say to Mother as he set off for the small church.

My introduction to this little white temple with its rows of wooden benches on either side and its plain-looking pulpit, took place when I was small enough to be carried part way by my father.

78

There was a division down the centre of the church between the benches marking the separation of the men from the women. On the left and the right behind the pulpit were doorways, one to the woodshed, the other to the Infant classroom. This classroom contained, for me, the most fascinating features of the building. Here I was introduced to religion as explained by a devout young woman through the medium of coloured picture cards with scenes from the Bible and a scriptural text below each picture which we were taught to repeat over and over with "teacher" until we could remember it. Simple texts, not too long for the memory of a child. "Lo, I am with you always." "Jesus wept." "Fear the Lord." "In my Father's house are many mansions." "Fear not, little flock." This was my favourite; it showed a shepherd sitting on a rock, his staff beside him, with a half dozen lambs clustering near and one in his arms.

Little benches followed the line of the wall in two and two. Those against the wall covered a row of tiny tubs. The use of these tubs was unknown to me and I coveted one for my doll's washboard. I mentioned this to my mother. She told me then that the tubs were used for the washing of feet, done in remembrance of a similar act which Jesus had performed in service to His disciples. I was not unduly impressed, not having attended a church meeting when "feet washing" was done. I continued to covet one of the little washtubs but with a sense of guilt.

It was in this Union Service that Tillie and I became convinced that we were sinners.

Tillie's family consisted of a father and mother, two brothers and an older sister. They lived in a beautiful house overlooking the river. George Tilt was a familiar figure in the village as he strode along, a well-dressed, well-built man who always carried a cane. He used the cane with a swinging motion as if indicating that it really had no purpose except as part of his rather formal attire. He was a cattle dealer and much of his time was spent driving from farm to farm buying and selling. Pauline, Tillie's mother, was a dainty, attractive woman who made me welcome whenever Tillie chose to invite me there for a week-end. Tillie's brothers were young men and Louie, Lill's friend, was a young woman of stylish charm, popular, and with a special attraction for children.

Louie, after a conversion and reception into the Baptist faith, became our Sunday School teacher. We had now graduated from the Infant Class. We were the Sunbeams. Encouraged by Tillie, I began to examine carefully the words of Louie as she sought to guide us in the direction of conversion.

It was an autumn Sunday afternoon when Tillie and I engaged in a whispered conversation after the lesson was over.

"We must become converted," I said.

"Yes," Tillie agreed, "we must, and the sooner the better."

I don't know how Tillie proceeded with her conviction but the seal was upon us both. As I walked home from Sunday School alone, with the sun's rays misty in the October air, I was surely Saul of Tarsus. The voice had spoken.

The house seemed quiet when I entered. Da was in his favourite chair, reading. Mother was writing a letter to Will at the table. My sisters were preparing supper in the kitchen. I went at once to my parents' room which I no longer occupied with them. It was such a secluded small room, with only one west window. I felt sure of privacy here. The beams of the sun were finding the window and reflecting from a mirror on the wall. Without delay I knelt by my parents' bed. I don't know how I couched my dedication but it was sincere. I rose from the bedside and as I did so the setting sun came into direct contact with the window and the mirror. To my eyes the effect was that of a halo.

I had been accepted.

There was a sequel.

"People who are converted must try to save others, Louie says," Tillie confided next morning at school. "A lot of people in this village don't go to church. That means they need saving. What are we going to do about it, Jessie?"

Tillie and I had many discussions about our new responsibility that week. We decided to tackle the problem systematically. We made a list of all the people whose names we knew in the community and we divided the list into two, those saved and those unsaved. Those saved, of course, were represented by the church-goers. This left a very lengthy column of sinners for our considera-tion. We started by examining those in our schoolroom.

"You pick a name and I'll pick a name," Tillie said. "Then we'll write letters. It will be easier to know what to say in a letter and it seems more polite, don't you think?"

I fully agreed, in fact I was relieved, for I felt an embarrass-ment when I thought of approaching anyone in person.

80

Tillie chose a roguish curly-haired boy several years her senior as a likely prospect. He was a favourite in the classroom and never, never attended Sunday School. I chose a studious well-behaved boy of my own age who resided on a farm not far from our own. We had never been friends and at school we were competitors. Sometimes he stood head of the class, sometimes it was I. I do not recall what my letter contained but I placed it upon his desk with an unsteady hand. Nor did Tillie confide in me what words of persuasion she had employed. The important thing was the outcome.

The following day a letter was placed on Tillie's desk. At recess time, huddled in a corner of the school yard, she shared it with me. It said, "If I go skating on Saturday afternoon, the answer is yes. If I don't go, the answer is no."

At thirteen, this young man expressed himself well, and he went skating. So it was that Tillie chalked up one on her list of converts.

Alas for me, I did not receive a reply to my letter and the shy, well-mannered boy whom I had thought to impress refused to face me on the country road. Whenever we came close to meeting, he climbed the fence and crossed the field. I felt dejected and a failure in my efforts as a missionary. Not so Tillie. That week-end, after school on Friday, she announced to me that she was going to drive me home and bring me back to stay with her over Sunday. Tillie's family were not poor like mine and Tillie owned a pony and cart. In a way I owned them too, for we shared them in many of our adventures.

When I spent a week-end with Tillie, most of my detachable possessions went with me – dolls, boxes of dolls' clothing and a carriage, games and writing materials. For it was a common entertainment in the evenings to jointly devise musical dramas which, in sole possession of the big parlour and a real piano, we enacted without interruption from anyone. But on this particular occasion we had a special duty to perform.

"My brother," Tillie confided, "goes to horse races and smokes. I think maybe he likes wine and things like that, I don't really know – but he never, never goes to church. I heard Mama scolding him about it. He is twenty. She said, 'You're not a little boy any longer and I shouldn't have to tell you what to do.' But

Jessie, we're going to have to tell him what to do. I'm pretty sure he's a sinner and he needs converting."

Tillie's brother was charming to look at and very gay but I could not think of him as a sinner. When I visited the family and he was at home, he was thoughtful of us as children and I delighted to hear him laugh and joke merrily during mealtime.

"I could never say anything to him," I told Tillie.

"Then you ain't a Christian," Tillie replied, "for Christians ain't afraid of anybody. Remember the story of the pilgrim that went through the dungeon where dragons chased him?" she persisted.

I was not afraid of dragons. I had met them many times in pages of books and I rather liked them but I was afraid of the challenge which Tillie had placed upon me.

"We could write him a letter," I said hopefully.

"That's the best idea yet," Tillie concurred, "and we can do it tonight, Jessie. Tomorrow is the Guelph Fair and he's going. He gets up about five o'clock to go and we won't be awake then so we won't have to see him. Mother's going to let us sleep together in his bed tonight and he's going to sleep in the single bed next to our room. We'll ask Meta to put the letter on his pillow after we get it finished. He always goes out on Friday night and stays real late. I think he's got a girl. You'll have to write the letter, Jessie, because you're good at things like that. I'll help you. We'll think of something very special to say."

We did. With secret intentions we went to bed early after taking Meta into our confidence. Meta was a maid in the house. She was a willing accomplice. I do not know in what way we began or finished our letter to Tillie's brother but I am sure that it was an outpouring of genuine concern in simple words. I remember only one phrase, of which I was inordinately proud:

"Our hearts bleed," I wrote in firm resolve to Tillie's brother.

We slept that night convinced of achievement and of purity of purpose. Surely Tillie could never say again that I was not a Christian.

It was five o'clock the following morning when we were wakened by stirrings in the next room – Tillie's brother dressing to go to the Fair. Tillie put her arms around me. She whispered, "Jessie, Jessie, wake up. He's leaving. He must have got the letter. Oh, isn't it exciting?"

Tillie's brother had forgotten his tie. He had left it hanging on the mirror of his dresser – the dresser in our room. When a hand touched the doorknob, Tillie and I feigned the deepest sleep. There was a tiptoeing from door to dresser and back again. We looked through our eyelashes, aided by a ray of light falling through the opening from the hall. At the foot of our bed, with a broad grin on his face and a twinkle in his eyes, stood Tillie's brother.

Aware that we were awake but saying not a word, he reached with each hand for one of our big toes under the covers. He shook them heartily and went out.

It was difficult to decide whether we had succeeded or failed but we favoured the former belief and sighed happily as we snuggled down to sleep again.

In the full examination of the event later that day I pondered Tillie's encouraging words, "You see, Jessie, he wasn't mad, he was happy. That means you – I mean we did, that's half for you and one-and-a-half for me. He liked being saved, Jessie, you could tell by the way he smiled, couldn't you?"

I didn't answer Tillie, for that mischievous smile troubled me. It was not my impression of the happiness expected from a sinner redeemed. I did not confide in Tillie the fact that I continued to pray for the salvation of her brother. But there were so many to pray for, I stopped naming them finally and turned my attention to considering my own waywardness. Despite conversion I was still a sinner.

Ah me!

Following the week of evangelistic services in the little white church, the baptism of eighteen converts took place by immersion in the lovely Grand River.

Arrangements for this solemn event engaged the attention of the entire village. Those not participating would be onlookers of two minds – the reverent and the scornful. Of whatever opinion, those present would restrain their feelings.

Tillie and I were not permitted to attend. My mother was opposed to sensationalism in religious practices, and "Children can't understand properly," she said. She added that some might think it an amusing affair, which would be "shameful."

It was my sister Lill who went with Louie on that Sunday afternoon, following a pathway extending from the road across the flats to a small wooded area where a dozen or so trees higher up the bank gave shade for picnickers. Here those not participating took their position.

In white robes under a clear blue sky and a smiling sun the converts marched to the riverside along the west bank, led by the evangelist, a man of slight stature. Among them were the young and the mature. A woman of middle age with greying hair stood slightly apart from them, leading the singing. First there was the solemn command,

Rescue the perishing, care for the dying,
Save them in pity from sin and the grave.

The minister took his place before the waiting line, turning to face them when at knee depth in the water.

One after the other they answered the motion of his hand and joined him, and after their immersion he led them back to the shore line. The singing went on, and as the final baptism was taking place it was followed by the lilting and triumphant promise:

Sowing in the morning, sowing seeds of kindness,
Sowing in the noon-tide and the dewy eve,
. . . . . .
We shall come rejoicing, bringing in the sheaves.

At our supper table that night, it was Lill who told the story of that day.

All had gone well and the mood of everyone was that of reverent participation until something happened which no one had foreseen.

Among the converts was a woman of unusual build, heavily overweight. The slim young man whose earnest preachings had brought about a turning point in the lives of many undertook a physical effort which brought about disaster. The woman, weighing well over two hundred pounds, was too cumbersome for his hold. While the singers raised their voices in praise, two figures disappeared below the surface of the water. The singing stopped and there were cries of terror but the water was shallow with a firm bottom. The minister and his convert regained their foothold and rose above the surface unharmed.

"Don't laugh, Lill," Mother said, when the story was finished and my sister was carried away by mirth.

"I can't help it, Mother," Lill protested. "It was the funniest thing I ever saw in my life. You were right to keep Jessie at home. It was no place for children."

84

IX

An Imaginary World

And as imagination bodies forth
The forms of things unknown, the poet's pen
Turns them to shapes ...

William Shakespeare

The lawn before our house was bordered on three sides by a decorative wire fence. There was a gateway beside the house and four steps leading down to the level of the road. The house faced south and on the west side it was shaded by an immense elm tree just beyond the fence under which was a stone building about twelve feet square. At one time there had been concrete troughs within the building and a steady flow of cool spring water keeping them at a proper temperature for the immersed covered tins of milk. From this use the small house had acquired the name "The Milk House." The building had lost its usefulness when the advent of the cream separator had provided a means of withdrawing the cream from the milk. The latter was then used in plentiful supply for mixing with various chopped grains as food for livestock. Calves were fed whole milk, of course, and some of this was saved for table use and for cooking. When I was a child, separators were common to most farm homes and my father had purchased a large wooden ice-box or refrigerator. The ice supply was contracted for from an enormous ice storage plant built beside a dam in the village. When the temperature was at its lowest point the water of the dam was sometimes frozen to a depth of two or three feet. By means of powerful saws it was cut into huge blocks and removed to be stored in thick layers of sawdust in an ice house.

We too had an ice house in which each winter with the same insulation a supply of ice was purchased to be used in our refrigerator. How amazing it was in those days to be able to acquire small pieces of this frozen treasure while our men chiselled it to the proper size for use. Brushing specks of sawdust aside, it was thrilling to pop the portions from finger to mouth, in and out, until the tongue and the roof of the mouth became accustomed to the frosty treat. I am not sure but I think that we were the only family with provision for ice storage in our community. It was an exciting day when our men with large wagon sleighs drove in line up our hill and through the driveway toward the barn near which the ice house waited. From the window of The Room I watched the great tongs clasp and lift through the open door of the building huge blocks which men inside placed in orderly layers, with packing between.

The little stone house was no longer needed, for the refrigerator was built in an extension to our kitchen on the west side of the main house. There were steps leading from this extension into a carriage house which protected the ice-box from the direct rays of the sun.

I took over the little stone house as a dwelling place for the Hafer family.

I am not sure when Alice Hafer with her mother and father, brother Tom aged twenty-one, Nellie eighteen, and Mary not yet a year old, came to live under the elm tree but to me their existence was as real as my own. It was fitting to my need for variety in experience that Mrs. Hafer should be a Christian woman while Mr. Hafer was an infidel; Tom was an intelligent hard-working young man while Nellie was a frivolous, dangerously gay teen-ager. It suited my requirements that Mary could be represented by my favourite doll, an Eaton Beauty which had sat beside my first Christmas tree looking so faultless that for some time I had difficulty in establishing any relationship with her whatsoever. I preferred my kid-bodied worn "Daisy" with hair which I could wash and braid in pigtails and eyes slightly crossed because replaced with packing by my sister Jean after Tillie in a fit of temper tossed Daisy over the veranda railing onto the hardened path in front of our house.

I believe that I was scarcely six years old when Alice, of similar age, entered my life. So real did she become that I confided her existence to my aunt-by-marriage Elizabeth, a cripple for twenty years, who visited us frequently. Sitting in a small rocker by her wheelchair I recall telling her in the deepest confidence the trials and errors of the Hafer family. Aunt Elizabeth's interest was consistent, so much so that on my birthdays and at Christmas I received two gifts, one for me and one for Alice Hafer.

When I started to school, Alice became conveniently unable to accompany me beyond the crossroads where I was joined by other children. She had acquired maturity and left me each school day to take over the duties of a private secretary in some imaginary position of importance. Her hours of work were so arranged that when I returned from school and my companions left me at the turning of the road she walked on with me to her home under the elm tree.

I was never lonely. Each new interest which entered my life at school I was able to discuss with Alice, until the time came when the images of Alice and her family were no more.

I had a new companion whose personality, contrasting sharply with my own, took her place. Tillie and I became bosom friends and together we created a new world of the imagination which in delightful companionship we shared for many years.

It was a wonderful new world which we found between the covers of books. There was first of all the Sunday School library with its saccharine and incredible stories of vice and virtue, the former punished by suitable disasters and the latter winning excessive rewards. We stepped from this collection into an enlightening choice of stories and poetry where we met and reflected upon an entirely new set of values. An enterprising young teacher at our public school, H. L. Smith, had bought for the use of his pupils a collection, suited to their various ages, of what might be called the classics. It was a never-to-be-forgotten day when a glass-fronted bookcase was set in the corner of our schoolroom. It had two sliding doors. The teacher held the key but one could marvel and make a choice through the glass. Books were loaned for a period of one week, and by this gesture of understanding a young man will be honoured in memory by many of those with whom he shared this treasure.

Every book in that collection was read and re-read by me,

from the fairy tales of Hans Christian Andersen, Grimm and Hawthorne to the works of Dickens, Thackeray and Scott, from the magic stories of *The Water Babies* and Maurice Maeterlinck's *Blue Bird* to Shakespeare and the Romantic Poets.

But while we developed our minds through this more classic channel of intellectuality, while the characters of Oliver Twist, Sydney Carton, the Knights of King Arthur and the Kings and Queens of the world's monarchies became so real that we half expected to meet them in our roamings through woodlands and unfamiliar places, we did not desert Elsie Dinsmore. However, it was when reading E. P. Roe's *Barriers Burned Away* that we adopted an almost day-to-day dramatic career. In Tillie's garden was a latticed summer house. Its sides wore an alluring wealth of grape-vines bearing fruit which we were permitted to enjoy, but it was the flat rooftop of about twelve by fifteen feet which became the centre for our imaginings. To clamber up was simple enough by means of the criss-crossing laths. Once atop the house we became actor and actress, sharing the honours of both sexes according to the nature and requirements of the play to be enacted. Tillie favoured the female role, which secretly annoyed me because I, too, should have enjoyed a suitor kneeling before me and pleadingly seeking my heart and hand. Nevertheless it was something for a child in delicate health to be assigned the part of an angry father, unchristian of course, faced by the loss of papers of fortune, while his weeping daughter in her sister's negligee pleaded with him not to enter a mansion tottering to its destruction under earthquake and fire.

Grasping the sturdy cane of Tillie's father, I shook it in the face of Heaven's decree and shouted in as masculine a voice as I could command, "I shall have certain documents though the heavens fall." Then, releasing myself from my daughter's trembling hold, I stumbled into the crumbling doorway and fell, of course, a victim of my own sinfulness.

I had the satisfaction of hearing Tillie say, "That was swell, Jessie," as I fell. She paid not the slightest attention to the fact that my nose in colliding with the floor of the stage had begun to bleed. As I applied my handkerchief and rose to my feet, she merely patted me on the shoulder, predicting, "You'll be an actress some day."

Probably the most dramatic experience in my life as an actress at ten was the undertaking of a sentimental scene from a love story which I had read secretly in my sister's magazine, the *Ladies' Home Journal*. A royal prince had fallen in love with a beautiful girl, but she was a commoner. There had been a morganatic marriage, and the birth of a child.

It was the word morganatic that fascinated me, as well as the unusual nature of the plot. The next day at school I confided my discovery when Tillie and I were sitting under a maple tree eating apples at recess.

"The mother died," I said, "when the little girl was three years old, but the father didn't want another Princess for a wife. The mother really had been a Princess, you know, in his mind; and of course, because the father was a Prince, the little girl was really a Princess. She was beautiful too and she looked like her grandmother, the Queen. The Prince was a scared man. His mother made him that way and now he was scareder than ever of her. He gave the child away to gipsies. I don't know what happened after that because it was a to-be-continued story and I couldn't find the next magazine. It was such a grown-up story, I knew if I asked Jean for it she wouldn't give it to me. But we could make up what we think must have happened and then I will be the Prince if you like and you can be the Mother."

"But what about the little girl?" Tillie wanted to know. "We can't take anybody else up the summer house. It's too small. They might fall off."

"We don't have to go up the summer house," I said, "we can play at recess and noon hour and I know somebody to choose for the little girl."

"Who, silly?" my companion wanted to know.

A new girl had come to school a few days before. She was five and very pretty, with large velvet brown eyes and a velvet dress to match. She had long golden curls. Her name was Vera.

"I know who," I said confidently, "and she won't have to do anything. We can do the pretending."

Under the trees of the school yard as Prince and Princess we gave Vera every attention. We told her stories, we took her walking. With a dainty comb provided by Tillie we curled her lovely hair. I saved her the piece of cake from my dinner pail and Tillie brought her an all-day sucker. But somehow or other the addition of someone else to our world of make-believe dulled the charm of play-acting. After three days the morganatic marriage came to an end, but the word repeated itself in my memory for a very long time like a mysterious whisper.

We went from one extreme to the other. Sometimes we were the Babes in the Wood, in fear of destruction by our imaginary captors. Sometimes we were devout leaders of a missionary movement among the natives of distant Africa. Neither of us enjoyed taking the role of the male, but Tillie was the stronger of will and I succumbed more often than she.

Perhaps the most absorbing period was our enactment of "Ceres and Persephone." This tale we shared in producing during school recesses. We chose a worn spot in the sod of the playground for the arrival of the wicked king who had stolen Persephone, driving his black steeds out of the bowels of the earth. After reading the story countless times with delight and awe, we had only to blink our eyes and there before them was the chariot of the king with its evil black steeds. Alternately Tillie and I played the part of Persephone who ran searching through the playground for her mother. It happened that a large shrub grew close to the area from which the king emerged, so true to the text of the tale. We never tired of producing this absorbing myth and it was easy to believe ourselves, especially in springtime, capable of bringing to pass the revival of natural life on the surface of the earth.

"When I have a baby," Tillie confided to me, "I'm going to call her Persephone. But I told Louie and she says there are two ways that she was named. The other way was Proserpina. Sometimes I think I like that name better. What do you think?"

"Persephone is like singing," I said, "Proserpina is like talking. I like singing best."

Every year in springtime, our Union Sunday School in the village was visited by a sober-looking man who represented what was called the Canadian Bible Society. We listened in awed attention to the stories he told about the parts of the world where the heathen lived and where savagery was practised. Our part of the world seemed very small and fearfully obligated as we listened to him. Those who were "heathen," of course, did not believe in our God and for that matter, many did not know of His existence. There would be no heaven for them, only a horrifying place mainly occupied by fiery furnaces into which they would be cast. This was God's plan for His world, we were informed, and it was our duty to

90

make known to these condemned sinners the contents of the Holy Scriptures, by means of which they would be saved from the fires of hell. While he talked to us he held a Bible in his hand. By making this Book available to them, he said, we would save our own souls and save them from eternal punishment.

This was a staggering challenge indeed to those of us still engaged in a happy world of childhood pleasures. We were made to feel that we had no right to such a world while "out there," a region left to our imagination, many millions were facing eternal destruction.

At the end of his dissertation, an unsmiling period of probably half an hour, he reminded us of something which had been lying heavy on the hearts of Tillie and myself since our recent conversion – that there were many heathen within the confines of our own country waiting to be saved by us. The way to salvation lay through the covers of the Book which he held. Of course, money was required to print such Books in sufficient quantity to reach around the world. All persons might have a part in bringing this to pass.

This appeal was supported by the Sunday School Superintendent, who announced that there was a need for persons willing to collect from every household if possible, even if only a small sum of money, yet something to add to the contributions required. Who would make themselves available for this undertaking?

Tillie looked at me and I looked at Tillie.

"We could have Jeff and the phaeton," Tillie whispered.

This was true. Jeff was ours for the asking, and when again would we be eligible for such a perfect type of Christian effort? I could see, and I am sure that Tillie could see, the poor naked heathen running about like loose animals in the jungles and deserts, waiting to be saved by us.

We put up our hands.

For the first time a broad smile crossed the face of the man in black. The Superintendent coughed a little. My sister Lill and Tillie's sister Louie were sitting together on the left side of the Sunbeams. He looked at them and Louie looked at Lill inquiringly, then both gave an almost imperceptible nod of the head.

The Superintendent said, "Praise the Lord, we have what we need."

He repeated our names, a little timidly I thought, and added,

Oil painting by Jeanie C. Beattie.
"The road ran through a thinly wooded
sunlit hollow with a wide trickling
stream...." Tillie and I stop for lunch.

"These young ladies have offered themselves to serve this holy cause."

It was settled.

No one questioned our eligibility. No one voiced a doubt that we were capable of what we had offered to do. We were given a month to complete our canvass of the village and the surrounding country communities. The Superintendent presented us with a little black book marked off for names, and there were two columns for contributions received.

"We can do the village after school hours," Tillie said. "The days are getting lighter and lighter, I mean longer. We'll have Saturdays for special times when we can drive Jeff and maybe take our lunch and have a picnic somewhere. I asked Mother and she thinks it's a good idea."

At the end of a week of collecting in the village we had acquired the handsome sum of eight dollars and seventy-five cents, but of course, the village people were closely associated with the Sunday School and very sympathetic to our cause. Calling upon the farming people was a different matter. The sight of two children, ages nine and ten, knocking upon doors and asking for contributions for whatever cause, was not always acceptable to the country residents. However, with few exceptions, our reliability was trusted but the giving was in small silver pieces, and after what seemed a long day, from nine until three, Tillie and I drew Jeff to a halt where the road ran through a thinly wooded sunlit hollow with a wide trickling stream and patches of blue pools here and there ringed around with lush marsh marigolds. We found a dry log near the fence side. We vaulted the fence, leaving Jeff to munch on his bag of oats at the side of the road where Tillie had skilfully tied the reins to a small poplar. Breathing a sigh of relief, we sat down on the softly rotting surface of the log. Our backs were to the sun and we faced the woods and the trickling stream. Neither of us owned a watch and we could only guess the time of day by the location of the sun.

"If we were tramps," Tillie said, "somebody would have asked us in for dinner. I smelled roast chicken at one place. That was when you were holding Jeff and didn't come in with me. The woman there was fat and she had just taken a strawberry pie out of the oven. It was all bubbly. She could have spared us pieces of that."

"But maybe they had a lot of men like we have," I ventured. "Maybe she couldn't spare any."

We opened our lunch boxes.

"Well, anyway," Tillie said, "I got plenty and it's nicer here than in somebody's old kitchen. Mother gave me extra to treat you. She made strawberry tarts for us and I'm sure she's a better cook than the big fatty who didn't give us anything."

I didn't presume to contradict Tillie. It was scarcely my place to do so as she gave me an enormous saucer-sized tart and a juicy orange from her basket. For my delicate digestion Mother had provided bread and butter sandwiches to be eaten with a jar of baked custard. There were, however, the famous cookies for both Tillie and me and a banana for my dessert.

I did not eat the banana but I shall never forget the flavour of that strawberry tart. Perhaps it was the sunshine, perhaps it was the billowy sky above us or the trickling green of the irregular stream not far from our feet, or the marsh marigolds and the wild iris, or the delirious song of a male robin on guard near the nest of his family, or the unusual notes of a wood thrush coming from a thicker woods on the other side of the road – it was just everything contributing to a perfect June day which made life so wonderful in the present that for the time being I forgot about the heathen and the savages.

We lingered there lazily. We did not collect from the houses which we passed by that afternoon after turning Jeff toward home. We were happy children again, believing in a God whose mercy was too great to consign anyone to the tortures of hell fire.

X

A Teacher for a Day

Obedience became a habit
And duty grew from there . . .

The author

I was eleven when our teacher was overtaken by a severe attack of
influenza. His landlady's small son was then in the First Book. As I
approached the school that morning he came running to meet me.

"Teacher's sick," he said, "and he wants to see you."

I was astonished, even slightly alarmed. I was being summoned – for what, I did not know. Had I disregarded an order or
unconsciously performed some act which had called down upon
me his disapproval?

In this state of questioning I took the hand of the small
messenger and walked with him to the boarding house which was
kept by his mother. The latter met me cheerily at the door.

"Come in, Jessie," she said. "Mr. D.'s got the grippe. The
doctor says he's got to stay in bed for a couple of days. He wants to
talk to you. Go right up them stairs. His room's at the top, straight
in."

I went, lagging a little as I approached the top of the stairway,
wondering and swallowing hard. Obedience was a lesson which I
had been well taught before school days and thus far I had not
suffered the reprimand of a teacher. What was coming?

Mr. D. was sitting up in bed with the covers clutched around
him. His face was red, his round dark eyes unnaturally bright.

When he spoke, his voice was little more than a whisper. He motioned to me to come in.

"Thank you for coming, Jessie," he wheezed, "but don't get too close to me. Sit on that chair beside the door."

I sat.

"I have a list here," he said, "of the work for each class to do. I can't come myself but I know that you will write my orders carefully on the blackboard. I have divided the work, starting with the first class. You will have to tell them what they are to do – read it to them, I mean. Instructions for the others you can put on the board and if they have any questions, or don't understand, I am sure you will be able to explain. Tell them that I have asked you to do this, and that I expect them to obey orders. I hope I'll be well enough to come back tomorrow. There should be enough to keep them busy for one day. I'm sure their parents will co-operate."

I do not remember speaking as I took the sheets of paper from Teacher's hand, there was such a swelling of pride and excitement within me.

I went down the stairs, ushered out by the smiling mother of Johnnie. He ran to keep up with me as I hurried along the snowy street and up the hill to the schoolhouse. The husband of the teacher's landlady had unlocked the doors and built the fires early that morning.

In a kind of dream I went into the hallway where pandemonium reigned. The children were all talking at once and chasing each other up and down the aisles of the classroom, which was a forbidden pleasure.

With dignity and a stern expression as one in command I reached for the bell rope and pulled vehemently. Then I proceeded, followed by the gaping children, into the schoolroom and took my place behind the teacher's desk. I waved my hand peremptorily for everyone to be seated. Now it was their turn to obey in amazement.

"I have a message for you," I said. "Teacher is sick but we are to behave the same as if he was here and I will tell you what you have to do."

It may have been my solemnity, my complete belief that I had been given command, which brought about the instant silence as each boy and girl sat staring at me as if at an apparition. A school day began with prayers. When I bowed my head everyone stood beside their desk and solemnly repeated with me the Lord's Prayer. Then everyone sat down again. I gave to the small children verbally the directions which Mr. D. had outlined. Then I turned to the board and began to copy as clearly as I could the instructions which had been prepared for the other classes. When this was accomplished, I faced the orderly classroom and said words which, even as I said them, I found difficult to believe:

"I am to be your teacher for today."

Classes were called by me in the order which was common and I was not questioned. For reading we were required to form a line before the teacher's desk according to our Grades and from right to left we read aloud while the teacher listened. This usual program I found easy to follow. Spelling came next, given from a Spelling Book conveniently divided into columns of words suited to our classes. Questions in Arithmetic I copied from the teacher's notes onto the blackboard.

It did not seem long until the big clock at the back of the room folded its hands together at the number twelve. Most of the children remained in the classroom after claiming their lunch pails and boxes from the freezing atmosphere of the unheated hallway. In recalling that noon hour I remember that the food in my own dinner pail, which I ate alone at the teacher's desk, was not particularly palatable to me. I felt apart and rather uncomfortable. Some of the children had scampered to their village homes and it seemed to me that they scampered back again sooner than usual, eyeing me with an unfriendly curiosity. But when the hands of the clock reached one, at the ringing of the teacher's bell every child took his or her place at the desks and obediently waited for further orders from me. I had come almost to the end of Teacher's directions but a bright idea presented itself. I would tell the entire classroom a story which I had recently read in the *Wonder Book* of Nathaniel Hawthorne, from which book Tillie and I had read of Persephone and the story of Jason and the Golden Fleece. My aunt had given me the book the previous Christmas and I had read it and re-read it until the contents were well known to me. I told the story and followed it with this order:

"Now, you can all write a story of your own."

I did not collect the stories, and as the afternoon dragged on I puzzled how to fill the balance of time, for to dismiss the school before the usual hour would be to disobey my instructions. There was, however, the permitted period for singing which Mr. D. was careful to preserve for Monday and Friday afternoons. This was Monday. On the final note of a newly learned rendition of the Lord's Prayer, it seemed a suitable time had come to end that memorable day.

They were an orderly forty children in the village schoolhouse on that far-off day, with one exception. The only son of a trustee delighted in performing calisthenics during recesses and noon hours. He was six years of age and possessed of not only an active body but a very active mind which in later years won him a high professorship. But on that winter's day under the unfamiliar rule of another child, female and only a few years older than himself, he could not resist challenging her authority. With a terrific bump he rolled from his desk onto the floor and began a series of original gymnastics which bade well to turn the tables for me. It was I who had taken him to school on his first day. We had worn similar small capes with velvet collars made by our friendly mothers from our fathers' discarded overcoats. But such memories bore no significance to him.

Realizing the seriousness of such a challenge to my temporary position, with every eye in the classroom upon me and the teacher's pointer in my hand, I walked down the aisle to where he lay wriggling like an enormous caterpillar, watching me come. What prevented me from using the pointer upon him I can only assume was good judgement on the part of a child. I used it only to direct the attention of the onlookers.

"You will sit in the dunce's chair for this," I said. "Get up and go there this minute."

My eyes must have contained incredible confidence, for he rose and without even a giggle walked to the corner of the room where the dunce's chair was kept. It was a tall chair almost like a high chair and stool combined. I had only once before seen anyone placed in it. As he pulled himself up and faced the gaping pupils, who no doubt had expected a conflict, there was not a sound. I turned and called the Third Class to the front for a Reading Lesson. The poem was "Somebody's Darling" which in a few minutes had conveyed me into the world of dramatic poesy far beyond the touch of anyone in the room.

The day passed without further incident but I did not call the culprit from the dunce's chair. He remained there until the tapping

98

of the bell on the teacher's desk – my desk – and the singing which concluded the most challenging experience of my years at the village school.

Even Tillie had looked at me with some reproof that day as if I had overstepped my authority. I walked home through the gathering drifts of a fresh snowstorm, my face sheltered by a green nun's-veiling scarf to protect it from the bite of the frost, my solemn eyes looking ahead with gratitude that the day was over for me and that the shelter of home and a return to normal was near.

Contrary to expectations, the teacher recovered sufficiently to resume his duties on the following morning.

Many years later, when I had grown to young womanhood and he had become a prominent physician, Herbert Detwiler and I laughed over the story of my one day as teacher while I learned that his intention had been only to provide his pupils with work to be done at home. How careful one should be in the wording of instructions given to a child!

XI

A Feud and a Fire

The love of money is the root of all evil.

Scriptural text

The sun came up that morning with a special brilliance and laid its June beams across the flowing river. June it was, with the air a fragrant pot-pourri and every leaf on every tree bordering the roadway over the hill to school glistening with its own particular beauty. On one side was a hedge of lilacs behind which a row of hardwood – oak, maple and poplar – stood guard. A well-worn path had removed the sod along that side of the roadway, pressed down by the hurrying feet of children on their way to school. On the left before the land dipped down to the flats and the flowing river there were clumps of swamp willow.

I was alone that morning on my way to school. Lydia and Willie had not met me at the corner because Lydia was suffering an attack of measles. My feet did not hurry. I all but stood still when I reached the hill-top. The lure to remain with nature outside the cold brick walls of the schoolroom was upon me as I listened to bird songs from tree and shrub and followed the manoeuvres of a little grass snake keeping pace with me as it wriggled along the wheelway of the road. Then the summons came, drowning out the notes of an oriole balancing upside-down on a branch of wild rose which had somehow crept in to share the hedge with the lilacs.

Ding-dong, ding-dong.

Teacher was pulling the rope of the bell and I took to my heels and ran. I must not be late. To my conscience, being late was a form of disobedience which would bring a sense of guilt.

"Tell me and I won't punish you," my mother had advised us, and there was no excuse that morning for being late because I had started for school earlier than usual.

When I reached the gate, a sight met my eyes such as I had never beheld before. Our school yard had become a battle ground. It almost seemed to me that the number of the pupils was equally divided between the south side and the north side of the yard. Between the assembled armies was a long stretch of green grass with a bare patch at dead centre – the home base for competing ball teams.

But even as I reached the gate, astonished and subconsciously aware of the presence of trouble, the bell stopped tolling and the teacher took his place on the sandy base. No one was actually speaking but there was a rumbling sound of repressed anger from both sides. Some of the older boys were attempting to spit across the open space, and a few small stones were hurled. I went into the deserted hallway and placed my dinner pail on the shelf. I hung my sailor hat on a peg and my school bag with it. Bewildered, I went to the door. Teacher was speaking. His voice was strong and commanding.

"This is the most disgraceful thing that has ever happened here," he was saying. "You should all be thoroughly ashamed. Your behaviour shows me that none of you have said your prayers this morning but we shall repeat the Lord's Prayer now and while you repeat it I want you to remember that you have need to ask forgiveness for this ridiculous behaviour. If such behaviour occurs again you will go home, every one of you suspended for a week. I mean what I say. This is not merely a warning. It is a warning and an order. Take your places in the classroom, but first repeat after me – "

Then he saw me standing mute and not a little frightened in the patch of grass a few feet from him. He put out his hand. The memory of that moment has never left me. The angry mutter which passed through both sides of the divided company changed to silence.

"Our Father which art in Heaven," said the teacher, and it is my belief that every boy and girl recited after him. My own voice

101

was a whisper but the kindly clasp of his hand with the Amen assured me that he had heard it.

That was a day never to be forgotten by any of us. Shortly before, a death had occurred in the community, and in the settling of an estate two families with children at school had been involved. Feelings had run high and had been transferred, unwittingly perhaps, from parents to children. Those who faced each other across the green school yard were the fairly well divided allies of one family or the other.

Lessons proceeded with solemn order that day and it was a subdued assembly of children who left the security of the little school where there had been the firm unfearing condemnation needed to quell an uprising.

I wandered home alone. The sun was falling now toward the west and a soft coolness was creeping up from the valley as I passed by the mill and the mill pond before turning the bend which brought home in view.

I sobbed out the story of that day to my mother who was able to explain something of its cause to me.

"Nobody likes me at school anymore," I said, "nobody but Teacher. Even Tillie was mad at me because I wouldn't take sides. Should I have taken sides?" I wanted to know. "Is it going to be like this all the time? If it is, I don't want to go to school."

"We should only take sides," my mother said, "when we know what is right or what is wrong. You didn't know what it was all about, and if you had known, it was not your quarrel. Never take sides," my mother said, "without knowing why. In a few days the children will forget all about it. You'll see, the teacher was wise and they will remember his words."

Mother was right, but months passed before the children of the two families involved did more than treat each other with civility.

During this period I was coolly accepted as a neutral.

Three events of dramatic significance took place at school during my eleventh year. Two of these affected all of us in attendance there: the feud, and a fire. The third was important to myself alone.

It was September and a hint of change was upon field, shrub and tree. Green still predominated, but the meadow grass was browning with a touch of purple in the hollows. Here and there a

102

leaf of maple was showing red. The harvest had been garnered. It had been bountiful and the barns were filled to capacity with sweet-smelling hay and golden sheaves of grain. In a week or two, threshing would begin.

The weather remained hot and thunderstorms were frequent. This was a time of concern for the farmers of the district because of the danger of spontaneous combustion in overheated mows. A fire after the harvest had been garnered spelled disaster because usually it resulted in a complete loss of profit after a year of industry.

It was mid-afternoon and the sun blazed through the west windows of the schoolhouse with an almost insufferable heat. There had been ten days of wet weather during which time some uncertainty had prevailed as to the advisability of "taking in the grain" even after a few days of clear skies and a drying wind. Fearing a second period of saturation the farmers had taken advantage of the sunny days to bring in the late grain crops. "Too anxious is too soon," as my father often said. During the following two weeks three barns within a range of two miles burned to the ground.

One of the senior pupils was reading from the Fourth Reader. The selection was a poem of Archibald Lampman's entitled "Heat." I was not yet in the Fourth Book but the poem was loved by me:

> From plains that reel to southward dim,
> The road runs by me white and bare;
> Up the steep hill it seems to swim
> Beyond, and melt into the glare.

The sound of the reader's voice, to which I had been listening with pleasure, was suddenly drowned out by the rumble of heavy machinery up the school hill. There was a moment of hesitance before the teacher said: "School is dismissed, but don't leave the yard."

Flinging the doors wide, we ran out to see a great fire-engine, with attached wagons containing ladders, pails and other equipment, climbing and passing westward along the road. It was followed by a wagon bearing many firemen with rubber capes and helmets. All too soon the procession passed out of sight down the other side of the hill and the dong of the bell called us back into the classroom. We all knew the meaning of what was happening. Somewhere behind the bend in the road, where we could not see, an entire harvest, perhaps livestock and other valuables were being consumed by flames.

The news of the fire spread quickly. By the time I reached home my father and my two brothers had joined the firemen in a hopeless effort to save not only the barn but the house of a neighbour half a mile southward. Standing on our veranda with my mother and sisters, I watched the continuing rise of thick black smoke over the edge of a distant hill. The air smelled of burning grain and wood. It was late that night when my father came home. There had been no loss of human life, he told us, but several animals had perished.

We gathered in The Room to sip hot chocolate and hear the frightening story. Everything possible had been done to save the house, my father said. Blankets soaked in water were spread over the roof, and when the water supply ran low the neighbours brought pails from their wells and dashed the contents against a clapboard shed on one side where heavy sparks had come to rest. There had been an attempt to remove furniture before the flames licked through the blankets, but the wind had joined in to make it a losing battle for the farmer's family.

Nothing was saved but a cow and calf that had been let out for exercise in the yard and two Buff Orpington chickens, pets of the farmer's small son who held them protectively in his arms all during the holocaust. Neighbours offered beds for the night and shelter until plans could be made for rebuilding.

I did not sleep well that night. The air was rank with drifting sparks, ashes now but smelling strongly of the destruction. The wind was unrelenting and fragments of ash lay on our veranda roof below my window. Would one of them suddenly become a small tongue of flame? This I feared and dreamed.

But for me, out of the ashes of the fire, a happier dream was to be realized.

It was the morning after the fire – Friday – and "Composition Day" at school. Mr. D. had been our teacher for more than a year, but never once had he assigned to our class a subject for an essay or story which had stirred my imagination.

Today was to be different.

"Today," he said, "I want all of you in the second, third, and fourth classes to write the story of a fire. Not necessarily the fire which took place in Dumfries yesterday but any fire which you have heard about, read about, or better still, that you imagine. Imagination is a useful thing, you know. It can protect us from disaster, save us in the midst of disaster or, more important still, it can prevent disaster from happening."

Mr. D. continued with his explanation, even consulting the enormous dictionary which reposed on a slanting table near his desk to read aloud for us the exact meaning of the word.

But to this I did not listen. Pencil poised on a page of my scribbler, I was already at work.

It was Mr. D.'s regular routine to assign the subject on Friday and to allow us the week-end in which to complete the assignment. The scribblers would be collected by him after prayers on Monday morning. The day of their return to us would depend upon the amount of time available to him for reading what we had written.

The devastation which had occurred in our community on the previous day was fully made use of by me. As well, it was extravagantly embroidered by dramatic detail. Two children had been rescued unconscious from the burning house, a pony had pawed its way to freedom from a locked stall, a small boy had entered the flaming barn loft to rescue a nesting pet bantam and her brood of newly hatched chicks. A dangerous criminal hiding and half-asleep had been carried to freedom and, acknowledging his identity, had turned out to be an early lover of the farmer's wife, through whose pleading he was allowed to go free. Crime, romance and violence were there when with a great sense of achievement I handed my composition scribbler to Mr. D. on Monday morning. Eleven closely written pages, and but for the time limit I should have made it more.

That I had written a story of eleven pages was not surprising to me. Ever since writing had become possible for me through the kindly guidance of my elder brother Will, I had been writing stories and verses but no one else had seen them. Each time Aunt Elizabeth visited us she gave me a dollar when she left, with these words:

"Now Jessie, I want you to spend this on anything you would like to have."

As early as I can remember, I spent her dollars on scribblers and pencils. Even before I could read and write I filled hundreds of blank pages with illegible words. Only in my mind did they have meaning. Therefore when Mr. D. paused at my desk as he returned my composition book to me, when he looked deeply into my eyes and said, "Jessie, this is a remarkable story. I believe that some day you may become a writer," I replied unashamedly:

"I am going to."

For a minute he hesitated, then he continued.

"You must keep on learning how to put your thoughts into words," he said. "You must think sometimes without talking about it to anyone. When you have ideas or feelings that you want to tell someone or that you don't want to tell anyone, put them in your diary. You keep a diary, don't you?"

I nodded. The previous Christmas an older cousin who was a school teacher had sent me my first diary and I had written in it faithfully each night. Sometimes the writing had sprawled over from the space allotted, to a length of two or three pages. I had merely changed the dating and gone on as before. Yes, it failed to surprise me when Mr. D. spoke as he did, but my reply had surprised him and I left the schoolroom that night feeling a sense of humiliation. I had boasted.

XII

Pets as Friends

I found a kinship with each living thing.

The author

From my earliest years I was encouraged to have pets. A farmer with a flock of a hundred and fifty sheep, at least fifty of them ewes old enough to breed, was certain of at least one motherless lamb every spring or at least one for adoption if a ewe failed to have enough milk for triplets. This lamb became mine. My father would buy it back from me in the fall when the flock was housed in pens for the winter, the best rams and the ewes together and the others to be specially fed for fattening.

It was probably owing to my father's desire not to hurt me that a pet lamb of mine was never placed with the fatteners. After a few weeks in the large protective pen with only occasional visits from me, it adjusted well. At first it would leave the others, pushing its way to me for attention. But with time it didn't do this, yet I could identify it because it would shake its head as if tossing off ticks and give a short plaintive bleat as I leaned over the wooden fencing by the entrance.

"Don't make too much of it now that you can't keep it near you," Da said. "Remember the three little pigs? When they were big enough to look after themselves, their mother sent them off on their own."

I obeyed him rather sadly. Whenever I went to the barn in winter, I avoided looking over the pen wall where my lamb was housed, but unfailingly I trained my eye to a crack in the boards of the wall. Pets were like people, I learned. They differed in their degree of attachment. The habit of raising a pet lamb by bottle-feeding was discontinued when I was ten. The orphan or triplet was merely transferred to another mother who had lost one or both of her offspring at birth. That final year of pet-lamb-raising by me was harder to bear than any when the parting came, for this little ewe had been permitted to enter the house and tumble up the stairs to my bedroom when I was ill. After allowing me to cuddle it, nuzzling its nose with delicate licks into my hand, it would leap down and lie still like a puppy on the bedside mat, with little bleats when I talked to it. It was never ill-mannered in the house.

We were such friends. It was really too small for lamb-breeding but my father kept it even so for that purpose, because I was ill in bed most of that fall and winter. Once in a while he would carry it up to see me. It would bleat its pleasure as they came up the stairs and in spring at lambing time, a miniature of itself was born. I was able to return to school after Easter, and one day when I came home my pet lamb was waiting for me at the gate of the pasture west of the old house. She was standing with her pretty face against the gate, wagging her tail and bleating for my attention on shaky legs. The newly born stood nuzzling her for the milk of which she proved to have a rich and plentiful supply despite her small size. Half laughing and half crying I hurried to open the gate and to put my arms around her.

Ellen Walker, the wife of my father's cousin Joe, raised peacocks and turkeys. The Walker farm was on Sprague's Road about three miles away. One lovely summer evening my parents took me with them to visit the cousins. The sun was setting with that rare opal afterglow which is called a watermelon sky – filmy wands of pinky rose on a startling greenish-blue background. The colours glorified the whole expanse of the sky, west, south and east, with even a hint on the north horizon.

We were travelling east. The farm was on the south side with a deep lawn and a windbreak of pines bordering the lane.

Ellen was a very tall thin woman with a pale face, her blond hair sparse and drawn back. She had eyes so friendly and so blue, her smile was so free, that I felt at ease at once.

"Well, well, well," she said as Mother and I met her on her

way to greet us while Joe showed Da where to tether Nell. "Come and see my peacocks."

As we went she picked up a feather from the floor of the lane, which was brown with pine needles, and handed it to me.

I had never seen a peacock feather before and the beauty held me speechless. Then I saw them, the birds themselves, dignified, quiet, while the "gobble gobble" of turkeys disturbed by strangers led us on to their fenced yard. I went home with two of their eggs, and one that Ellen said was laid by a peacock.

"Put them under a setting hen, Jessie," she directed me. "In a few weeks you'll have little turkeys and maybe a fluffy peacock."

Mother entrusted the three eggs to a clucker with seven other eggs, but she pushed them away from her warm body. In three weeks she walked proudly through the farmyard with a brood of fine young Buff Orpingtons but the three alien eggs lay rejected in the abandoned nest.

I kept the peacock feather for a long time and Jean tried to carve the root into a pen for me. But I laid the tufted feather in a drawer of Mother's bureau, allotted to me. I rescued the three unhatched eggs and laid them beside it but one day during fall housecleaning they disappeared.

I did not ask about them. The feather was still there but I did not often look at it. I was saddened by the whole incident. The clucking hen had raised her chickens and begun to lay again, but a prowling sly fox got her one autumn night while she slept outside. She insisted on sleeping outside although there was plenty of room on the roosts.

I had never forgiven her for rejecting those not of her feather. According to my religious teachings we might expect retaliation if we were unkind to others.

I was sure that the fox had been sent by God to punish the discriminating hen.

A week later, Cousin Joe arrived. He drove his team into the free space near the barn where the threshers always took up their position. He came to the house carefully carrying a big cardboard box with a few round holes in it.

I was brushing Teve on the veranda but Teve didn't bark. He knew Cousin Joe and wagged his tail.

"Good morning, Jessie," said Cousin Joe. "Here's something for you. Ellen was sorry that damned old hen wouldn't hatch the eggs for you. Better keep these little fellows under your eye for a while when they ain't under cover, or they might run away. They move fast, disappear like lightning, but once they get tame they make good pets."

Cousin Joe left me with the box and went off to visit my father who was repairing a fence beside the barn.

I don't remember thanking Cousin Joe; after all it was Cousin Ellen anyway, wasn't it? I undid the string and opened the box. Huddled in one corner were two brown and beige striped chicks so small that I thought there was only one until they drew apart and looked fearingly up at me with bright dark eyes.

Mother came out in answer to my excited call.

"Baby bantams," she said. "How nice of Ellen. Da will make a house for them and you can keep them in the carriage shed where you can look after them."

In a few weeks Christina and Richard (Teanie and Dickie for short) had the run of the lawn and adjoining yard where my father set the coop for them. At night they were protected from the claws of prowling animals by removal to the shed.

I was ill and a cot was placed on the veranda for me. My new pets were never far away. Often they flew onto my bed and cuddled into my hands. When I was well enough to play under the russet and St. Lawrence apple trees in the outer yard bordering the main orchard, they perched on my shoulders, flying up and down at will.

One afternoon when I was playing on my swing, which was under the roof of the veranda, my mother came to the door of the kitchen. I had taken a loosely knit bedspread from the cot and had draped it over my head. A bird cooed from each side.

"Whatever are you doing, Jessie?" Mother asked. "It's time for your glass of milk."

"Sh," I whispered, not moving, and my pets silenced their gentle twittering.

"Jessie," Mother ordered, "come and get your milk, dear. It's hot. You'll smother under that thing."

How was she to know that I was an Egyptian Princess in a harem with two cooing doves?

Regretfully I emerged. Teanie and Dickie got down obediently to follow me into the kitchen. They were welcome, for – as in the case of my pet lamb – they never at any time had forgotten their manners.

110

Teanie was close behind me. She hopped up the step with me and I thought Dickie was with her. But he moved more slowly. I released the door, which had a strong self-closing spring.

Death was instantaneous for Dickie and I shall never forget the sorrow of that day.

Tillie came up to see me after school and her presence somehow helped to assuage my grief.

"We'll have a funeral," she said dramatically.

We did have a funeral. We lined a candy box with pink and white balsam flowers, and we used a lace cape belonging to one of my dolls for Dickie's shroud. With Tillie as master of ceremonies, Dickie was buried in a small grassy plot under the Duchess apple tree. We marked his grave with a ring of small stones and carved his name on a piece of lath discarded by the carpenters who were repairing the summer house at Tillie's home.

The next spring my father bought a new companion for Teanie – a dashing young male bantam with the most attractive variation of colours in his feathers that I have ever seen. I chose no name for this replacement of my beloved Dickie but this did not affect his adjustment to his new surroundings. One day Teanie arrived on the doorstep with five newly hatched babies. It did not occur to me that the handsome stranger had been responsible, and I continued to treat him with a certain amount of reserve.

As a family we gathered a number of unusual pets, among them a lone baby chipmunk, the only survivor after starvation had stolen the lives of three brothers and sisters. The mother had been killed by a weasel. My mother lined a small Indian basket with cotton wool for Chippie, who was fed with an eyedropper until he opened his eyes and was ready for solid food. He was very tame and one of his favourite occupations was to whirl around my mother's finger like a small wheel on a pivot, stopping once in a while to nibble the tip of it but never to bite. Chippie outgrew us, however, and chose as his home the wooded slope behind our house. He paid us frequent visits, never refusing to stay for a meal of nut-meats or oatmeal cake.

Timidity prevented me from making friends with a crow which my brother Al brought home from the fields. One wing had been damaged by the shot of a hunter. The wound would heal, my father said after careful examination, but it would take a long time. Al built a wire pen for his pet in an empty hay loft of the barn.

111

Sometimes he brought the crow, which he called Happy, to visit us in the house. I kept my distance but I listened, for without altering the bird's tongue as some have done, Al taught Happy to speak and even to attempt to follow a tune. Al would play a simple melody on the violin while Happy sat on his knee watching every move of the bow. He would not sing unless Al carried the tune for him. One day he laughed, and so merrily that I was never afraid of him again. When the wing was healed and the spring came back to call all things to their native haunts, Happy flapped his now strong wings and flew cawing over the green meadows to join others of his kind in a newly planted cornfield.

"He'll never come back again," my father said, "we can't expect it."

My brother Al's face was sober as they stood on the veranda, watching.

"He'll come back again," Al said, "he won't forget."

Perhaps he did not forget, but my father's words were true.

The vegetable garden, which included an acre of tomatoes on a sandy hill, presented problems although it was a profitable enterprise. The tomato worm or caterpillar demanded quick removal when it appeared, for the plants could be stripped of foliage in a few days. It required sharp young eyes to find the creature, which resembled so closely the green stems of the plants. My father usually posted a sign at the village store and explained the equipment needed. Eager to earn the five cents per worm offered, the schoolboys arrived with pails and Da provided them with thin spatula-shaped wooden sticks with which they tapped the stems of the plant on which the worm was feeding, holding the pail in a manner to catch it when, unprepared, it lost its hold.

One afternoon before the fruit had begun to ripen, Mother sent me to fetch enough green tomatoes to use as a vegetable for supper. Sliced, rolled in bread crumbs and fried in sweet butter, they were a favourite dish with us when used as a second vegetable.

The day was Saturday and schoolboys from the village had been picking worms all afternoon. They had done a good job, my father said, but when I asked him what they had done with the catch, he hesitated and looked at Mother before replying. Then, "I sent them to the far field with them," he said. "It's heavy with mulleins that need stripping. They won't starve, that's certain," he ended a little grimly.

I did not further question this method of disposal but I wondered about it. My father loved animals and birds, but did his mercy include all forms of life? Of course I was old enough to realize that crops must be protected.

But when I went at mother's bidding to the tomato patch and found an escapee wriggling in between two rows of plants, half buried in sand, how could I leave him, the sole survivor of an attack, to a life of lonely fearing for existence?

I loved most creations of nature but worms were not included. However, I had to admit that he was a beautiful specimen of his kind.

He seemed to sense my pity. As I left the row I turned for a last look. He was following me. I ran home.

I was breathless when I arrived there.

"What's wrong, Jessie?" Mother asked. "You didn't need to hurry. These only take a few minutes to cook and it's only twenty to. The men won't be in till six."

"It was the worm," I said. "The boys lost him. He was in the sand and I think he wanted me to look after him."

My brother Al had been mowing hay east of the road behind the garden. He had finished mowing and was early in for supper. Al was a sober young man with surely a grievance unexpressed, for although he had a keen sense of humour and was fond of dry jokes, he rarely smiled and I had never heard him laugh. If provoked to laughter he had the habit of putting a hand over his mouth.

Al was washing for supper at the sink basin.

"You watch out," Al said with a wink at Jean but a solemn shake of the head to me, "he'll find you."

I didn't believe my brother but after supper as he left for chores at the barn, he called me from The Room where I was reading a book from the Sunday School library, *St. Elmo* by Augusta Evans Wilson. I was deeply interested in the book because the hero was so worldly. Wicked characters were always more interesting.

Al was standing by the kitchen door. On the upper panel of the screen, firmly attached through the minute gaps by his many tiny feet, was my lonely friend.

I began to cry.

"You won't send him to the far field, will you Da?"

My father looked at my mother and mother nodded.

113

"No, we won't send him anywhere," my father promised. "There's a big cardboard box in the shed that the motor for the ram came in. We'll put it beside the back steps, but you must not forget to feed and water him every day. We'll put some grass in the bottom and a few branches of green stuff for him to fasten on. Leave him where he is till I get it ready."

Before going to bed that night I watched my father tickle the worm with a grass stem through the screen, holding a piece of broken flower-pot into which it fell. It was then transferred to the new home which my father had prepared. I named my strange pet "Charlie." I was faithful in my attentions, and he seemed quite happy. But one morning when I went to feed him a branch of aster and a twig that had been broken by the wind from a climbing rose, I found the box empty.

I went to school with an unhappy heart. No one could find a reason for Charlie's disappearance except my mother.

"I saw the white Rock hen sunning herself on the path yesterday," she said. "Maybe she flew onto the box and saw him. Maybe not, though. He could have crawled away. It's about cocoon time."

I knew what she meant by cocoon time for we had lessons in nature study at school.

"What kind of cocoon would Charlie make?" I asked.

"A pretty big one," Da said, "for he's a good fat worm, but I don't see any sign. Besides, it's rather early for him to make ready for the winter."

But that is exactly what Charlie had done. It was Jean who drew my attention to the cone-shaped object firmly fastened to one of the veranda rafters.

I could hardly wait until the spring. I really missed Charlie. But I knew that a wonderful transformation was taking place, all unseen by me.

It was the first week of May and a sunny warm day for that time of year. I opened the kitchen door on my way to school. The storms had been changed for screens and there, clinging to the screen with soft velvety feet, with a five-inch spread of wings, was the most beautiful moth I had ever seen.

"You see," said my father, "Charlie came back to thank you."

But as I went to open the screen he fluttered out and away into the sunshine.

114

XIII

Winter Celebrations

Ca' the ewes tae the noes,
Ca' them where the heather grows
Ca' them where the burnie flows
My bonnie dearie.

Robert Burns

Grandfather Fleming was not the only one to remind us as children that we were of Scottish ancestry.

Every year when the January snows were hardened under the passing of the sleighs along the country roadways, when February was just around the corner, Da brought home a sheep's stomach from the butcher's in town and Mother got out her cookery scrubbing-brush and washboard. After the scrubbing was thoroughly done, the stomach was washed in clear warm water and put to steep overnight in cold brine. In the morning it was transferred to clear cold water, carefully dried and then filled with the famous haggis mixture. The process of cooking was long and gentle. The birthday of Robert Burns was celebrated by a genuine haggis and the entertaining to dinner of two Scottish families in our community – the Kings and the Olivers.

It seems to me that everyone in our household planned some contribution to that event. Mother prepared the haggis, Jean the currant scones and the Scotch pasties, Lill organized a program for the evening. Of course Grandpa prepared to render his favourite songs, practising them with one finger holding down a key to mark

The Olivers. Jimmie was the fiddler.
1902.

the chord on the organ. Al got down his violin and tested the strings. He added a fresh coating of resin to the bow. My brother Will was no longer with us. The Kings did not wear costume for the occasion but the Olivers did, Jimmie donning the kilt, Mrs. Oliver with a broad band of plaid ribbon as the collar of her dress tied in a flaring bow at the front, and Mary, their pretty daughter, with her dark hair arranged in a pompadour decorated by sprigs of purple and white heather at the crown. My sisters devised costumes to represent the characters in "When ye gang awa', Jamie," becoming Jamie and Jeanie and changing to fisher-folk dress for the rendition of "Wha'll buy my caller herrin'?" I had a plaid dress of Royal Stewart tartan made by Jean, and my curls were tied with a matching ribbon.

No one present possessed a set of the bagpipes, therefore Jimmie played the haggis in on my brother's violin. The haggis was plump and elegant on Mother's ironstone platter with its bevelled row of Scotch thistles.

By such simple celebrations the people of Scottish ancestry remembered the past.

After the organ became a part of our home furnishings, Grandfather Fleming was often found sitting alone before it in the cold little parlour where fires were not kept on in winter except when company was expected. More than any of us, Grandpa mourned the past, having so early lost contact with other members of his family. Often, with my brother Al's violin under his chin, he sawed away on such tunes as the Highland Fling and the Burns Ballads. The expression in his eyes was of far-away things and although he was not a man to show emotion easily, those eyes were sometimes moist.

It did not really matter what the weather. On Burns' night, as we called the occasion, all who were invited arrived. The Kings had taken over the pioneer home of my father's parents, which was several miles away. To reach us they had a choice of two ways to travel. One was by a winding road through what was called Whistle Bear, a section piled with drifts in winter. Here quantities of gravel had been withdrawn for use on local masonry and the wind carried the snow from the top levels into the viaduct. It was well for any travellers in winter to carry shovels in snowy weather if they planned to come by way of Whistle Bear.

"How did the place get its name?" I asked my father.

"Because a man called John Baer lived at the end of the upper level and he was said to whistle from sunrise to sunset, especially when his wife was with him. She was known to be a woman of many words."

"You see," said Lill, including us all in her remark, "men like to talk but they don't like to listen."

"That statement doesn't apply in our house," muttered my brother Al under his breath. "Nobody talks around here more than you do."

I looked at Lill a little anxiously but she was happily smiling.

The other road which could have been taken was level and straight from the gateway of the King farm to a crossroad named the Town Line. This Line brought one to the V where the traveller took a sharp turn to the right and followed a curve up the hill to arrive at our gate.

The level roadway was narrow and penetrated a swamp which covered many acres, with trees reaching out from the fence sides as if hungry to recapture the slashing through which the road passed.

The dusky stillness which permeated this man-made opening held a special charm for me. On Christmas mornings after breakfast and when presents had been examined, my father hitched the team of bays to the big sleigh, covered the sleigh bottom with sweet-smelling hay, brought blankets from the stable and added extra bells to the harness of the horses because it was Christmas. We climbed in, and in easy comfort started on our annual Christmas sleigh-ride. As we entered the swamp, a light wind shook the boughs of the evergreens and the air which passed over the sleigh laid miniature flakes of snow on our faces. On either side of the roadway, snow filled the slashing and hung heavily upon dried reeds and grasses. As the sleigh-bells tinkled a warning, a red squirrel scurried along the snake fence, leaving a path of footmarks and dark bare spots from the swish of his tail. A clump of what appeared to be snow by the side of a cedar bough suddenly came to life and leaped over the fence, disappearing into the swamp.

"A hare," Da said, adding, "You seldom see a wild white one nowadays."

From a dead branch of tamarack a crow lifted its wings and flapped after the hare, cawing as it went.

It was so still in the swamp. No one wanted to talk or to

118

destroy in any way the peace of that silence. There was of course the soft jingle of the bells and squeaking of the runners on the sleigh as they passed over the snow. Once in a while a collected ball from a horse's hoof was tossed back onto our blankets. Halfway through the swamp we crossed over a wooden bridge so small, and over so small a stream, that it had no protecting sides. The stream, partially covered with ice and snow, had yet a few open spaces which caught the blue of the sky and morning sunlight slanting between the trees. Then the sharp report of a gun broke the stillness.

"Too bad," Da said. "Somehow it doesn't seem right to kill anything on a morning like this."

Even as he spoke there was a brilliant flash of colour through the air above the heads of the horses.

"Pheasants," Lill said softly, as if her voice might frighten them still more. "I hope that shot was a miss."

"You can't stop a man from destroying nature," Da said.

"But man is really part of nature," objected Lill, who enjoyed nothing better than an argument.

Perhaps that is why Da didn't answer. We moved on slowly toward the south exit. A cluster of hardwood trees inside the fence of a pasture lifted barren beauty to the cloudless sky. Not entirely barren. I noticed a single dead leaf stubbornly clinging to its place on an overhanging bough. We passed within a few feet of the trees and the dead leaf which had withstood the storms and the winter weather for so long became the victim of a sudden quick breeze which lifted it from its place, defeated at last, and tossed it down onto the snow near the edge of the road. It was then that I saw a small dark patch underneath the overhang of a narrow drift. Even as it fell the wind lifted the leaf again and laid it neatly over the patch of dark.

Da pulled the horses to a halt.

"There is something under there," he said. "It may be alive. It may be half frozen or in need of food."

Al was out of the sleigh in a minute to investigate. He waded through the heavy snow of the roadside to the place which had arrested our attention. He bent for a moment over the dark patch but came back to the sleigh without touching it. He climbed in.

"You might as well drive on, Da," he said. "It's finished, the poor thing – a mouse, frozen to death. We'll leave the leaf where it is to cover it. The snowdrift will keep the wind from moving it, I think."

We drove on but I looked back sorrowfully at the dark patch on the snow. A mouse – I was glad that the leaf had covered it. The episode had placed a touch of sadness on my Christmas morning. Years later I wrote verses in memory of the small mouse, a part of nature which nature had destroyed.

With Grandpa Fleming, Mother and Jean had remained at home; there were things to be done, and a goose was roasting in the oven. The sleigh-ride had been pleasant, but thinking of the happenings that morning, I was thankful to be again safely in the shelter of the old house.

I place here the last four lines of the poem which I later penned in memory of the little field-mouse:

Down from its place by the wind set free,
The dead leaf fell from the bare old tree
And over the snow like a small dark cloud
It made for the sleeper his humble shroud.

On Christmas afternoons, filled to capacity with roast goose and chestnut stuffing, followed by Mother's steamed Carrot Pudding with Lemon Sauce, we made off to the nearest far hill, a perfect place for sleds and sliders. There is no way to describe the exciting moments of adventure and the periods of lone silence, as the one left behind waited his or her turn at the top of the steep hill. The reflected flame of sunset behind the pine-clad pinnacle, laying a soft hue of rose over the snowy meadows, reminded us that supper time was near. Home we went.

Supper was a simple meal. The first course was always Da's famous celery, the striped red with its dark green tops and the white with goldy leaves. They came from a special storage pit built for their protection when removed from the black loam, but buckets of black loam were added to the sand of the pit into which, with roots still unharmed, they were replanted. Da's celery crop was the most valuable harvest taken from our land and the finest bunches were kept for our own use. Mingled, the stalks were piled generously into Mother's long Limoges celery dish. On the table with them was the all-important wedge of cheese, freshly cut from the wooden-boxed Cheddar at the bottom of our cellar steps. For

Christmas supper no one was restricted as to the amount consumed. To my recollection there was a plentiful supply of Mother's home-made bread and plate-sized scones cooked in an iron pan on the top of the range. The final course was, almost always, home-canned immense purply-red raspberries, topped with whipped Jersey cream and attended by platters of Christmas cake and Scotch shortbread. A simple menu but never-to-be-equalled in flavour through the passing years.

The topic of conversation often reflected our morning contact with the Big Swamp through which we had passed on our morning ride. The swamp was a never-failing area of mystery, for strange happenings had occurred within its territory. There was, for instance, the autumn when a hunted fugitive vanished while being pursued along its border. Although posse and police dogs were used in the search, the hunt was unsuccessful. The wanted man had murdered a companion while engaged in a logging operation many miles away. All through that autumn and even after the onset of winter when the swamp was crossed and re-crossed by those in search of deer and rabbit, no evidence was noted of the presence there of any human being. But three years later, when a party of berry-pickers carefully blazing their trail made their way through the western portion of the swamp, they found several felled trees which had been roughly hewn into lumber and a small low hut carefully concealed by the tree tops. Inside the hut was a pile of rags and horse blankets evidently used for a bed. There were shelves placed high enough to avoid thieving by prowling animals and a few hand-made wooden containers with lids, in which food had been stored. But not a vestige of food remained. By what means the fugitive had kept himself alive none could tell. There was of course the sheltering effect of the thickly wooded swamp and the warmth of snow, if piled against the hut. The hunted was never found and his fate never discovered. It is said that a perceptive examiner of the interior read a few words carved into the wood which had escaped the attention of others. These words were:

"Get me if you can, but you won't get me. I know where I am going but you don't. Good-bye."

Little Sister at thirteen.

XIV

A Dream Realized

Love is a jealous mistress.

The author

When I assumed the nom de plume Myrtle Millson, I took on also
the role of an artist. In the window of a small empty room upstairs,
I hung a self-designed placard with name and occupation. The
room had a desk-like pine table and a battered and abandoned
high chair with a broken back and one rung at the front on which I
could rest my feet.

I knew that the animals with which I decorated my landscapes
were interchangeable, with the probability of mistaken identity if
named. I could not draw nor sketch, but I loved colour. With an
horizon line to divide sky and earth, I indulged my taste by
generous splashings.

I was going to school now and had many distractions, for life
had become more exciting with the departure of Alice and the
advent of Tillie. However, there were long weeks when, stricken by
ill health, I sought for ways of passing time in a kind of magic
solitude. At school I developed a new thought about how my way
of life could be improved. It was at this time that considerable
discussion was taking place about a recently formed agency, the
Children's Aid Society. There was also an orphanage for English
boys, the Barnardo Home, passed by my father and me on our way
to town. If it were Saturday he took me with him; my mother

seldom went but Jean frequently accompanied us. Da pointed with some pity to the drab building in which the children were housed.

"I would like to take one of them," my mother said, "but there really isn't room for a boy."

Max and Grandpa were still with us. But there might be room for a girl, I thought, and the more I thought about it, the more eager I became.

"I would like a little sister," I told my mother.

"Mercy on us!" exclaimed Lill who was listening, "you must think your parents are magicians or something."

"Why?" I asked indignantly.

"Lill," Mother warned in a low voice, "be more careful what you say."

Such remarks returned to me for further examination. I mentioned the subject to Tillie and Tillie mentioned it to Louie.

"Louie says," said Tillie, "your mother is a normal woman and your father isn't a monster. Only monsters go on having babies after they get old."

"My father isn't old," I said haughtily, "and you don't have to do anything at all about having a baby. You can adopt somebody and that's what I want to do. I want a little sister."

"Your father is as old as my father is," Tillie stormed, "and we're not going to have any more children. I heard him say that adoption causes an awful lot of trouble."

I asked Mother about this that evening. She was mending a pair of socks and held the needle suspended as she answered me.

"If your Da and me weren't here to look after you," she said, "and there was nobody else in the family to do it, I would want somebody to adopt you."

A terrible fear came over me. I said nothing about it but that night after I repeated my usual prayers, I asked God to save me from adoption. But the idea of finding a little sister grew upon me.

There were a number of immigrants from the British Isles seeking new homes in our part of Ontario. There was, for instance, the pair of twins, Elsie and Annie Vanner, who had just started to school. They were English and very shy children with blond hair and brown eyes. They always wore dresses the colour of their eyes. Sometimes during recess they were the only listeners I had, as I told fairy stories which I had read, adding other exciting details.

I loved Elsie and Annie. I heard that they were very poor and I invited them to come home with me from school to be viewed by my mother. Would they like to have a mother like mine? Would they like to live in our house? To these questions they made no answer, but I was not discouraged. Each time a new resident came to our village I looked upon any attending children as probable prospects, an addition to our family. Again and again I invited them to come and play with me. Again and again I made the same suggestion to my mother. Her reply was always the same:

"These little girls have homes of their own, you know. Nobody wants to leave their own home, however poor it is, if they can stay there."

My enthusiasm began to wane. I passed my eleventh birthday, still a lonely child. With the precious dollar given to me by Aunt Lizzie I bought myself a new box of paints. That night as Jean watched me painting blue mountains against a ruddy autumn sky, I looked up and said to her, "I'm not going to pray for a little sister any more. I have decided instead to become a great artist."

Jean's brown eyes smiled into mine with the understanding which was never lacking.

"That's good," she said, "but keep on wishing."

It was during that summer that my father decided to install a Government drain from the swamp land of a new farm property which he had purchased to a suitable place of outlet.

This required the employing of a half dozen men from the nearby town to act as diggers. Most of the men were housed by the villagers and did not object to a long work-week which extended as late as dusk on Saturday. They were paid according to the amount of time they spent at work. Among them was a slight young Englishman, small of feature, with a waxed moustache. He had a very serious expression. The men ate their noon meal at our house and Mother remarked that she had never heard him laugh.

"There's a reason for that," my father said. "He has just lost his wife. She broke her leg. It was a very bad break and infection set in. She died two months ago. They came from England and before they left they adopted a little girl. She's only six and now she's without a mother."

"However does he manage?" Mother exclaimed.

"He does his best," Da said. "He boards her out while he's here at work but he would like to go home on Friday instead of Saturday because the neighbour who takes care of her wants to be free on week-ends. I told him he could go but it's hard for him to get there because the other men get a ride together. They've made arrangements with the storekeeper. He drives them to the trolley at Preston."

"It must be hard on the child," Mother said, "not to be in her own home. I wonder . . . " She paused and looked at Da.

"That's an idea," Da said. "I'll look into it."

That night when I went to bed I puzzled what Da was going to look into.

Holding his hand I had peered down at the men working in the drain. The top of their heads did not reach the level of the earth. It was an awesome sight. *What* was Da going to look into? I went to sleep wondering.

Perhaps it was midnight. Perhaps it was later. I awoke with a start and looking from my window into the sky it seemed to me that the stars were nearer than I had ever seen them before. I blinked my eyes and remembered the little girl without a mother somewhere in the town. I got out of bed. Jean caught me by the skirt of my nightgown as I did so.

"Jessie, Jessie," she said in a low voice, "are you dreaming or something? Get back into bed." I climbed in but I did not lie down. I threw my arms around Jean and in a burst of excitement I whispered back.

"I'm not dreaming," I said, "I'm not dreaming at all, Jean. I'm wide awake as can be and I want to tell Da. It's about the little girl without a mother. I want her for my sister."

Jean slipped an arm over me and in the dark she stroked my hair.

"Maybe," she said. "I was going to tell you in the morning. She's coming to stay with us for a while anyway. Da spoke to her father last night. Now go to sleep and don't do any more thinking until morning."

I was eleven on the second of October that year. On the ninth, I stayed home from school by special permission. Beside the kitchen stove I set my small rocking-chair with one of my dolls in it. I spread out a set of doll's dishes on a stool nearby and I carefully made up my doll's cradle and placed it beside the range. The morning was cool.

The doctor who had attended the now deceased mother was

caring for our neighbour on the next farm who had been kicked by a horse.

"He's coming out to see Mr. S. this morning," Jean said, "and he's bringing Edith with him."

Edith was the little girl's name.

"Put on your coat and bonnet," Jean said. "Then you can go down the hill a little way and watch for her until she comes."

I counted the number of times I walked up and down the hill. The ninth time, when I was near the top and almost at our gate, I heard the fast trip of the trotter and rolling of wheels. Close behind me the vehicle slowed up. We reached the gate together.

Edith was a small six-year-old. She looked much younger. She wore a blue velvet coat and matching bonnet. Bits of shortly cut brown hair pushed out from the bonnet's edge. But it was her eyes which drew attention. They were violet blue and edged with long, dark, curling lashes. Her eyebrows were beautifully curved and well marked. She was like a frightened little bird – her hand was cold in mine as I led her into the kitchen. I don't remember what either of us said as I removed her coat and bonnet, placed the doll in her arms and set her into the rocking-chair.

The oven door was open and there was a mild heat escaping into the room, pleasant on that cool autumn morning.

I was so overwhelmed with joy by her presence that I do not recall how she was greeted by my mother and sisters, but soon she was provided with a mug of cocoa and a piece of toast. I sat on the wood box partaking of the same although I had eaten breakfast, but to share with her was a token of welcome, it seemed to me.

Although the period of Edith's visit had been limited to the time of her father's employment which was to end three weeks later, there was never a more firm decision made by me than the determination that she would remain forever.

I had found a little sister.

We did not have a bathroom in the old house. Baths were taken by each one in turn in the privacy of the old kitchen, warm in all seasons.

The tub was large, a wooden washtub which was stored in a deep closet between kitchen and carriage shed, along with the icebox.

Grandpa Fleming had his special bath time – usually on a Saturday morning. With all doors closed, Mother took over the responsibility of the bathing. Grandpa, minus all clothing except his trousers, sat backwards on a chair while Mother with the reliable Lifebuoy soap and wash cloth did service.

When she had completed everything including the washing and drying of Grandpa's hair, a mop of white without a sign of baldness, and after soaking his feet in a large metal basin, she would say, "Now, Father, here is the cloth and here is the soap. When you've done the rest I'll be in The Room."

Into The Room she went and closed the door. Wherever I might be it was not in the kitchen but often I heard Grandpa's comment as he took over the ablutions of what was under the trousers:

"Ah, Cissie, that was grand. You keep my skin as soft as a baby's."

The night of Edith's arrival the washtub was set on two chairs in the kitchen and half filled with warm water. The Lifebuoy soap was in evidence and a much too long nightgown of mine was ready for the newcomer's tiny figure after the bathing was done. I was allowed to remain and my heart warmed to the gentleness with which my mother thoroughly washed my new sister. For that was what she was to be. My resolve was adamant.

We were to sleep together that night on the feather bed in our guest room. I can still feel my excitement as I led her up our narrow stairs, holding for her the too-long skirt of the gown that she might not trip on it. Her little feet were bare, for she had no slippers in her small valise and mine were twice the needed size.

Every article of clothing that was washable would that night be so treated and hung to dry on an outer clothesline where the fresh frosty air would act as a disinfectant, so I heard Mother say. Once in bed, I claimed the little stranger as permanently one of the family.

"We are sisters now," I said, "so put your arms around my neck and say 'Good-night, Sister Jessie.'"

She obeyed.

"Now we'll say our prayers," I ventured. "We won't get out of bed to say them because you haven't any slippers and the floor has horrid cold linoleum on it. When you have slippers we'll kneel to say them. You repeat after me."

The simple four-line verse was accomplished in unison. But with a lonely little head on my shoulder and a protective arm around a thin little figure I could not sleep. My excitement was too great, and my satisfaction.

Like a weary babe, secure if a little bewildered, Edith slept soundly.

The pattern of my planning was followed to the letter for three days. Edith was not going to school with me as yet, but I all but ran home each night to be greeted by a watching little figure at our gate.

Edith fitted into our household easily, for the security of her surroundings and the knowledge that she was wanted there brought about a happy child's easy relaxation. On our big lawn with Teve she romped and whistled and sang while I was away. After school, in the evening, lessons forgotten by me, I devoted myself to fully acquiring her and to her entertainment.

This was accomplished by orders delivered by me and followed by her. At mealtime she was set on a cushioned chair between Mother and myself at the corner of the table.

"Say, 'Thank you, Mother,'" I whispered each time she was served.

In the evening my father occupied his usual armchair in The Room beside an oval table where books and papers were handy and close enough to the heater, which was always lighted after early fall brought a chill into the old house.

I had outgrown my little rocking-chair and now Edith enjoyed its possession. I sat where I could observe her and the way her violet eyes were fixed upon the burning coals inside the mica. But I had designs beyond her possession of my rocking-chair. I motioned her to me and whispered:

"Run and jump on Da's knee."

Edith obeyed me. I had formerly instructed her to call him by that name and this she did freely.

He had stopped reading to smile at her. She put an arm around his neck and I heard her say in a tranquil voice of satisfaction, "You're my Daddy now, ain't ya?"

I watched my father's arm go around her. He laughed a little at what he supposed to be her uninhibited ways.

"Well, well," he said.

He did not say "Yes I am," but a kind of coldness crept over me and I felt a sickness which I cannot describe. I was not aware of the reason but only of the effect upon me.

It was soon bedtime. Sleeping arrangements had not been decided upon as yet, and Edith and I still occupied the feather bed. It was Jean's habit to tuck us in and to kiss us good-night. I turned the wick of the lamp low until she would come, when she would extinguish it.

When she came that night, I was overcome by a desire to cry at the sound of her footsteps on the stairs. I closed my eyes and feigned sleep without really understanding my own emotion.

Jean tucked the blankets snugly about us both. I felt, rather than saw, Edith's arms go up and around Jean as the latter kissed her.

"Now it's Jessie's turn," Jean said softly.

I made no sign.

"She's sleepin'," said Edith.

Jean waited another half minute, then she extinguished the lamp and tiptoed softly out and down the stairs.

I opened my eyes, which were wet. No one could see me now nor the tears which were falling. But as I moved to put a faithful arm around my little sister, she said, "You ain't sleepin' at all, you know you ain't."

I wiped away my tears on the sheet which was over us and turned to receive and to give a good-night kiss. A terrible sickness was upon me and it was still there the next morning.

I tried to conceal my desire to weep by special activities while we dressed and after going downstairs to the old kitchen. But Jean's eye was upon me and when I sat up to the table before a steaming bowl of porridge I lifted my spoon and laid it down again. I could not swallow. The tears were coursing down my cheeks. Jean had read the signal.

"Aren't you feeling well today?" she asked me, and I shook my head.

"I think you'd better stay at home from school," she advised.

Edith was eagerly partaking of her bowl of porridge.

Jean directed me away from the table and into The Room. Mother and Lill were at the barn doing the milking. There was no one in The Room except Jean and myself. Our men and my father had already gone to the fields. Jean picked up Mother's shawl from the couch and wrapped it around me.

"Lie down and rest for a while," she said. "It's a nice day. Edith will play on the lawn with Teve, that is what she likes to do. Later on you may feel like having some breakfast."

I did not eat breakfast that day and I was still lying on the couch when the men came in for the noon meal. Mother brought me a bowl of bread and milk and feeling somewhat foolish and ashamed, without knowing why, I tried to eat it. The food choked me and again I burst into tears. After the noon meal there was a quiet conference in the kitchen between my parents and my sisters. What was discussed I never knew. But that afternoon, before supper, Jean came in and sat down beside me. Her long slender fingers touched me gently.

"Edith's having a good time, isn't she, and it's nice for you to have someone to play with. But there is a special place in our hearts for you and a special place in our hearts for Edith. Nobody can take special places away."

Perhaps it was an inadequate explanation but it carried the message that was needed. Since I had encouraged Edith to replace me my father's knee where, big girl though I was becoming, it had been my habit to sit in that intimate hour after supper, I had not been able to take my place there even when Edith was absent and otherwise occupied. Now, when Da came in, smiled at me and prepared to read the evening paper, he sat down, laid the paper unopened on the table beside him and turned to look at me again. Dusk was falling and somehow the absence of bright light in The Room, for there was only one lamp burning, seemed to soften the sense of tragedy that only a child can experience. Da understood. He opened his arms wide. I flung off the shawl and ran to him.

That was the first and last time I suffered from jealousy after the arrival of my much wanted little sister who became, by her father's consent, a member of our family and who was to remain with us until her marriage in young womanhood.

XV

A Trip to Town

He came and went,
But there was left behind
A change of vision
And a breadth of mind.

The author

When Uncle Andrew, on furlough from China, spared the time to cross the continent from California where he would temporarily reside, to visit his one brother in Canada, this was an event. My father belonged to a closely knit family. Canadian born, only one sister and himself had remained in Canada. Although at long intervals the California relatives, as we referred to them, came to see us, the arrival of Uncle Andrew was an occasion different from all others. He was close to retirement after many years in the Orient. But when my father urged him not to return there, Uncle Andrew smiled tolerantly and replied, "But China is my home."

He respected and admired the Chinese people and although his visits might extend to less than a fortnight he left an impression which remained with all of us – a new awareness that we were of one creation and an understanding of "the foreigner" which we did not acquire from the written word nor the teachings of church and school.

Aunt Nellie had come with him. She was a quiet-spoken, thoughtful woman of small stature. Her parents had been Southerners but she had been born in China where her grandfather and father, the Hartwell family of missionary fame, had lived for two generations.

Uncle Andrew was tall and very thin, but the jolliest of all my uncles and somehow the easiest to understand. They had three children, two sons and a daughter, who had been placed in boarding schools in the eastern States. It was difficult to be separated from one's family, they admitted, but an accepted restriction in the normal way of life if one believed in dedication to the missionary movement.

When my father indicated his intention of going to town with an order of celery and harvest apples, Uncle Andrew expressed a wish to accompany him. Perhaps Da noted my look of longing as they prepared the democrat for the journey. There was a hasty low-spoken conversation with my mother. Then:

"Would you like to go along, Jessie?" she asked me. "You don't need to change your dress. It's fresh ironed and clean, but ask Jean to brush your hair and you'd better put on your sailor hat because the sun gets very hot in the middle of the day."

It was July. I sat between my father and my beloved uncle on the wide front seat of the democrat. Behind us was a hamper of apples, a bag of potatoes and some bunched fresh vegetables.

It was a beautiful morning with a clear, almost cloudless sky and a gentle wind which relieved the intensity of the sun's heat.

We followed the winding road to the village and from there through the valley of the Grand River. On the south, the land rose into well-populated hills. On the north and east it sprawled into narrow flats and on the other side of the water one could see the outline of the town of Preston. Before us the road wound slowly upward, through a viaduct over which passed the main branch of the C.P.R., and on to the tip of a steep hill. From there it descended rather quickly into the thriving young city of Galt. So recently had it reached a size earning for it the name of city, that many people continued to speak of it as a town.

Most of the residents were Britishers at that time but one or two Chinese families had recently come there, undertaking to make a living by opening a laundry and a Chinese restaurant. The marketable produce which we carried in the back of the democrat had been ordered by two greengrocers on the Main Street. We crossed the wooden bridge while I clutched my father's coat sleeve with one hand, a little frightened by the gushing water flowing over the edge of a breakwater and swiftly onward, under the bridge, to follow what was known as the river road on the south side.

Old Nell, our bay mare, disliked the roaring water as much as I. She announced our location by pricking up her ears and crossing the wooden bridge with nimble feet and increased speed, showing relief when we reached the pavement on the other side.

Uncle Andrew and my father had seemed to forget my presence as we passed over the four miles of roadway from our gate to town. Their conversation was of things past and of people whom I knew only by name, their brothers and sisters, and the days when all had been together in that cosy pioneer home near the great swamp. Da would drive Uncle Andrew to see that home before he returned to California and thence to China. The barn had been built in 1864.

"You can still see John's initials carved into the concrete," Da said. John was their brother.

Both were very quiet for a few minutes after that. Then, "There's no way around it," Uncle Andrew commented. "Times have to change and we can do nothing about it."

We stopped half-way along the first block where there was a hitching ring in the cement of the sidewalk. Uncle Andrew picked me up like a feather and jumped down over the wheel while Da, descending more slowly, tied Nell to the ring, allowing her plenty of head play.

"I've got to deliver this stuff," he said. "It won't take me many minutes. Keep an eye on the rig and I'll make a sign to you when I've finished."

"We'll have a look at things while we wait," Uncle Andrew said to me, taking my hand and moving toward a window which had engaged my curiosity each time I accompanied my father to town. After hearing my uncle refer continually to China as the Orient, I now read with new understanding the gold lettering of a sign hung by attractive chains across the window of the shop – The Oriental Bazaar. Below this capitalized advertisement, in small letters was a name, "Francis J. Brown."

The window revealed a display of such magnificence that the individual objects were lost sight of in the over-all picture. Models in teak wood; gorgeous fans, their panels carved and inlaid with mother-of-pearl; statuary, vases, and numerous articles in lacquer and bronze. I looked from them to my uncle who was sharing with me a close examination of the decorative arrangement.

"I'd like to go in here, Jessie," Uncle Andrew was saying, when a man stepped from the doorway. They stared at each other in utter astonishment. The man was of medium build with a fresh boyish face and sweeping moustache. He was hatless but wore a rather stylish cut of suit and shiny patent-leather shoes.

The hands of the two men were clasped in front of me. I stepped back a little.

"My word alive!" the man with the moustache exclaimed. "Andrew Beattie, or is it his double? I haven't seen you since I put into Hong Kong five years ago. What in the world are you doing here?"

Uncle Andrew's laughter was always hearty and pleasant to hear. He laughed as he answered.

"I might ask you the same question, Brown. Don't tell me this is your shop."

Francis J. Brown laughed too.

"Because I told you that I hated shopkeeping?" he said. "Well so I do, but you see, I leave that to my worthy family. They do it well and make a pretty penny out of it. I only provide the goods. If you lived in this town you wouldn't see me here very often. But let's come back to how you happen to be here – on furlough, I take it."

Uncle Andrew nodded. "And you?" he asked.

"The same," the other man answered, "only I take mine when I feel like it. I've had a strenuous year. Saigon, India, and the Philippines. You're never your own boss at sea, although some people think it's the freest life in the world. In one way it is, but in another – you daren't take your eyes off the horizon for more than a minute."

"Things are almost as difficult on land, right now," Uncle Andrew answered. "But I'm glad to see you, Captain. How long will you be home?"

"A month or two." He crossed his fingers. "If all goes well."

At that moment Uncle Andrew caught sight of my father undoing Nell's hitching line.

"I suppose you know Frank," he said in parting. "We must be off, Jessie and I. I see he's ready to leave. We are enjoying a wonderful reunion."

The man in the doorway nodded and smiled to my father who was looking in our direction.

"Hello, Frank," he called brightly, and "Good-bye, Andrew – and Jessie. Maybe we'll meet again."

It was approaching noon when we rejoined Da who stood waiting beside the democrat. Uncle Andrew said:

"Let's make it an adventurous day, Frank. The little one will enjoy it. You say there's a Chinese restaurant in town. Suppose we have dinner there. It's a hot day and you've been working. It would take us an hour to get home, wouldn't it? I say dinner first. Where is the place?"

"The place" was a very small café on Water Street, only half a block away. Da replaced Nell's hitching line in the ring and we walked the short distance. This was indeed an adventurous day for me. When we entered the doorway, a series of small cubicles could be seen on either side of a narrow aisle. By each one stood a wooden bar decorated by several hooks. At the foot of the bar was a shining metal receptacle, for what use I did not know. I sat with Da on one side of a small table and Uncle Andrew on the other. They hung their hats on the hooks but although Uncle Andrew put out his hand for mine, I shook my head. My sailor had long ribbon streamers and I was very proud of it. Placed on a hook, no one could tell what might happen to it. It was safer on my head, thought I.

Bowing and smiling, the proprietor of the little restaurant, wearing an enveloping white apron, came to receive our order.

Uncle Andrew winked at Da, and turning soberly, he addressed the man in a flow of singing syllables, unintelligible to me.

But not to the proprietor. He dropped to his knees, caught the hands of my uncle in his and bowed his head on them.

The effect of this astonishing act left me breathless. I looked at Da and saw his amazed expression. I put my hand in his, under the table. Indeed, I was a little frightened, without knowing why.

But my uncle was speaking again in the same singing manner, and the Chinese rose to his feet and with his own hands now clasping and unclasping in ecstatic delight, he spoke with such fluency and rapidity that I heard my father suppress a laugh as Uncle Andrew answered slowly in English.

"We must speak the language of our new country," he said.

"We are hungry. This is my brother and my little niece. May we have dinner?"

The feast spread before us was an indescribable presentation of the best that the humble café could provide. While we ate, Uncle Andrew explained to us that it was natural for a person far from home to be thus affected when hearing his native tongue spoken by a stranger.

I was able to absorb only a small portion of the great significance of events which occurred that day.

It was difficult indeed for my uncle to break away from such an overwhelming display of happiness. While he and Da were in some way presenting parting words and at the same time edging toward the doorway, I had stepped outside. I turned, waiting, and as I did so, from an alleyway by the side of the building a small boy ran toward me. I still wore curls. He caught one in each hand and gave them a merciless pull. What he said to me sounded like

Hong, Hong,
Chippity hong.

That evening when I told my uncle what the boy had said, he laughed heartily and I knew that my interpretation was at fault. However, he was able to explain to me the meaning of the small Chinese boy's command:

Get along, get along,
Stranger, get along

was what he really meant, Uncle Andrew said.

The days of my uncle's visit passed all too quickly. As gifts from Aunt Nellie and himself, my sisters received sterling silver brooches with a filigreed inscription in Chinese, myself a silver three-leafed clover with a long stem, really a sugar spoon, matching a larger serving spoon presented to my mother. But the most treasured gift of all was that from Uncle Andrew to my father. During the former's ministry in Canton, an immensely rich man had been converted to Christianity. He had been a teacher of the doctrine of Confucius. After his conversion he had presented my uncle with a magnificent replica, decorated in lacquer and gold leaf, of the Guardian of Little Children. This statue is a family heirloom.

After the work day was over, during Uncle Andrew's visit, the brothers sat together on a cushioned bench facing south on our veranda. I sat on the veranda step, unable to refrain from listening in while the famous visitor told stories, the like of which I had never heard nor was I likely to hear again.

Before us stretched broad fields growing a purple grey in the falling dusk. Then there was a bush land in a valley. Only the tips of its trees could be seen like a fringe along the southern horizon. Behind them was the row of knobby hills which changed appearance with the changes of sky from daylight through sunset to semi-darkness. To me, those hills were like a hand beckoning a welcome to some distant country – a boundary beyond which I had never been. From the left the moon rolled up and under its light the scene became even more mysterious and alluring.

Uncle Andrew was talking. He and my Aunt Nellie, who could be heard in low-toned conversation with my mother in The Room, had barely escaped with their lives during the Boxer Rebellion in China. The houses there, at least that in which they lived, Uncle Andrew said, had a flat roof. The ceiling was composed of bricks. During the rebellion a small company of rebels, unable to force the gates in the walled enclosure, had vaulted the wall and, finding the house doors locked firmly and the windows barred, had clambered onto the rooftop and with deft fingers had taken it apart.

"When they had a hole big enough," Uncle Andrew explained, "they dropped down one by one, so fast that in a couple of minutes the house was full of them. They wired me to the bedpost and Nellie to me, wrist to wrist. Our Chinese nanny began to plead with them. Because she was of their own race, they listened. She urged them not to harm anyone, declaring that we were the friends of their people and not their enemies. While she talked, she stood beside the crib, holding one child in her arms and guarding the other, who had been put to bed. The whole house was ransacked. A circle of Boxers bent over the crib. The children were too young of course to recognize any danger but the robbers were fascinated by the 'little foreigners.' There was a white woollen blanket on the crib. I heard one of them say as he felt it with his fingers, 'We'll take this, it's woolly warm.' And I heard the nanny protesting, 'He's just a baby, leave it for him.' And to our amazement they left it.

"In the meantime, I was working on the wires to free myself. The men were so thickly packed in the room that they did not

138

notice me. I then freed Nellie, and while more and more of them gathered, until the house wouldn't hold another one, I got down on my hands and knees and crawled between them. It was a chance I had to take, and it worked. The door was open and I slid through it unseen. The night was dark. I reached the wall and vaulted it. I ran for help. The American Embassy headquarters was not far away and they were on the alert. They sent a contingent, but the Boxers had left with their loot. My heart was filled with terror in case they had harmed Nellie, but she met me at the door, tears streaming down her cheeks. They had taken everything movable, including her wedding ring.

"'I'm glad it came off,' she said, 'for if it hadn't, they would have taken my finger to get it.'"

I could have listened all night to the strange and exciting stories which Uncle Andrew had to tell, but Mother had not forgotten that it was more than my bedtime. She came to fetch me.

"Good-night, Jessie," Uncle Andrew said, and reached to kiss me after Da had done so. "Don't have any bad dreams. Just be thankful that you live in Canada."

XVI

It Was the Time of Autumn Rains

But of all pains, the greatest pain
It is to love, but love in vain.

Abraham Cowley

Mother was standing at the door of the old house looking southward. Her eyes were not upon the impressive greenhouses, three now, on the left side of the road, nor was she rejoicing that the old buildings of barn and stable had been replaced by modern structures. Yes, the mortgage had been paid off and my father was now looked upon as a very successful farmer. Even the ribbons tying my braids of hair could compete in width with Tillie's which I had coveted for so long.

I was at home from school with one of my "spells" as the sudden attacks of illness and pain were called from which I had suffered since the age of seven. It was the beginning of June, haying time, and as I lay on the old couch under the south window, the smell of hay drying in the sun drifted to me through the open door where Mother stood.

She was silent as she looked, and her sorrow-touched countenance troubled me. Out there somewhere I could hear a vireo repeating his melody over and over. I could hear an oriole moving from one octave to another with perfect timing, and a bobolink spilling his rounded notes into the fresh air of morning as he dipped and whirled over the meadow.

In the meadow the half-grown lambs with their mothers were

nibbling the tasty grass. It was long past lambing time. The hay was cut and lying in rows ready for coiling. What did my mother see to bring such a look of sadness? I rose up from my pillows and peered from the window, following the direction of her looking.

With his hay fork over his shoulder, my brother Al was limping along the road toward the hayfield.

It was a perfect morning for coiling. There had been two days of sunlit drying weather after a rain. This climate accounted for the heavy sweet of the air being blown by the wind from the clover field, for the hay was a mixture of clover and alfalfa.

It was now two years since my brother had come home from the town in eager longing to become again a tiller of the soil. The new barns and stables, additions to thoroughbred livestock and the purchasing of a second mare of dappled grey, almost due to foal, had added to his enthusiasm in accepting again the supervision of that part of Da's property known as "the farm." The installation of machinery to raise the basket of the hay-wagon to any desired level in the barn for unloading had been the most recent addition to modern equipment there. Installed at the end of April, the first year, Al had demonstrated its usefulness for the benefit of uncles visiting us from California. During the operation Al had slipped from the wagon when it was almost at roof level and had fallen to the floor of the barn.

My Uncle David, a doctor and Da's youngest brother, had examined a very painful injury to Al's ankle and had recommended further medical attention. The uncles had left us to visit other relatives and my father had driven my brother to town the following day to be re-examined by our family doctor. He declared that no bones had been broken and had bandaged the ankle, advising that Al keep it bandaged until it ceased to trouble him.

"He should have required an X-ray," my uncle said when he was informed of the outcome, but such attention was not yet common in our town.

Al continued to bandage his ankle each morning and to remove the bandage each night. It was now a year since he had fallen and only the determination not to leave his beloved occupation kept him ploughing, harrowing, seeding and harvesting while he suffered agony which changed his happy satisfaction with life to an attitude of stubborn endurance.

"There must be something wrong," my mother said, as if to

141

herself, as she watched him until he turned in to the waiting field. "If his ankle was only sprained, why doesn't it improve? He limps as badly now, almost, as he did a year ago."

It was true. Perhaps it was fear of discovering a condition which would alter his way of life that prevented Al from taking advice to further investigate the year-old injury.

But one morning he did not leave the house. He sat after breakfast in the old kitchen with his head in his hands. Out there the golden wheat was beckoning him to the harvest. It was the end of July.

"I can't make it," he admitted. "Dog-gone it, I can't make it, Da," he said to my father.

The other men had left the house; only members of our family were there to hear him. My father sat down beside him and put a hand on his shoulder.

"This is the time to think a bit," he said, "and not only about what's to be done in the fields. Find out what's wrong, boy. Use common sense. Don't wait any longer. Drive into town and face the doctor with what he said. He was wrong and you can tell him. That's a message from me. It's time somebody spoke up. I'll go along if you want me."

Al shook his head.

"No, I'll go myself," he answered in an unsteady voice, whether from grief or pain it was hard to say. "I'm going to get to the bottom of this, Da, I promise you."

That seemed a very long day to me and nothing which I did affected me as of importance. My father went back to his work in the garden. Mother and my sisters found housework to keep them very busy, but the house was quiet. I knew that they were thinking about my brother who had driven away to town and I, too, was thinking of him. I had been writing an exciting love story the day before. It was only half-finished but when I sat down at the small table in The Room which I had dignified with the name of desk, I could not think of a word to add to it.

This was the way of life in our house. The trouble which affected one, affected all.

One year after Al's accident, the doctor who had examined him at that time and had pronounced his injury a sprain admitted his error; a central bone in my brother's ankle had been fractured.

For the rest of his long life of eighty-three years he was to walk with a limp and suffer at every step.

The intestinal trouble which had followed after the appendix operation did not again affect him, but one day in a burst of confidence, when I was a mature woman, he told me that he had been haunted from the time of that illness by a fear entertained in our family that he might have inherited the disease which had been responsible for the death of my mother's favourite brother – Johnnie – a disease known in those days by the terrifying name of "galloping consumption."

Al had "a girl" when in his early twenties. She came sometimes, invited by my sisters, to visit us. I remember her very distinctly. She was a tall handsome young woman with clear brown eyes and wavy dark hair arranged in a French roll. Theirs must have been a very restrained courtship, for her visits were few and I was a woman grown before I knew that when Al was twenty-three and Addie was twenty-one they were engaged to marry. Then there fell the event of that winter day when the ambulance had carried my brother away to our town hospital. His recovery from the then rare appendix operation had been considered little short of a miracle, but the after-effects had so discouraged his hope of good health that the engagement had been broken by him, much to the grief of Addie who loved him dearly.

"That is one young woman who would have cared for him in sickness and in health with her whole heart in the caring," Mother said sorrowfully on the day of their final parting.

The words were spoken to my sisters but in my presence. Al, coming unexpectedly into the house by way of The Room, heard them. He stood in the kitchen doorway with the most resolute, most unhappy expression, which even a child could never forget.

"I heard you, Mother, and what you said is true," he told her with a tremor in his voice. "I didn't want that to happen, if you can understand what I mean. She deserves a better life."

We never saw Addie again and my brother went on, grimly bearing his physical disabilities and turning more and more to his other love, that of the earth of which he was made. As the years passed, other sorrows were to affect the course of his life.

Several years after the broken engagement with Addie, when Al's health had improved noticeably, he showed a special interest in a blond fräulein whose family moved to our community. Her strongly built young body was complemented by regular features and heavy fair hair, which she wore parted in the middle and wound gracefully at the nape of the neck. Her eyes had a levelling look, as if no emotion in the world could move her to tears. Perhaps it was her physical strength and her consequent composure and confident manner which drew my brother's attention. But the association was short-lived – why, I do not know – and Al went on again after meeting another challenge to his emotions, alone with his disillusionments and his ever present gnawing pain caused by the rubbing together of the unjoined areas of the fracture.

The affair with the blond fräulein reached the proportions of a serious attachment before it came to an end. Hannah had accepted a ring prior to an absence of several months while she took what was known as "the short course" in sewing offered at that time by a clothing factory in a town thirty miles away.

It was late September. The drizzle of rain which had begun before daybreak had developed into a torrential downpour with an increasing wind driving it against the windows of the old house. Occasionally, as night fell, it was accompanied by hail which rattled against the panes.

Mail routes were not common in country districts at that time. After supper that evening, one of our men who enjoyed a daily nip had gone to the village. Before returning, he had called at the post office.

When he returned, Mother was saying, "Time for bed, Jessie."

Most of our men had already retired. My sisters were examining an Eaton's catalogue at the table in The Room. Da was in his usual chair reading *The Farmer's Advocate*. In the kitchen, Mother had been preparing the yeast for tomorrow's bread-baking while Al and I shared the lamplight at the kitchen table. I had been doing my homework; Al was writing a letter. I replaced my schoolbooks in their bag in obedience to Mother's words. The man was dripping with rain. He returned outside to give his hat and coat a strenuous shake, after laying two letters on the table beside Al.

"Both for you," he said, and went on upstairs to bed. From where I sat, I could see that one letter was an advertisement from a flour and feed company. Al raised thoroughbred cattle and was a good customer. The other envelope was addressed in a woman's

144

fine writing. Al picked it up quickly and as quickly opened it. His usual weekly message from Hannah, thought I.

When I had hung my schoolbag on its peg placed low enough for my use, I turned to kiss Mother good-night before going upstairs myself. Al was still reading. Mother accepted my kiss but did not return it. Her eyes were on Al. The open letter was still in his hands. His face was ashen. His eyes had a fixed expression. I looked from him to Mother and back again.

"Al," Mother said in a half-whisper, "what's up?"

Al did not answer her. He did not move. He continued to hold the open-faced letter in his hands. He was not reading now. He was as one who had died instantaneously. He did not move because he could not.

Mother pushed me before her into The Room.

"Upstairs," she said, and I went, but my brother's face was before me.

I slumped onto my bed without undressing, aware of an impending calamity. As I went up the stairs I had heard Mother call: "Girls – Da!" I had heard a rush of footsteps, then the closing of the door between the kitchen and The Room. I began to cry. Then I heard my father open the door, and the burr of the telephone on the wall as he turned the handle. I heard his voice. He was speaking to the doctor. He was asking for help.

It was four miles from the town to our farm but the doctor had a motor car now. The agony of waiting was shortened as it whirred up our hill.

Dare I go down or must I stay alone in ignorance of what was happening? All voices were quiet-spoken in our house that night and told me only of disaster, of what nature I had no clue.

Then Jean's quick steps on the stair sent me to meet her.

"Sh," she said. We entered the bedroom. She kept her arms around me as we sat together on the side of my bed.

"Al is very sick," she told me gently. "The doctor says it is shock. He can't move and he can't speak. The doctor will stay with him for a while. There is nothing we can do except wait. It was the letter from Hannah that did it. I'll tell you about that another time. Just go to bed and lie still. Don't be frightened. You will hear Da and the doctor. They are going to carry him into the downstairs bedroom. He can't move by himself."

Jean buried her head on my shoulder.

"Oh, Jessie," she said with a half sob, "it's so cruel. Al feels everything more than we do. He always has. He'll be all right, but don't forget to say your prayers."

She hurried away downstairs and I did not forget. Two hours later I could bear it no longer. I, too, went down. The doctor was still there. He was in The Room talking in a low voice to my mother and sisters. Da was in the bedroom with Al. Al had not moved and he had not spoken.

"This is critical," the doctor said. "Shock beyond my power to deal with it. Where is the girl? She must be brought here. He is in a state of unconsciousness. The girl is the only hope." Later, Jean told me that Hannah had confessed her engagement to a power-operator in the factory, a man ten years her senior. Her marriage to my brother was to have taken place the following spring.

Mother's reply was, "She is thirty miles from here."

"We'll send someone to get her," the doctor planned. "I'd go myself if I hadn't a patient expecting a baby. Al needs his father with him." He turned to Jean.

"If someone could drive *you*," he said, and paused.

Our most trustworthy employee, who was also Al's helper on the farm, stood fully dressed at the bottom of the stairs. He looked at Jean and Jean returned the look.

"It's a terrible night," the doctor went on, "but that boy is in a terrible condition." Then he lowered his voice. He turned to Mother.

"If you have any fire-arms in the place," he said, "hide them."

"If Tom will drive me," Jean said, "I'll go for her."

The gathering of people in The Room disbanded. The doctor left with the promise to keep in touch by telephone. Mother went to join Da. Jean and Lill went up the stairs together and Tom to the stables to prepare for the journey.

I was left alone. I knelt on the couch by the window facing the barn while Tom hurried to bring the buggy from the shed. He had harnessed Nibs, the favourite of Al's two colts which Al had raised and trained. When the horse and buggy stood waiting at the gate, Jean came down the stairs to me. She put her arms around me while Lill took an oilcloth cover from the table and stood waiting to wrap it about Jean.

"Everything's going to be all right, Jessie," Jean said, and kissed me. "Just be a good girl and don't make any more trouble for anybody. Tom's a good driver and we'll soon be back."

Lill and I watched as Jean ran to the waiting buggy, Lill holding a lantern high that the beams might light the small path to the gate. The rain continued to fall and the wind howled in wild gusts. The water-drenched top of the buggy and the curtained sides looked like blackened glass and already the horse was tossing his head to shake off the collecting rain, a cold autumn rain, which went on until early morning.

The buggy rolled away into the darkness. Lill, crying openly, drew me with her to the stairs. I undressed but I remember that she did not. I slept but I am sure she did not sleep.

It was noon of the next day when Jean and Tom drove up our hill with Hannah between them.

The doctor had returned. There had been no change. Da came out of Al's room and waited with the rest of us while Hannah went in alone.

"It would be better if you went too," Da said to Mother, and she obeyed him.

It was years later before I learned what took place.

"Hannah went up to the bedside," Mother said, "but she couldn't seem to find her voice to speak to him, at first. She just laid her hand on his forehead. When his eyes stayed looking right before him, when he didn't seem to see her, she spoke his name. She said, 'Al, Al ... it's Hannah.' There was no response and he kept on looking past her and what he saw we'll never know."

The treatment had failed.

Hannah returned as she had come, without a sign of remorse, without a word of sympathy, Mother confided when I was old enough to understand "the greatest pain."

Unresisting, Al was taken by ambulance to a hospital where emergency treatments were administered.

"He will have special nursing care, both day and night," the doctor told us, "until he shows signs of a normal recovery."

But before two weeks had passed, weeks during which as a family we suffered together, sometimes certain, sometimes uncertain of our absent brother's recovery, as quickly as it had come, the strange spell came to an end.

One evening when we were gathered in The Room, when the chill of approaching winter required the lighting of fires, and the bringing in of the harvest was over, the door opened and Al stood before us. He had walked twelve miles in hospital slippers, in his night clothes, with a blanket to shelter him from the chill of autumn. In the temporary absence of his guardians, he had forced the window of his room. From the window sloped the roof of a dormer, and from there the down pipe of the eavestroughing brought him to the level of the street.

"It was easy," Al said later.

How can I describe our reaction? Almost it seemed as if my brother had returned from the dead, and, in a measure, this was true.

My father was the first to reach him but there was yet a battle to be won.

"Don't touch me," my brother stormed. "Why did you let them take me away? Why did you let them shut me up like some crazy person? I'll never forgive you."

"It was a normal reaction," the doctor explained, when Da went to him for help, heartbroken.

Al could speak now but he would not speak to his father.

"It will pass," the doctor consoled Da. "Give him time. He's suffering from the prevalent opinion that all types of nervous trouble, including mental shock, are symptoms of mental disease or insanity. Some day we'll laugh at the idea, but for the present we have to cope with it. Treat him as you have always treated him and don't show you're hurt when he tries to hurt you."

Da did not show his hurt but he grew older-looking and more quiet. Then, after more than a year, one winter night Al did not go to his room after supper and chores as had been his adopted habit. No one was in The Room except my father when Al came to him.

"I want to talk to you," Al said.

Da, sitting by the fire in his favourite chair, stood up. It was the first time that Al had directly addressed him since the day of his return.

"I blamed you for treating me as if I were crazy," Al said. "Well I was crazy not to realize that you only wanted to help me."

Al's arms met around the aging frame of the one who had suffered with him. It was Da who could not speak now, while tears coursed down his cheeks, but Al's tears were falling too. Then Al laughed, a healthy, hearty laugh.

"Can you imagine anyone with guts," he said, "losing his mind over a girl like that?"

And the stars danced,
And the little rabbits in their burrows hugged each other,
And the whole world sang for joy.

XVII

We Choose Careers

Woman's place at home should be;
None so fortunate as she.

Jarcie Lee

My Uncle David was a prominent surgeon in California. He had two daughters with a space of seven years between them. When the elder was entering her teens my uncle decided that a trip around the world would be an excellent introduction to her further education and a well-earned holiday for my Aunt Agnes and himself. Life as a medical missionary in China had seriously threatened his health. The necessary homecoming to America had merely plunged him into a round of services which his exceptional abilities and humanitarian nature could not refuse to assume.

On the return trip, the family spared time to visit with us. Excitement ran high within me as I listened to tales of far-away lands and the mention of ways of life which were little more than words to my restricted understanding.

My sister Jean, whose quiet beauty was undeniable to the most casual eye, was invited by my aunt and uncle to visit them with all expenses paid. Jean, the support of my mother in work and in decision-making, the confidante of Lill and the one person to whom I had, from early childhood, poured out strange thoughts and questionings, how could we do without her? However, all were agreed that Jean must be permitted this opportunity to take part in a way of life unfamiliar to us, a farming family, and to gain the

150

benefit of journeying into a different country. Shortly after our relatives reached home we received the exciting news that another child was expected. It was Aunt Agnes who wrote to my mother as follows:

"David is sure," she wrote, "that it will be a boy this time and I am inclined to agree with him."

A boy it was, and now a second invitation was sent to Jean. It said, "We really need you. Please come."

Without a sign of jealousy or fear of becoming a substitute, as well as carrying her own responsibilities, my sister Lill shared in the preparations for Jean's exciting adventure.

Careers for women were still uncommon in our land. They were more common in the United States of America. Before a month had passed a letter reached my parents from Uncle David offering my sister a complete sharing in their family life and assets, and an education of her own choosing, if permission were granted for the separation which would be necessary.

"Our daughters need an older sister," he wrote.

Permission of course was not a requirement, for Jean was twenty-five – not a requirement, but a matter of filial loyalty and personal choice. The choice was made and Jean came home after three months to be the strong influence and support of us all and to contribute the quiet devotion which made her presence necessary to our happiness.

Jean did not, however, come home with empty hands. I do not refer to the generous and numerous gifts which relatives in that far-away state of the Union had lavished upon us all. There were ten children in my father's family. Seven had emigrated to that state, had married there and were established in business or professions. At one time, restless and lonely for his kin, my father had laid plans to sell out in Canada and to join them. I was a very small child at the time but I can remember my mother and sisters packing large cartons and barrels with clothing and china. The time of preparation may have been a week or two. It may have been a month. Then the unpacking began. Everything was returned to its place in the old house and life as usual was resumed. I do not know why and I cannot recall any discussion of the going or of the turning back. Perhaps my parents could not face the division which would have taken place in our family, for it was certain that my brothers would remain in Canada. Al would purchase the farm. Will would continue in his prosperous occupation in town. It is my belief that the very thought of separation was a deciding factor.

However, the visit which Jean made brought about many changes in our family life. American women were becoming career women and some of their ambition had spilled over into Canada. But, as yet, few country girls could be spared from home duties; therefore, except in marriage, few had broken away from their home life.

The first sign of change was Jean's decision to enter the hospital in town for a nurse's training. I remember the day her decision became final. As was common, I was at home from school following two weeks in bed. It was a warm day in late September. Most of the birds had migrated but a robin sang softly and haltingly in the elm tree above the little stone house, as if mourning their departure yet feeling, for some reason, unwilling to follow them. I had slipped out onto the veranda. I sat down on the upper step leading from the front door. I folded my arms across my knees and laid my head on them. I felt strong sympathy for the robin, who surely must have been feeling something of what I was feeling at the thought of Jean's leave-taking. Of course the town of Galt was only four miles away and she would, she said, have "time off to come home at least once a week." I knew that it was foolish of me to want to cry, but coming home would not be the same as being at home.

Unfortunately for Jean, during the month of January, scarcely five months after she had entered her training, she suffered from an illness which left her with a noticeable heart murmur. Termination of work as a nurse was recommended and Jean came home, quieter perhaps but with no other sign of discouragement nor bitterness. Was it selfish of me, I asked my conscience the night of her homecoming, as I rejoiced in secret? Again I was able to depend upon the touch of her gentle hands when I suffered attacks of pain, *my* nurse, if not permitted to train for that profession.

It was Lill who took advantage of the change in plans as soon as Jean was able to resume her duties in our home; and it was Jean who urged Lill to do so.

During Jean's absence we had employed a maid, the daughter of a farmer in an adjoining community. She was entirely happy to be so occupied and was delighted when she learned that Lill intended to follow Jean's example to prepare herself for a career of some sort.

Although Jean could not endure physically the strenuous routine of a nurse's training in those days, she was soon to resume her former responsibilities at home, but she remained a career woman nevertheless, and I overheard a conversation which may have affected my own way of life later on.

Certainly the influences upon Jean of our relatives in California had presented a new picture of woman's role in a changing society. Among the cousins there, Isabella was teaching in High School, Margaret planning a professorship, Emmaline to be a concert pianist, and, later, Helen to become a social worker in Hawaii. Young women were realizing that life could hold for them a choice of occupation without denying them the dream of happiness in marriage, but there were other reasons for Lill's restlessness.

My friend Tillie's middle name was Lillian and mine was Louise. In this way our families acknowledged the close friendship between Lill and Louie.

"Louie says we'll never get anywhere if we stay in this old dump," Lill was heard to say.

The "old dump" was our village, loved by me.

"It's good to have ambition," answered Mother, "but not to let it run away with you. What would you like to do?"

From Lill's expression one could see that she had expected opposition from Mother and was taken by surprise.

"Why, I don't really know," Lill faltered, "but I'm pretty certain. Both Louie and I would like to take a college course, maybe at Macdonald Institute. You can become an Institutional Housekeeper or a Dietitian after two years there, and you don't have to be a high-school graduate to get in if you're well recommended by a minister or somebody who knows you're decent and all that. Of course, it costs money. Louie doesn't have to worry about that, but I do. There's really no difficulty though, if somebody will lend it. For it will be easy to pay it back. The girls who graduate are getting as much as fifty dollars a month and their board. Louie and I have counted up and we think we can make the two years on five hundred dollars. Jean, why don't you say something?" Lill said petulantly, turning to Jean who was mixing the ingredients of a suet pudding at the kitchen table.

"All I can say is," Jean commented, "that I'd like to see you go, but I haven't the five hundred dollars to lend you."

The previous year had been one of unusual prosperity in both farm and garden.

"I'm going to ask Da if he'll lend it to me," Lill declared boldly, "and I'll pay him interest too."

That evening, as my father was reading the *Family Herald and Weekly Star* while I sat beside him discussing an advertisement offering a trip around the world with a sure plan to finance it, Lill made her appeal.

My father folded the paper and laid it on the table beside him. When disturbed, his brown eyes had red lights in them. The red lights were in them at that moment as they met Lill's large blue ones. I noticed Lill swallowing nervously as she explained her plan, but she looked so capable and her face was lit by a dream of success.

My father murmured something under his breath, looked hard at her and asked, "Do you know what becomes of girls like you who set themselves up to handle their own affairs and spend a lot of money getting ready to do it? They no sooner get what they go after than they turn around and marry somebody. Then what?"

Lill's eyes flashed fire.

"Then what?" she repeated. "They know a lot more than they would have known without an education and so they make better wives and mothers."

Da got out of his chair and took off his spectacles. He laid them carefully on top of the folded paper.

"This takes a bit of thinking about," he said, and went out.

Mother came in from the kitchen. Lill was sitting in Da's chair and she was mopping her eyes.

"Don't cry, Lill. You heard what he said, and I say the same thing. But you must give us time. You know we want what's best for each of you."

"Old-fashioned, that's what everybody is," Lill stormed. "Just plain old-fashioned. How is it that every girl's expected to get married. Look at Cousin Grace and Cousin Mary. You're always telling us what wonderful people they are. It doesn't make sense."

She marched off to the kitchen and soon the dishes were rattling in the pan.

"Go and help her with the dishes, Jessie," Mother said.

154

Cousin Mary, while caring for an invalid mother, had become a teacher of piano and had remained at home. She was pointed to as a model of heroism and self-sacrifice. Cousin Mary, it was said, had been deeply loved, but had refused marriage, preferring to devote herself to duty. Cousin Grace, who could speak four languages, had taught in Trinidad for thirty years. Cousin Grace was single also.

I began to think about the conflicting impulses which made saints of some and sinners of others. My own ambitions, at the moment, were twofold – I would become an author at all costs, but I had every intention of fulfilling my womanhood. The thought of following a career only was a very unattractive one indeed.

Lill got her wish, but the time of realization was delayed. The condition of my health deteriorated during that autumn. The "spells" became more frequent and the need for prompt action became a certainty. The nature of the plans which developed as a result required Lill's presence at home.

XVIII

I Enter a New World

> ... Common as light is love,
>   And its familiar voice wearies not ever ...
>
>   Percy Bysshe Shelley

The fortunes of our family seemed to be improving. It was the summer of 1909 and I was approaching thirteen. After six months out of school I had managed to pass my Entrance as the title for admittance into High School from Public School was called.

Examinations were tried in Tassie Hall, an impressive grey stone building with long bare corridors. Da drove me to Galt in the buggy and I came home on the "Grand Trunk" which dropped me off at the village station, a small shabby building reaching the edge of the narrow wooden platform. This seemed to all but precipitate one onto the tracks.

It was a close summer day with threatening storms along the horizon and a humid mist on the hills. Summer had only begun and there were weeks of vacation to enjoy before High School would open. High School – how often intermittent sicknesses during Public School days had caused me to fear that I would never reach there. Although discussions of my frequent illnesses were carefully omitted from conversations among members of my family, their attitude of concern for me was ever present. This attitude created in me a doubt that I would ever become a woman grown. I did not admit this doubt to myself but it was in my

156

subconscious, causing me to dwell unnaturally upon the uncertainty of life and the certainty of death.

I had been writing verses from the time I could write words. I had been composing them before that time but, as the years passed and the attacks of pain, or "spells" as they were called, became more frequent and more severe, my verses developed into poetry, apprehensive and sorrow-filled, unlike the expressions of a healthy child. During winter, when the small-paned windows of my room became decorated with prongs of frost, and the sun turned the frost tips to rose as it fell in the west, I lay alone while other members of the family were busy and in the ever-present scribbler I wrote, at twelve years:

Flame of life in the east at dawn,
Flare of death in the sinking sun
Both are one.

Neck to neck, never knowing rest,
Life and death at the King's behest,
Forward pressed.

Coming silently as the rose,
Gone as dew on the petal goes,
Tide that flows.

Fading rays on the western hill,
Promised morn in the east fulfil,
By His will!

Lill's light footsteps on the stairs announced the arrival of the supper hour. Lill was a healthy young woman and she rebelled at my unexplained state of ill health. She brought in my tray. In one corner lay a flower and leaf from Mother's Patience plant. The tray was daintily arranged. I looked up to thank Lill as she set it down before me, but her hand was on my notebook. Her alert eyes were scanning what I had written even as she said, "Poetry again?"

I flushed a little. This poetry was of a private sort and I had not intended that it should be read by anyone but myself. Lill raised her eyes from the book and gave me a long sober look. Then she laid the book down where it had been and left the room without a word. Later that evening my parents paid me a good-night visit together. Da sat down heavily in a chair. Mother, sitting on the bedside, took my hand.

Dr. Sylvester Edward Charlton. Daily he
drove a distance of ten miles to visit a
sick child. 1908.

"Your Da and I have been talking about the doctor," she began. "He doesn't seem to be helping you very much."

At this point my father spoke.

"No, he doesn't, but his intentions are good, I'll admit that. Intentions aren't enough, though, and I think we'll try someone else."

I looked from one to the other in surprise, rather nervously.

"But I don't know anyone else," I protested.

"Sometimes it's good to have a change," Da continued. "Will and Oma like the one they've had very much and now he's opening an office in Galt. Maybe he would have a look at you, and if you like him he might come out to look after you. He takes country patients. Everybody that I've spoken to has a good word for him. The next time I go to town I'm going in to see him. His name is Sylvester Charlton – a good name."

"I think it will be kind of interesting to have a new doctor," Mother put in.

I thought about what they had said after they had gone to bed and my sisters came upstairs.

Jean slept beside me whenever I was ill, alert to every move which I made on occasions of restlessness. Lill slept in the single bed. Jean was twenty-seven now and the beautiful eloquence of her dark eyes was never without a hint of sadness. We did not talk about the reason for this. We had been forbidden by Mother to talk about it and we obeyed, but it seems to me now that the extreme solicitude and tenderness which my sister Jean showed for an ailing child through my years of illness may have been a form of release for the pain in her own heart.

I may have been ten years of age, I may have been eleven, when I stood at sunset on our old veranda looking southward. We had had a guest for supper – a friend of my brother's who was attending college. He would become a teacher someday soon. He was a handsome young man, tall, dark, and with a special dignity matching well the dignity and charm of the young woman now walking hand in hand with him up the country road. Even as a child I was aware of Jean's beauty. As I approached adolescence, I was moved by pride and some envy when I looked at her. There was a hint of resentment in my feeling now, coupled with an awareness that some new feature had been added to my sister's life

– a new experience. To my possessive eyes she was, if possible, more beautiful than ever.

"We're going to have another brother," Lill said one day, coming to stand beside me, as the couple set off for a drive through the country with his horse and buggy. Motor cars were not yet in evidence. Restraint, respect and repression were still features of a man's wooing. This man was wooing my sister, I knew it, and now Lill's words confirmed my conviction.

After graduation, he took a position as an educator in a distant province. Jean was to follow him there. How could I part with her, thought I, and by some turn of fortune this was not to happen.

I do not remember who brought the news of his marriage. I do not remember whether it was received by letter. About that tragic happening in my sister's life, I remember only two evidences. Shortly after the news reached us, I woke one night to find my mother standing by our bedside, a small lamp in one hand and a cup of tea in the other. I have the memory of my sister sitting up in bed with a Bible on her knees. Her face, in the half light, was pale and her dark eyes darker with tragedy. I was half asleep, but before I slept fully again, I heard my mother say, "Jean, you mustn't go on like this," and I heard Jean answer, "I must know what's right."

Shortly after, when I was again well enough to be downstairs, I was playing the organ with Lill singing to my accompaniment when Mother suddenly appeared in the parlour doorway.

"I thought Jean was here with you," she said. She looked from the window and Lill and I found ourselves looking too. It was a beautiful day in early spring. The sky was billowing with pearly clouds and birds were singing everywhere. Jean stood alone on the veranda, her hands clasped before her. We could not see her face but we knew instinctively the emotion that would be written there. My mother turned to us.

"Never speak his name again in this house," she said, in a voice of command. "Never!" Mother's command was obeyed.

It must have been fifty years after that time. As I was coming down the steps of a funeral home after paying my last respects to a dear friend, a grey-haired man, tall and erect although surely more than three score years and ten, was coming up the steps on the other side of the rail. He stopped when he saw me. His dark eyes behind thick glasses registered incredulity. Then:

160

"My God! my God!" he muttered, continuing in full voice to me, "you must be – you must be Jessie."

"I am Jessie," I said.

"But you look like her – like Jean, I mean."

I continued on my way.

The autumn of my thirteenth year, I realized my dream – I became a High School student. During the summer my health had improved. For two weeks I rejoiced in the companionship and the surroundings of a new type of education. Da drove me to the trolley each morning and I returned home by the train at night. I was in a state of high excitement. Every feature of my new experience delighted me. Then, early one morning, I woke with a spasm of pain which could not be ignored. The new doctor was called and somehow I realized that the end of my school days had come.

The new doctor early admitted his inability to diagnose my case. He recommended my removal to the Hospital for Sick Children in Toronto, there to be placed in the care of a specialist in Internal Medicine, Dr. Alexander McPhedran.

"He's one of the best in the land," the doctor said. "If she were my own child, he would be my choice."

I was not told of the doctor's decision until a family conference had been held. I had been allowed downstairs to lie on the couch under the south window of The Room. There I seemed to be one of the family again. But that first evening, after I had been served supper and our men had returned to the barns to do the usual last chores of the day, my parents and sisters told me what the doctor had said. Lill sat cross-legged on a rug by my couch. Jean took a chair close to me and her hand found mine. Mother and Da stood together and it was Da who broke the news to me. At first I burst into tears and then I heard Mother's voice, cheerful and confident.

"Jean will go with you," she said, " and she will stay until you are able to come home again. Da will go along too, and so will the doctor, but they will come back after they hear what the specialist has to say. I've written to Cousin Jeanie McGowan and she wrote me back. There's a house across the street from the hospital where they take boarders, and a nice room with a window next to the street. She's spoken for the room so that Jean won't have to do any looking. You won't be alone, you see, and there will be lots of new things to learn about, kind of like going to school."

161

Jean's smile of reassurance, Lill's affectionate arm thrown over me, the combined concern of all was like the sudden burst of sunlight through a clouded sky. I was not alone. I would not be alone. Recalling this moment, I realized the great good fortune of a child with a loving family. I struggled with tears but I no longer felt afraid.

There was also the new doctor. He was a man who had inspired me with confidence from his first visit. His expression was one of concentration and deep concern. His love for children was evidenced in his gentleness of manner when speaking to me, in the way he included me when speaking to others.

"He's an unusual fellow," Da said. "Not many doctors would leave their practice and go with their patient. He will meet us at the train in Galt and we'll all travel together. It will take up his whole day and that's a sign of his interest. You'll be in the best of hands and as Ma said, Jean will go with you."

At that moment Al, who had come in by the kitchen door, overhearing the conversation, poked his head into The Room.

"So you're going for a train ride, Kid," he said, with a twinkle in his grey eyes. "Maybe the engineer will let you have a whack at driving the train. I'd like a chance at that myself."

The others laughed with him but the laughter did not sound merry. I was not deceived. A few days later, Al drove us to town in the democrat, for there was not room for four people in the one-seated buggy. Al tied the horse behind the station where it would not be startled by the oncoming train. He waited with us until we were joined by the doctor and then, from the left on the other side of the long bridge across the Grand, with cautious speed, we saw the train beginning to approach. Excitement now overcame apprehension. The train puffed and snorted to a standstill. With a good-bye kiss, Al was gone and we were mounting the steps into the coach, so unlike that small chugging Grand Trunk on which I had ridden home from school for those two short weeks.

A new experience of life had begun for me.

XIX

That New Experience

I carry my lamp into a room
Where new experiences wait.

Jarcie Lee

It was late September when, as a party of four, we set out on our
train ride to Toronto. It might have been a pleasure trip; there was
no hint of gloom.

The doctor selected two seats facing each other. He stood
aside until Jean and I entered and sat down; then he and Da took
the remaining seats.

The train puffed and wheezed for a long time, it seemed to me,
before it whistled sharply and the wheels began to turn.

A brakeman was making signs to the engineer. He stood close
to our window. Da was watching every move he made. "We're
off," Da said, with a wave of his hand to the man and a smile to
me. What was it about Da which made one so comfortable when
he was present? I smiled too and glanced shyly at the doctor. He
was still new to me, but I felt quite comfortable with him.

"Toronto's a big city," Da commented, as if in preparation for
our arrival there, almost two hours away.

The doctor nodded. "Big," he agreed, "but the same people
live in every city. Just more in some than in others. Boys and girls
too, lots of them, Jessie," he added, and his dark eyes smiled into
mine. His voice, too, was reassuring. The thought of Toronto no

longer frightened me. I would just be as other girls – and Jean would always be there. After a consultation between Dr. C. and the specialist, the former would return home and Da with him.

Except for the visit to the John A. Bruce seed company when I was nine, I had never been in the city of Toronto. Since the business of market gardening had been entered into, Da had gone each January for a supply of seeds and to place an advertisement in *The Globe* for hired help. The city was not new to him nor to Jean, for she had visited cousins there several times.

But I, scarcely remembering the former occasion, viewed the maze of tracks, as we approached, with fear. Trains, I thought, might appear from any direction to threaten the position of that on which we were travelling. When it crawled to a stop, the doctor proceeded toward the door and we followed him. Accompanied by shouts of orders from the red-faced conductor, we prepared to descend. Leaving Da and the doctor on the platform to claim our luggage, Jean and I made our way down a stairway leading to a tunnel-like corridor into the station. I clung to Jean. The confusion alarmed me.

"Don't go home, will you?" I begged, near to tears. "You won't leave me, will you, Jean?"

We turned a corner and there was a railway station with long bench-like seats with backs. Jean drew me close to her on one of them, partly occupied by an old man with his coat rolled under his head for a pillow. He was asleep and did not stir. "Of course I won't go home," Jean said. "Not until you do."

Soon we were joined by Da and the doctor, accompanied by a boy with a red cap carrying our two valises, Jean's and mine. He led us through the great station to a street where horse-drawn cabs and two motor cars stood along the curb. The doctor chose one of the cars and gave the driver orders. Soon we were whirling up the city street – my first ride in an automobile.

The hospital was on College Street – a red brick building with many windows, each one with a small iron balcony.

Da and Jean sat down in a large hallway to wait with me while the doctor gave and received orders. Then we climbed a long stair. A nurse went with us. She opened a door into a room with pale green walls and a snowy white bed and dresser. It had a fireplace with a long mantel, and two rather narrow windows facing the street.

164

"This is your room, dear," she said to me, "and your sister's room is right across the street on the third floor. Isn't that nice? The lady who owns the house came over to see us. She was thoughtful, wasn't she?"

Everyone was concerned for me – this certainly drove out fear and inspired confidence.

That afternoon, our doctor and Dr. Alexander McPhedran held a consultation. Before my father and Dr. C. caught the late afternoon train home, it was decided that an operation should be performed to determine the cause of my recurring attacks of pain. A doctor was named. "The best in the land," Dr. C. reassured us, "Mr. Cameron – he doesn't like to be called doctor. He specializes in surgery. He's from England. I favour the gentleman except for one thing – his fee. And it has to be guaranteed, but I told McPhedran I could vouch for payment, Mr. Beattie." Da's nod was firm. "You can," he said. "But you'll be here with him?"

The eyes of Dr. C. were watching me; there was an appeal in mine, I know. He smiled into them. "Of course I'll be here," he said. "Jessie is my patient. You're staying, Jean. That's good. Perhaps it won't be long until we can take Jessie home again."

They all left then, Jean to claim her room and the doctor and my father to the train.

But with perfect timing, a nurse came in with an appetizing supper tray and a cheery "Hello."

I began to feel important and a little excited. I remembered the directions on etiquette in the *Ladies' Home Journal* which I had never failed to read. After Jean's visit to California Aunt Agnes had entered for us a subscription to that magazine. I was very hungry, but I ate daintily, enjoying creamed chicken, a baked potato, a wedge of squash, and, for dessert, orange ice and a cookie. I had never tasted water-ice before.

But when the nurse hurried in to take the tray away, she left the door of my room ajar. I heard the crying of children and an occasional scream, as of one in pain.

Dusk was creeping in and the lights came on. There was a shaded lamp on my dresser. I felt a sense of the bigness of the place, the strangeness and impending challenges, only words as yet, but conjuring up images of Al in the ambulance (though years had passed), of his stomach treatments and of his limp of pain. I examined the windows across the street. Each of the four small

165

ones on the third floor was a dormer, and they were unlit. I buried my face in my pillow and sobbed. But, when I looked out again, the flame of a lamp glowed in the centre dormer and there was a hand holding the lamp and another hand waving.

Every night at dusk, for six weeks, the lamplight glowed and a hand waved to me. Soon, after I grew accustomed to the distance between us, I could see Jean smiling to me in the reflected light and I was at peace.

After three days came the operation. Mr. Cameron was a red-faced man, dark of hair and eyes, with a small, sharply-pointed beard. He called on me three times before the operation and three times after. He did not converse with me, but he said on the final morning, "You heal well." His orders were that I should lie very still and on my back for ten days. Small wonder that a course of castor oil in a cup of warm milk was given to me each morning. Lill once declared that each one of us in our family had been falsely promised the same shining half-dollar for the taking of a dose of oil. It had been my lot to receive the fifty cents for I was the youngest. I took no pleasure in the payment, nor did I ever remove the sum from a china cup in our cabinet.

Every week-day a pencilled letter had arrived from the anxious and faithful members of my family at home. By the time I was served a cup of warm milk before breakfast each morning, with bubbles of yellow floating on the top, I had accumulated a pile of letters in their envelopes. But now the envelopes disappeared, one by one, formed by me into a spoon-like tool with which I removed the oil, letting it soak well into the paper, then placing the latter in the iron basket of the fireplace near my bed.

A few days after the specialist's order, as he examined me, he turned with a look of satisfaction to the nurse accompanying him. "Ah," he said, "she's better, much better. There's nothing like good old castor oil," adding, "Continue the treatment." The treatment was continued as formerly.

Despite my childish behaviour and the loss of "good old castor oil," I made excellent progress toward recovery. But, really, what did this recovery mean? It meant that after an exploratory operation in search of the cause of my "spells," after the removal of a healthy appendix, the cause remained undiscovered. "We made a snip here and a snip there," Dr. McPhedran said, "but actually, we found nothing out of order, and guessing in surgery is a poor business."

At the end of three weeks, I was preparing to return home when an epidemic of diphtheria developed within the hospital, and I was one of eight patients so affected. Now Jean's daily visits ceased. I spent three long weeks in isolation. The nurses and doctors who took care of me came robed in long white gowns, wearing caps and masks.

In those weeks of enforced loneliness, a young English nurse, Louie Ruth Bryce, showed a special interest in me. She now provided a service which introduced me to a new kind of experience. When I was released and permitted to go home, there were twenty-eight books on my mantel, all brought to me by her. "They will be burned after you leave," she said. "A friend of mine in the library gave them to me." Although classified as worn-out copies, the texts were intact. I made the acquaintance of countries about which I had known very little. There were books about England, several of which portrayed the countryside and the people so clearly that for a long time when people talked to me about England, I half believed I had been there. Most enjoyed of all was *Carette of Sark*, by John Oxenham. Miss Bryce later became renowned for her skill and devotion to the profession of nursing as an assistant to the famous Dr. Wilfred T. Grenfell in Labrador. A record of her experiences was later published in the *Nurses' Journal*, London, England.

And there was Mr. D., now a medical student at the University of Toronto. He had learned that I was a patient in the Hospital for Sick Children, and the location of my room. I came to watch daily for the wave of his hand and his cheery smile as he passed by my window, which overlooked the street.

Jean remained in her little third-floor room, faithfully waving to me morning and night. For the period of time when she could not visit me, she came to the hospital daily for a report on my progress, and to assure me of her presence I received alternately a fancy chocolate in a paper cup and a rosy Northern Spy apple.

It was now December. My window was raised a few inches for ventilation. There was no screen. Each "apple day" I set my prize on the window sill for cooling. How crisp and delicious those apples became when eaten at just the right temperature. By bending to one side, I could reach the sill from my bed, where I still spent most of my time. One evening, as my hand sought the cooling apple, I

167

accidentally touched it with the tip of my finger and it rolled out and along the balcony to the farther ledge where the railing prevented it from dropping to the street.

My heart sank. It was the largest and rosiest apple that I had received. The more I looked at it, the more certain I became that I must have it at whatever cost. And what would be the cost? I reviewed each possibility. I did not act without considering the consequences. I had not been out of my room for six weeks. The room was very warm. The weather was cold. I could contract pneumonia. I measured each movement required to retake my prize. I felt sure that I could be out and in again in less than one minute. No one could catch even a cold in one minute, I argued. The other danger was more difficult to estimate.

The balcony appeared secure enough for my weight, but who could tell – a loose portion, a faulty rail which a touch from me could precipitate into the street, taking the apple and me with it. What then? I might be killed or severely injured. I might never see home again. Home – the most precious place in the world, that I had cried myself to sleep in longing for. But such dramatization, such cowardice was mere foolishness. The apple was there waiting for me. It would wait for me until my hand grasped it. Without words, its very beauty told me so. I threw off the covers. I pushed up the window. I made a dash. Only two steps, only one carefully planned closure of the hand. I do not believe I breathed until I stood again with the closed window at my back. I turned to open it two inches – someone might suspect. Then I got into bed and, leaning against my pillows, I ate the sweetest apple I had ever tasted.

There was a covering of grey over the sky on the morning Jean entered my room for the first time in three weeks. The period of infection was over. I was free to go home.

Home. Where those waited who had endured anxiety and separation for six weeks. To aid my mother at the helm, there had been Lill, uncomplaining although deprived of entering "Mac Hall" for another year while she took Jean's place as the support of my mother.

Da and Lill met us at the railway station in Galt. "My goodness, you've grown a lot!" Lill commented as we all crowded into the single-seated buggy. "Wait until Mother sees you. She thought we should take the buggy because it rides easier than the

168

democrat, but she didn't count on the size of you." Six weeks in the hospital had brought out curves and increased my stature.

The first snow was falling as Nell trotted along. How precious every familiar thing was: the winding road, the thorn-apple trees, now bare of leaves and dotted with red fruit, the blue river, the watering trough where, half-way home, we gave Nell a long drink. Then the village, oh, so small to my eyes now, but how dear; the hill, the descent, and up and around the bend – the old house, with Mother, Edith and our dog all at the window. Da stopped at what we called the little gate. No one could wait to drive into the lane and yard. The tears on my mother's cheeks as her arms met around me were an unusual sight, for Mother did not often cry visibly; when deeply moved, she cried within. The six weeks of waiting had been hardest for her. Meanwhile, with jumps of joy, Little Sister joined in the welcome.

There comes to me many times that moment of return to the old house. Al had gone West that summer with the harvesters. But where was Grandpa? Then I heard a familiar chord coming irregularly from the little parlour. Grandpa's fingers were fumbling, but the notes were clear – "Be it ever so humble, there's no place like home."

XX

Christmas 1910

The quiet pool a while
If it must be . . .

The author

We were all at home for Christmas 1910. December was a
beautiful winter month with fluttering snowfalls and radiant
sunsets. Al returned from Qu'Appelle after remaining for the
threshings, so impressive in the great West. My brother Will with
Oma and their son Francis, a handsome dark-eyed five-year-old,
and baby Elizabeth, came to eat dinner with us and there was
Little Sister (Edith), prettier and healthier after two years with us.
There was Grandpa, of course, still able to dance the sword dance
and the Highland fling and two "winter help," as Da called the
year-round hired men.

I had been home for more than a month now and I was
determined that the operation had cured me. Certainly I had not
been harmed by it except for multiple adhesions caused by Mr.
Cameron's order to lie still on my back for ten days. The back and
the front of me had grown together, our doctor said, and I suffered
much discomfort. But there had been no "spells," so my family
believed, and I had grown too big to really sit on Da's knee now.
However, when evening came I was usually somewhere near.

During Christmas week I assembled my books for a return to
school in the New Year with Dr. C.'s permission. But I would board

in town, coming home for week-ends only. My mother accompanied my father to choose a room. I was affected by conflicting emotions. The thrill of attending High School in town was lessened by the necessity of living away from home. I had experienced enough of that during almost two months in the hospital, even with Jean always near. Home had never been so sweet, so love-lit as now after that absence. How could I leave it?

Beauty within, and without. From every window of the old house. Busy people with contented faces inside; Al and the hired men cutting wood in the bush, south-westward. Whack, whack. The smell of pine roots burning in the greenhouse furnaces where Da was warming and blending soils for seed planting. His clothing carried the pine smoke when he came in for meals, and especially at night when he stoked the furnace with heavy knots of hardwood to smoulder until 5 a.m., at which time he refilled the fire-pots with pine which flamed quickly after touching the embers.

In winter when the maples, elms and oaks on the knobby hills were leafless, one could spot the outlines of farm buildings; among them, just peering over the ridge, the house and barn newly built where a summer fire had left a path of destruction. The farm had been sold after the fire and it seemed strange to think of new people living there. I had never seen them and I wondered about them – a young couple with twin boys, Da said.

"English and very friendly."

Many country people had duck or goose for Christmas dinner. That year, because of the size of our household, we had both. There was mince pie, too. I was growing fast and I ate heartily.

I now occupied a single walnut bed in my sisters' room. On Christmas night I woke with that knife-like pain. It couldn't be true. I buried my face in the pillow to stifle the moans, which were uncontrollable. I told myself that what I was suffering had its cause in over-eating. For more than an hour I lay as still as possible and endured an agony even more severe than I had known before the operation. Finally, in spite of myself, I sobbed aloud. Jean was beside me in a minute.

"It's back," I moaned. "It's back again."

It was back again. Like some beast of prey, it had been lying in wait only. It had been there during the months of moderate comfort while I deluded myself in vain.

The return of the unidentified sickness cast a gloom over our entire family. I felt responsible for that gloom and ashamed that I had not been "cured." So many doctors had been consulted, so much money had been spent, and the normal routine of our family life had been interrupted. While we waited for the doctor to arrive, I sobbed as much from disillusionment as from pain.

Dr. C. came and went every day for six weeks. The return trip was a distance of eight miles and this had to be covered with a horse and cutter. The efficiency of motor cars had not extended to their use on snowy country roads. January passed into February and February was close to March before I was able to come downstairs to enjoy the cosy comfort of The Room and the companionship of everyone in the family.

Just as it had come, the terrifying "spell" had passed, but during the period I had been treated I was able to survive only by frequent injections of morphine. Dr. C. brought other doctors, he sought advice from some who could not come but were willing to assist, he read medical books late into the night until, he admitted to my father, Mrs. C. had found him at his desk, head on his arms, fast asleep.

Those were long hard weeks but the daily visits of the doctor brought more than security. They brought a warm friendship which supported my spirit while his skills sought to improve my health. He was a tall handsome man with kindly dark eyes and an expression of true concern for the welfare of his patient. Sometimes, when he stood with Jean at the foot of my bed giving her explicit orders, for she had become my nurse, I thought how alike they were. They could have been brother and sister both in appearance and nature. There was no hardness in either of them.

"I don't know what I would do without you," I heard Mother say to Jean many times, after an almost sleepless night.

"I offered to help her, Mother," Lill would say, and now I realize that Lill's voice had a little hurt in it.

Lill did try to help and her eagerness was apparent, even to a child, but her slender hands were hard-boned and firm as she stroked my forehead. Jean's were long-fingered and gentle of touch. I tried not to show that I felt the difference but Lill must have sensed it, because on one occasion she said, "Do my fingers hurt you, Jessie? Al and I were playing ball in the barn loft last night and I have some callouses."

"No, they don't hurt me," I said, but I didn't deceive her.

172

When she turned from me, she put her handkerchief to her eyes.

One late February day, the doctor's visit was prolonged by a consultation with my parents downstairs. He came up again.

"I wanted to say good-bye to you, Jessie," he said lightly. "I won't be here tomorrow. I have a consultation out-of-town but I'll telephone before I go to see how you are. We've been discussing whether or not you should go to school this winter and we all feel that it would be better to wait until the spring or even next fall. That will give you time to recover and I know you aren't wasting your opportunity to improve your mind in the meantime."

He picked up a copy of *Ivanhoe* by Sir Walter Scott, which was lying face down on my bed.

"Are you enjoying this?" he asked me.

"Yes, I am," I answered.

"That's wonderful," he said. "Keep right on with your reading, and your mother tells me you are writing stories and poetry. I'm sure that this year at home may be a good thing in the end. Learning is often better done out of school." He patted my shoulder and left me.

I lay thinking. The window of my bedroom looked out over snowy fields toward the west. Beyond the fields rose a pine-clad hill. The sun was declining and soon a ruddy glow would cover the sky behind the trees – the promise of tomorrow. There came a peace out of pain. A promise was what I needed. I picked up my book and began to read again.

I did not go to school that spring.

The autumn season entered with its usual beauty of sight and sound. Purple, scarlet and gold changed the trees into elegant shaded lamps. The stumps and the logs in the swamp and the grey fences were garlanded with coloured vines. Flocking birds stopped to voice their farewells as they travelled southward. The air was spiced with ripened fruit and shafts of late flowers.

Lill and Louie, delayed a year by my illness, left for Macdonald College, proud and hopeful.

Tillie entered High School that fall but I did not go with her. It was five difficult years before my secondary education was resumed – difficult but, in many ways, the most formative years of my life.

XXI

The Beginning of an Interlude

Our lives are merely strange dark
interludes . . .

Eugene O'Neill

How did my continued semi-invalidism affect the members of my family and my friends?

Before the death of my sister Isabella at the age of three, my mother had been a member of the church choir.

"Cissy had a voice like a bird," Grandpa said. "As a young woman she was always singing. But after the wee one died, she sang never a note. It was pitiful. Then, when you were born," he told me, "she began the singing again."

I had never heard my mother sing after the period of babyhood ended the necessity of lullabies. It was then that I first became ill and perhaps it was the presence of fear in her heart and the memory of Isabella's death which ended the singing again.

Instead, she could be found at the corner of the veranda where it crossed and turned along the side of the old house, found standing with her hands raised in an attitude of pleading, as if to repel the sound of wagon wheels approaching along the country road. After sleepless nights racked by pain, I would fall into the sleep of exhaustion. Would the passing wagon awake me? It was the dread of this which made her hurry to her place of watchfulness when she heard wheels nearing. The anxiety did not lessen but increased when months passed into years. Would I ever recover?

174

This must have been a question which she asked herself and for which there seemed no reassuring answer from the many who were summoned to diagnose the cause of my pain. Mother grew quieter and laughter became almost unknown to her. As I developed into adolescence this fact lay heavy upon my heart. Sometimes when the spasms came, I told no one. It seemed to me that by continuing in ill health I was deliberately causing unhappiness for those most dear to me.

My father endured the periods of pain by escaping from the sound of my voice.

"Whenever she is taken with it," I heard Mother telling the doctor, "her Da goes to the barn or to the greenhouses where he can't hear her."

If within hearing when the attack came on, he would be there beside me, long enough to assess its serious nature and to summon the doctor at once. After making the first telephone call, if the attack were a severe one, with unreasonable impatience he would make a second call, shouting angrily before the doctor had time to be on his way. He would then leave the house and follow the pattern of behaviour which became his common practice. When the doctor had reached me and was about to return, my father would reappear in time to waylay him and to learn his opinion. Often I would hear them talking together outside my door, and on more than one occasion, the words which were said supported me in my journey through the valley of pain.

"She has every faith in you, Doctor," my father would say, and Dr. C. would answer:

"That makes it all the harder, Mr. Beattie, and I curse my own ignorance."

Next to my parents, Jean, I believe, suffered most with me and the doctor turned to her for the carrying out of his instructions. She was my self-appointed nurse. There were times when, under the effects of morphia, which in my case produced stimulation although easing the pain, Jean would support me with her arms until I fell asleep from sheer exhaustion. I would awake to find her still there, sitting in a cramped position on the side of my bed, fearing to move in case I might awake. If her own health was endangered by over-fatigue, if her own life was sacrificed in nature by her devotion to me, I was never told. Perhaps, in so giving herself, she eased the hurt which she had experienced by the withdrawal of a dream unfulfilled. I do not know. But during the five years while I was intermittently racked by pain, she did not relinquish her post to anyone else, except for needed rest, when my mother took her place.

Excluding summer vacations and over week-ends, Lill was no longer at home. Topping her class at the college-on-the-hill she was quickly chosen for an institutional position. During brief periods with us she cooked and baked and cleaned, her agile strength giving of itself in the manner which she knew best, and showing the warmth of her attachment to home and to us all by the tears in her blue eyes when the time came to return to duty elsewhere. We waited for her homecomings as one waits for a cooling breeze on a hot day.

Lill's place was taken in the house by a woman whose contribution to the welfare of many families in our community was made without stint for many years.

Jennie lived just around the bend and had been bereft of parents in early life. She took over the duties of the home for two older brothers and, when not needed there, gave her services wherever an extra person was required to "help out" in times of emergency.

Jennie's sunny disposition was frequently a part of our home atmosphere. She was a big woman of middle age but with small deft hands in which, when not engaged in serving others, the tatting shuttle or the knitting needles moved continually in the making of dainty laces and homely woollen garments. Her voice was like a song, a treble voice which carried cheer wherever it was heard. Jennie could bake, cook, clean or nurse efficiently, but, to quote Jennie, "I never learned to milk and I never will."

It was her boast. We had a dairy herd and Mother frequently helped with the milking but Jennie was never asked to do so. When Jean could leave my bedside she assisted mother, although "Your pretty hands were never made to squeeze the teats of a cow," Jennie would tell Jean bluntly. Her words were straightforward and plain; they were also sincere.

My brother Al, who knew the meaning of pain, had learned a lesson of restraint which aided him while it hindered him. Because he had found it necessary to ignore the effects of an improperly set bone to carry on the work which he loved, he had developed a gruff defiance which sometimes seemed unfeeling. Al thought to cheer

176

me when he said, appearing at my door, "Hi, Kid. Still in bed, eh? I'm beginning to think you're lazy. You ought to be out in the field helping me to pull turnips."

Then his eyes would twinkle. There would be a wry smile. "It's tough luck, but oh, one of these days, you'll be fit as a fiddle."

Perhaps there would be a story then about some observation in the field or in the woods before he went on his way. Although I was young, I knew that among us all, despite his off-hand manner, no one of us could feel more deeply than could Al.

Meanwhile, Little Sister Edith was progressing at school. There was no longer any question about her becoming a member of our family. She was one of us. She, too, in her little girl way, attended to the wants of the invalid. In a miniature nurse's apron and devised cap, made for her pleasure by Jean, she was given the proud duty of carrying my trays from the top of the stairs into my room. Sometimes there was a small flower or a flowering weed laid in the corner as a decoration. Thought was given in the choice of dishes, however simple the meal, and simple indeed it was, for my digestion would not tolerate anything more.

One grief was the loss of Tillie. Our playmate years were over. Tillie was now a high-school girl as I had dreamed of being and her visits to me were only occasional, for she was healthy and attractive. Between studies and social activities at school, she had little time for me. We drifted apart only to find each other again in a lasting friendship many years later.

During this interlude in my life I acquired a new circle of friends through the medium of the written word and I became an observer, meanwhile, of those who came and went along the road which I did not travel but which brought strangers to our door.

There were intermittent periods of relief for me, some extending into months when a false hope was engendered that the strange sickness would never come again. There was, however, a fear which lurked at all times, even during hours of normal girlhood pleasures, a fear which set me apart in thought, as someone who could never share in the way of life which I was continually devising in verse and story.

It was the summer of 1912. Aunt Mary had come from Hamilton with her two younger children to pay us a flying visit on her way to the Fleming home at Puslinch where Alex, her brother, was a tenant of land still owned by my grandfather. Grandpa would go along with Aunt Mary for a few weeks' change and a renewal of contacts with pioneer families well known to him.

Aunt Mary was small and feminine in appearance but there was no mistaking her strength of character, shown by the way in which she walked. Aunt Mary did not march nor stride but her feet were set with firmness and revealed that she knew where she was going and why. Her visits were bright spots in a summer program of relatives coming and going – especially bright for me, because Aunt Mary had time and the inclination to entertain. The stories which she told often savoured of those told to me by Grandpa, for she had shared in the neighbourhood life at Puslinch during her girlhood days. Her ability to mimic was almost perfect.

"They lived not far away," Aunt Mary said, "and one morning the son appeared at our door. 'Sure, Mary Fleming,' he said, 'me father is sick with the liver complaint and we've been to take him on the stoneboat to the doctor.' I asked him what the doctor said, and he went on to tell me that his father's liver was dirty. 'Sure, Doctor, I explained, that may be for he was workin' in the peat bog. Can't you take it out and clane it?'"

I forgot my troubles when Aunt Mary came to visit. After her story, I joined her in peals of laughter, until she continued:

"But the poor man died, Jessie, and two weeks after, when his sons heard a noise in the apple tree beside the house, probably caused by a prowling raccoon, the one said to the other, 'Sure, don't bother a bit. It's only the old man come back to take his fill.'"

Death – the word was a threat to me. I laughed no longer. But there had been many unusual characters in the wide countryside known to Aunt Mary, and her ability to imitate brought them into my world.

It was during Aunt Mary's visit that summer that I began a six-thousand-word story of life in a country which I had never seen – Ireland. It was a story of mystery and romance, lightened with the introduction of such characters as Aunt Mary's depiction had combined with my imaginings.

Until this time, my attempts at prose had been few, for poetry was my first love during those early years. This was natural, surely, since my emotional life was the awakening in solitude of a desire for more than dreams.

One evening before Aunt Mary's departure, when I had

penned the last word of my story, I took her into my confidence. She listened with gratifying attention while I read the long narrative to her. When I had finished, she looked at me with proud conviction.

"Jessie Lou," she said, "you may be sick in the body but there's nothing wrong with your head. You keep on writing stories like that and I guarantee that you'll become a rich woman."

Such a comment lightened my spirits and sent me along my chosen occupation with confidence that what I was attempting would lead me to the field of authorship, although even at that time I was wisely doubtful of Aunt Mary's further prediction.

Whether in bed or convalescing on the veranda in good weather or in The Room during cooler days, I was attended by a growing pile of scribblers and notebooks and many well-pointed pencils. It seems to me now that I spent the better part of five years, when well enough to do so, in two occupations – the composing of music, never to be recorded, and the writing which led me to a career and authorship after I became a woman.

I received occasional visits from the young people of the village with whom I had attended school, but they came irregularly, and for the most part my contacts with the world outside the old house were limited. There was the coming and going of relatives as visitors, and of men from all parts of the world as workmen. There was the effect of the doctor's calls, which gave me support and confidence when my life was at its lowest ebb and at all times trust and a belief that in some way, sometime, a cure for my malady would be discovered. At sixteen there came the secret dreaming of a romance inspired by the visits in spring and in autumn of the pleasant Mr. Gray about whom I have written in *Along the Road*. The collapse of the romantic dreams took place when I learned that Mr. Gray was performing a salesman's duty to keep touch with a probable customer, for Mr. Gray represented a well-known monument company in a nearby city.

Of course there was the frequent presence of Jennie, our nearest neighbour. Her small house, which was immaculate inside and touched with the simple grace of Jennie's own nature, was little more than a shack outside. Unpainted, of weather-beaten grey, it stood under sheltering trees at the bend in the road toward the village. Jennie's windows always shone, cleaned by her capable hands and curtained in spotless white. From them she could see the

179

The author. SEVENTEEN. That was
the year I sold my first short story "The
Awakening" to the *Toronto Weekly Sun*.
Six thousand words in length, a tale of
unrequited love.

turn which the road made to the left and to the right at the bend. During my long illness, if Jennie was at home, she would appear at our door on the very heels of the doctor in a clean and starched gingham dress and a flowing white apron tied in a perky bow.

"I saw the doctor's mare taking the hill," she would say, "and I changed quick and came right up."

In her hand there was always some token of her concern for a sickly child – home-made jam, a slice of bannock with currants, fresh vegetables from her sunlit garden, or a bunch of quickly picked flowers that grew for her with abundant pleasure.

Our doctor called Jennie "the Country Angel" and that is what she was. Her face was rosy and her blue eyes very bright. When she talked, you were sure that what she said was cheering. There was no hint of gloom about her, and although my condition caused me to be fearful of strangers on duty in the sickroom, this was not so in the case of Jennie.

We were fortunate to have Jennie as a near neighbour.

"I'll turn my hand to anything within reason," she used to say, and she did.

On one occasion when I was ill over a long period, my mother and Jean became exhausted by night duty and Jennie relieved them.

A cot was placed at the end of my bed for Jennie. I did not sleep that night and neither, I fear, did she. I lay as quiet as possible not to disturb her, but regularly, hour by hour, Jennie's head would appear above the bed rail by means of which she would support herself as she asked, in a stage whisper, "Haven't you got there yet, Jessie?"

I would shake my head, and with a sigh she would lie down again, but I know that her keen hearing registered every movement I made.

Jennie never admitted that she was tired or depressed. Unless kept awake by someone who was ill and unable to sleep, I believe that her slumber must have been untroubled and deep.

Jennie's hair grew grey by the time she was middle-aged but the youthful tone of her voice and her cheery laughter did not change.

Then a new influence came into my life. I had begun to fear that, for me, there would be no opportunity for a higher education. Now, hope was reborn.

XXII

A New Influence

Perhaps the most valuable result of all education is the
ability to make yourself do the thing you have to do,
when it ought to be done ...

T. H. Huxley

When Uncle Andrew retired as a missionary from China, he and
Aunt Nellie joined the other Beattie families in California. His
children had come to the United States to be educated in boarding
schools. Ernest, the eldest, had attended Blair Hall Academy in
New Jersey from the age of eleven. When he was fifteen, he had
spent a summer vacation with us and had returned to join us at
Christmas.

The distance in age between my brothers and myself had
resulted in a limited intimacy. Will had married when I was seven
and, although he retained a warm interest in all members of our
family, he was totally separated from me by his absence as well as
the age barrier. Al was still with us but aloof in nature and entirely
absorbed in his great interest, farming and the raising of purebred
livestock. We shared a love of nature which brought us together
occasionally when he took time to show a deep concern for my
physical condition.

It was the spring of 1912 when a letter was received from
Uncle Andrew informing us that Ernest, now in his second year at
Stanford University, had developed an affliction of the eyes which

prevented him from continuing his studies for an indefinite period. An oculist recommended two years of eye rest and, if possible, outdoor life where green was the dominant colour. It was the opinion at that time that this colour had a healing effect and, to the eyes, was the most restful in the spectrum.

"Since his summer with you," Uncle Andrew wrote, "he has talked affectionately of you all, and we feel in agreement with his suggestion that he become one of your workers in farm or garden, wherever he is most needed. He will be writing to you himself to ask if you can make use of him, also to be sure of his welcome as a temporary member of the family, but Nellie and I wanted you to know our own feelings."

And so it was that we welcomed back someone who had formerly won for himself an occasional place in our family life.

Troubled that he must interrupt his education in order to spare his sight, Ernest brought with him many of the textbooks from which he had studied during his first year at college.

Ernest's disposition was cheerful. He was exceptionally thoughtful and serious for twenty-two. He represented to me much that I had longed for – boarding school, college, and the opportunity for companionship with young people of my own age. True, I was scarcely sixteen, but my aspirations were more mature, made so by frustration.

When Ernest appeared at my bedside one evening with an armful of books, it did not require his suggestion – "I wonder if you could educate yourself a bit, Jessie " – to create in me an eagerness.

Little did I realize the determination required to study alone, especially when the subjects represented in the wonderful volumes had never been explained to me. There was a French Grammar, a book of Advanced English, a Latin Dictionary, Higher Mathematics, and other texts, the nature of which I can't remember.

My days were spent in an endeavour to learn beyond my ability to understand. My attempts were toward the impossible but the effort influenced my future. Occasionally, Ernest inquired as to my progress but I was ashamed to admit my inability to understand. I pored over the books diligently but for some reason, the wording was like a blur to my mind. Assistance in this effort I felt I could not ask of my cousin. I remembered with some chagrin that Lill had been admitted to college without a high-school training and that she had claimed the highest honours in her first year. I mentioned this to her, honestly, on one of her week-ends at home.

"You forget, Jessie," she said, "that I learned from others who had learned from books as much as I learned from the books themselves."

But Ernest brought something into my life which was even more important than the suggestion of unassisted study. After a busy day with the men, where his eyes could benefit by the healing effect of the many-shaded greens of the countryside, he found time during the weeks when I was confined to bed to provide the young companionship for which I longed. Sitting by my cot on the old veranda or by the couch in The Room, he told me of a world rich with experiences – in China as a child, in boarding school and in college. The routine and the pranks were described with delightful pictures of group activities which I had never known. He was a serious young man with the aim of devoting his life to improving the welfare of others. He would be a doctor, he intended, which seemed a favourite profession among members of my father's family. I travelled with him along the avenues of possibility which lay before him, but which I believed were not for me. After a desperate effort to improve my mind by study, I laid the textbooks away sorrowfully. I did not confess this, but now, in reflection, I realize that my very failure contributed to an increase in my devotion to creative writing.

I was approaching sixteen and my thoughts were full of dreams. Ernest took the place of a brother who had died before my birth, but he also reminded me that sometime, somewhere, I should look for another type of experience – that of falling in love.

I wrote:

Somewhere in this great moving world you are,
To know where that may be!
For with the steady radiance of a star
You beckon unto me.

After five such verses, I ended the poem thus:

Soul, mind and body – mine affinity!
Meanwhile the years go by,
Meanwhile I hear you calling unto me
And I would fain reply!

During my sixteenth year I was able to share in the simpler duties of the house, and with each day free of pain, hope increased in me that I might yet become rid of the sickness which had hampered me from childhood. Occasionally now I attended community activities but always accompanied by someone of my family. On rare occasions too, I shared in visiting friends or relatives in the nearby town, but again, I did not go alone and never did I remain away overnight, for – who could say – even when I felt reasonably well, a "spell" might overtake me.

The safer way was to live through unusual experiences and to travel into distant lands by the use of my own imagination. Poetry was not enough; I began to write long involved stories in a prose decorated by outdated forms of speech and elaborate phrases. But suddenly, after a vain attempt to market such a story fifty-three foolscap pages in length, to the *Ladies' Home Journal* when I was thirteen, I seized upon the possibility of finding a sympathetic editor nearer home. We subscribed to a number of periodicals and newspapers. Among them was the *Weekly Sun*, published in Toronto. Sometimes it contained a short story as well as news items of special interest to country people. On my sixteenth birthday, I began a fictional tale of love. "The Awakening" reached a length of six thousand words. I had never seen a typewriter nor did I know of anyone in my world who possessed such a machine. I wrote in longhand. Parcelled in brown wrapping-paper, the manuscript went on its way. How long it took to reach the editor's desk I do not know, but I had turned seventeen when the letter came – the letter containing the incredible news that my story had been accepted for publication. A cheque for two dollars was enclosed. Never shall I forget that day. I looked the demon in the face who challenged my right to live, and lost my fear of him. I would live and I would become what I had planned for myself as a child. Sick or well, I would accomplish the feat of becoming an author.

Before this time I had received the encouragement given to numerous aspiring young writers by the issuance weekly of a page in *The Globe* (Toronto) known as "The Circle of Young Canada." For many this was probably the only published expression of their early attempts at authorship. Each contributor supplied a pseudo-nym and friendships were born through the exchange of letters by the young contestants. Well-known people began their attempts at self-expression by submitting work for publication in these columns. I was "Rainbow" and one of my correspondents through what we called "The Page" was Charlotte Whitton, later Mayor of Ottawa. Charlotte, then "Red Wing," was a student at Queen's University and her letters to me were as individual and forthright as the expression of her personality in later life. One letter described her experiences with a broken nose, brought about by a skiing accident. Another, written in April, was begun with four lines of poetry as follows:

> Spring is comin', spring is comin',
> For I feel the summer's zephyrs,
> Across the sky the clouds are flyin',
> And under them young heifers.

When I was fifteen a word of encouragement had accompanied a book prize (*The Black Tulip* by Alexandre Dumas) for a poem which I had submitted to *The Canadian Countryman*. I do not recall the title of the poem, but the first four lines were:

> Take me out into the country
> Where the west wind travels free,
> Where it bears the healing spices
> Of the fir and pine to me.

But now, incredible as it was, I had found a market, and in one year I was to contribute two continued stories, each approximately twenty thousand words in length, and several shorter pieces in poetry and prose to the *Weekly Sun*. I believed that my writing career had really begun. The stories were full of romance, mystery and melodrama.

Descendants of Grandpa Fleming's second family included three grandsons ranging in age from thirteen to fifteen. About this time they came to spend a week-end with us. It had been their common practice, when small boys, to arrive the day school closed and to remain until the day before school opened. We had been playmates at that time, and the serious concern for me which their faces expressed when they were ushered up to my bedroom by Mother, touched me very deeply. Also I was pleased by their show of interest in my budding authorship. It was Saturday morning when they arrived at the farm and shortly after the noonday meal, to my disappointment, they left, stating their intention of going to

186

town. This meant depriving me of their companionship and showing me, thought I, their lack of interest in a girl cousin who was also an invalid. The distance to town was four miles. A sister of my mother's lived there. Perhaps they had gone to visit her. Their brief call upon me and mysterious departure left me unhappy and dejected. I had never accepted that my physical disabilities placed me in an inferior position with robust young people.

But just as the sun was declining behind the pine-clad hill of our neighbour's pasture field, just as I was about to turn my face to the wall and to weep the tears which I had been choking back all day, I heard footsteps on the stairs. They were eager boyish footsteps. I could not mistake their identity. Eyes bright with accomplishment, smiling, three boys stood at the foot of my bed. The eldest stepped up beside me and laying a parcel where I could reach it, he said:

"We got you this, Jessie. It is nice to have an author for a cousin."

After the excitement of the presentation was over, after we had laughed together in mutual hopefulness, they answered Mother's call for supper.

I lay still in the gathering dusk. I was no longer as one set apart. My confidence had been re-awakened by three gestures of affectionate concern. Where had they procured the price of such a book as I now held jealously in my hands? True, it was holiday time, and they had been picking fruit for a neighbouring farmer. How many hours of work had they given to purchase a leather-bound volume with gold-tipped leaves and handsome design – the poetry of John Milton. My eyes smarted with happy tears and I could feel my heart beating faster with a sense of coming achievement. In my lifetime I have never been moved more deeply by a gift.

They would not know that while I read every word from the first page to the last, the genius of John Milton was to remain forever above my comprehension. What could I do in return? When they came up later to say good-night, I thanked them as best I could and I gave to each of them a sheet of paper – a list of books. They, too, had a future and whatever their chosen occupations, general knowledge and the development of literary appreciation would enrich their experiences. John Ruskin so advised. I was reading Ruskin's *Truth and Beauty* at the time. Jean had brought it to me from the attic, together with Carlyle's *Sartor Resartus* which I had not yet explored. There were titles which I remembered from hospital days to excite the imagination. *Swiss Family Robinson*, Jules Verne's *Twenty Thousand Leagues Under the Sea*, and Ernest Thompson Seton's *Two Little Savages*. Thoughtfully I included books recently re-read by me but earlier enjoyed – titles from Dickens, Scott and Thackeray. What influence was provided, who shall say? But I have a letter dated 1913, written by the eldest, asking me for a second list. The first had been exhausted. Carried forward by ambition and a staunch inheritance, these three boys surmounted many difficulties by determined industry. One became a school principal, the other two executives in the field of commerce.

Was it Grandpa Fleming's opinion of education which influenced his descendants to march to its tune?

In the dusk alone, I lay with a hand on the volume of poems, bound in the finest morocco. I smoothed its soft cover with the touch of dedication.

XXIII

We Leave the Old House

Naught may endure but Mutability.

Percy Bysshe Shelley

Concentration upon the condition of my health and plans for my future were temporarily lost sight of in the sudden serious illness of my mother. It was the month of August and I was secretly planning a return to school. There had been two months of reasonably good health for me with only one "spell." The stimulation of Ernest's presence, a daily reminder of a life still lying beyond my reach, had inspired in me a determination to go forward at any cost. If I did not attempt it, I would never know whether or not I could meet the test. A shuttle bus service had been opened between the town of Preston and our village. From Preston, a radial car took passengers from the terminal to the city of Galt and the route passed by the street on which the High School stood.

But early in August when the katydids were droning their enjoyment of the heat and a soft mistiness blurred the blue of the hills, a severe attack shattered my dream before I had given voice to it.

While I lay in bed, almost without hope of ever being well again, Mother was stricken. For weeks she hovered between life and death while Dr. C. came sometimes twice daily. There were two patients to be seen now and I was still too ill to be allowed the exertion of visiting Mother's room. When I did so, after almost three weeks, I scarcely recognized her. During that time she had

189

The Old House and The New House
(Willow Bank)

been unable to tolerate food and her wasted condition sent me back to my own bed tragically distressed. My mother would not live, I felt sure. Gone were all thoughts of a future in which ambition and personal experiences had meaning. It was as if an earthquake had shaken the very foundations of the old house. No one was heard to speak above a whisper. No member of our family rested comfortably day or night for five long weeks. Jennie came to help with the nursing. Intravenous feeding was unknown in those days. My mother was slowly dying of starvation, we knew, and we also knew that despite consultation with the best medical knowledge available, Dr. C.'s expression became more serious and his visits more frequent.

Meanwhile the farming and the gardening had to be attended to. Meals had to be prepared for our men and that all-important event, "the threshing," required the efforts of everyone able to assist inside and out as the operation moved from home to home in our community.

Lill, summoned by the seriousness of our mother's illness, remained at home for two weeks, during which time threshing at our farm took place. Jennie was by Mother's bedside most of the time, but I could hear her sharp short steps running up and down the stairs as she spared a few minutes here and there to help Jean and Lill. The house was in turmoil downstairs, for the threshers had arrived a half-day before they were expected. On a neighbouring farm the harvest had been lighter than estimated, which meant an additional meal with us for them and an overnight arrangement. There were three in charge of the outfit and the afternoon and evening of that first day were spent by them setting up the engine and the separator.

Meanwhile I could smell the cooking and baking which was going on in our kitchen. There would be crocks of smooth applesauce cooling in the pantry, the cookie jars would be filled and pastry mixed and stored in the ice-box ready for pie baking the next morning. My father made a hurried trip to town and returned with a roast so large that it had to be cut in half in order to fit into the oven of our range.

At the crack of dawn everyone would be up, my father and his men putting things in the barn to rights, milking the cows and driving them out of harm's way into the pasture field. Meanwhile the pile of dried firewood placed near the engine was sawn into

191

suitable lengths. The sound of the saw forcing its way through the wood was accompanied by the putt-putt of the engine which supplied the power for this operation.

In the morning cooking and baking went forward at full speed, for the noonday meal would be a heavy one. The smell of fresh apple pie and roasting meat filled the house. I knew that my dinner tray would be a special one with a currant biscuit of Jean's baking, a quickbread never missing from our table when the threshers came to us.

The doctor arrived before noon. After he had visited my mother there was a low-toned conversation with Jennie in the hallway before he entered my bedroom.

His eyes were bright and he was smiling.

"Well, Jessie," he said, with the warm sympathy which had often comforted me, "I know that this has been a very hard time for you, but I think that I can say that the worst is over. Your dear mother has taken a turn for the better."

I was crying but they were tears of joy and he understood. He took my hands in his.

"Now, if we can do as well by you," he said, "we will all be happy."

His encouraging words proved true; relieved of the fear that my mother would not recover, I was soon on the mend.

That threshing day was a happy one after all. The sun which had come up through a heavy mist smiled in through my bedroom window before noon. The threshers left us after the evening meal, and the rumble of their departure southward along our road had the sweetness of music about it.

That night I could not sleep but I was not kept awake by pain. The doctor had given me permission to visit my mother, and I had been to see with my own eyes the signs of improvement in her condition.

About midnight the moon came up like a kindly friend, pushing aside a misty veil and moving above a row of trees along the border of the east meadow and smiling in at me. The window was open and I could hear night sounds, comforting homely sounds – the neigh of a horse in the meadow, perhaps dreaming like the chirping robin in a far tree, the bleat of a lamb out of touch with its mother, almost fully grown and yet dependent, the rattle of a distant train on the Dumfries line, two miles away, the cooing of a

192

pigeon claiming a better place for itself on the roof of the barn, and the soft regular breathing of my mother, enjoying, I believed, her first natural sleep in many weeks.

I lay down at last. I had been sitting against my pillows while I watched the mystery of night enfolding the world. I did not lie down until the clouds touching the eastern horizon were touched themselves on their lower rim with a hint of gold.

"Thank you, God," I said, and slept.

Now a new challenge came and was met courageously by my father almost before he had recovered from the strain of anxiety caused by my mother's illness and my own.

Al's love of the land and his devotion to the development of modern farming was appreciated by my parents. It was understood that upon my father's retirement the farm would be sold to my brother at a previously stated figure. Now, from Al's viewpoint, the time for retirement had come. But neither of my parents wished to leave the home which they had occupied since shortly after their marriage and the land which they had brought into productivity by faithful effort.

Another farm had been purchased at the bend in the road. The land was richer and the house and other buildings were modern and of higher value. Al was offered this farm of equal size in acreage for an equal price. His indignation spilled over into anger. His heart was in the development which he had directed since he returned to the plough from his work in the city. Doubtless he had thought of this as his farm, his fields and woods. It was he who had helped to design the barns and stables which had replaced others of older fashion.

My mother's sickness had hampered open discussion with him and finally a property which formed a triangle between the two farms was purchased by my father. Here, in close proximity, a new house would be built and preparations were made for removal to this location.

"Fair is fair," my father said. "We won't be leaving the place, we'll just be moving off and taking life a bit easier."

There was a reason for my brother's demand. On a week-end spent with us early that spring, Lill had been accompanied by one of her classmates who had a teaching position in Toronto where Lill was now employed as a dietitian in the Toronto General

Hospital. Rebecca Nesbitt was to bring into my brother's life the release from frustration and the happiness to be found in the love of an unspoiled young woman which surely none of us could deny him. If he were to establish a home, the natural location, if permanent, would be the farm which had meant so much to him.

My mother's illness seemed to justify my father's decision. A new house was to be built, of modern design, on a site which still contained the foundation of one erected in 1803.

Jean became the architect. She appealed to my father for permission to design the house.

"I learned house planning when I took the three months' Homemaking Course at Mac Hall," she told him. "We had long discussions on the way to save space and steps at the same time, and each of us had to draw a plan for what we thought was an ideal house, at the end of the year. I knew Al would be buying the farm some day – you had told me, and I thought about the kind of home we should have. Of course I had no idea where it would be built, but now that I know, I'll make some alterations. Please trust me, Da," she ended, "for I really know what will make housekeeping easier for Mother."

My father looked at her and the red lights came into his eyes as they did when he was emotionally stirred.

"My goodness," he said, "I had no idea they taught such sensible things at that place. You have a good memory, Jean. Go ahead with this drawing business and when you've finished, let me have a look."

Jean set about demonstrating her ability as an architect. There would be a modern furnace, a bathroom, a serving cupboard between the kitchen and dining-room and many other features unfamiliar to life in the old house.

My father examined Jean's carefully drawn-to-scale plan and he did something which I had never seen him do before. He stood up and, handing it back to Jean, he placed a hand on her shoulder. The affection in his touch was evident to me.

"My girl," he said, "this is wonderful. Without being extravagant or investing beyond our means, it looks to me as if we'll be setting the style for a new kind of home in this community. Put that safely away until the carpenter comes. He'll be here tomorrow. There's not a thing that I can see could be changed for the better."

194

The carpenter came and within a week his men were at work on the skeleton of what was to become our pride. But when neighbours stopped to comment, their words contained some scorn.

"Frank Beattie," one said, "why are you bothering to build a house at all? From what I can see it's going to be a glass case."

"They're pretty disgusted with the number of windows," Da said to Jean, grinning.

"Wait until they see the finished product," Jean answered, returning his grin.

"I'm satisfied," was all my father said in reply.

But when the house was finished and I made a tour of it with him, he stood looking from a sun-room on the second floor extending over the flat roof of a wide veranda. The veranda was built almost to the edge of a wooded ravine beyond which stretched the rippling waters of the mill pond.

"It's like finding a picture and it's the same from every room," he said proudly. Then, with gentleness, "What would we do without Jean?"

This was a question which each of us in turn asked ourselves when we moved into the new house with most of the conveniences to be found in city homes. My father had co-operated by the installation of electric pumping from a well discovered not far from the house. The well was deepened and a supply of ever-ready hot and cold water was to be found in sink and bathroom. A hot-water tank had been installed in the basement and attached to the furnace. The old lamps were replaced with electric lighting and Lill bought a piano to grace the new living-room, and to make possible a continuing study of the music which both of us loved so dearly. But we kept the organ, and now and then Grandpa, who only half appreciated the change of environment, could be found on the organ stool, his fingers on the keys to make the chord while he sang to himself the Scottish ballads which he loved so well.

But there was one who never really removed to the new house in spirit. My mother avoided the west windows which overlooked the road that led up-hill to the farm which now belonged to my brother. Although she shared with us in our fondness for the gentle colleen who had become my brother's wife, although "Patsy," as we called her, rarely let a day pass without coming to take tea with the now-recovering invalid, it was two years before Mother could be persuaded to return her visits. Every part of the house on the hill held precious memories for a woman, now in her sixtieth year, who had come there at the age of twenty-one.

We called our new home Willow Bank, for it was semicircled by age-old willow trees. The slope to the pond contained other trees of sixteen varieties which were a lure to the birds. The wide veranda below the sun-room extended almost the full length of the house and it was easy to imagine, especially when alone, that one was in the heart of a woodland. That springtime the inspiration to write became more and more demanding upon me. It was encouraged by what we called "The Little Room" on the south-west with windows facing both directions. There were built-in bookcases and a colonial desk which had belonged to my father's family and which had stood in my parents' room on the farm. This was now the main article of furniture in what became my "sanctum sanctorum." It was a quiet room, reached from a doorway in the front hall. All through that first winter and far into the summer, I spent my days, when well enough to be out of bed, dreaming at the piano or putting my dreams into verse and story in The Little Room. I had found a new world and it carried me through another year of waiting before I returned to school, going and coming daily by the new means of transportation and thus continuing to keep in touch with the protective environment which had been mine for five years.

After several years of infrequent contact, Tillie and I met again at a boarding house for students across from the school. She was now in her fourth year and close to graduation while I, at eighteen, was a First Form student. We enjoyed a noonday meal together and something of the old intimacy returned to warm our relationship. But while Tillie was a part of the social activities with many friendships among the students, I was a shy country girl, matching wits with those who had passed directly from Public School studies to a review of the program followed there in the Fourth Book. In five years I had forgotten the simple facts of common subjects familiar to them – history, geography and arithmetic. I heard them glibly recite the names of the rivers and lakes of our province. I knew the name of only one river – the Grand – and one lake which I had crossed at fourteen from Hamilton to Toronto with Aunt Mary and my mother – Lake Ontario. The first few months were spent in painful knowledge of

196

my ignorance and in desperate determination to overcome it by studying far into the night. But I found a friend in the teacher of Composition, lost to me after six months when he secured a captaincy with a local regiment. World War I was now a horrible reality. Before he left us he spoke to me of my apparent interest in creative writing. There had been three submitted compositions – "Spring", "A Walk in the Woods" and "The Story of a Wanderer." He had returned them to me without comment but each one had been marked as "excellent."

I recall the day Captain George Marshall came to Galt Collegiate to bid us good-bye. He spoke briefly to us in the classroom. A number of the students approached him afterward in the corridor to wish him well and bid him a personal farewell. I longed to do so but instead, I stood alone at the other end of the hallway. He came to me.

"I am glad of an opportunity to speak alone with you, Jessie," he said. "I do not advocate partiality in a classroom, but I must admit that I have had a special interest in your work ever since you wrote your first composition for me. 'Spring' – do you remember?"

I nodded but I am not sure that I spoke.

"Was the poetry at the beginning and the end original?" he asked me.

I found my voice. "Yes, sir, it was," I said.

He made a gesture of belief.

"I was sure of it," he said, "and it has been my intention to discuss your future with you. But when I decided to leave civilian life, a lot of conflicting interests took over. Jessie," he continued, "unless you deprive yourself of that opportunity, you will be a writer. Your gift is special and you must never deny it expression."

He did not give me time to thank him. He shook my hand and was gone, but his words stayed with me and helped to support my faith in myself when a later teacher, who openly confessed that she disliked the subject which she was forced to teach, gave me such a low marking, coupled with the comment "too long and too serious," that my confidence was frequently shaken.

I was a grief-stricken schoolgirl when, less than a year later, George A. Marshall was a casualty in France.

Another change took place in our family life in the autumn of 1914.

Lill's success as a career woman had brought to our attention the need to consider a similar opportunity for Jean, who had been the staunch support of us all through years of trouble and sickness. A capable young woman was employed as a maid in our house while Jean, a little fearfully, but quietly showing appreciation for a new way of life, prepared at thirty-two years of age to follow Lill as a student of Domestic Science at Macdonald Institute in Guelph.

"I'm afraid to leave Mother," I heard Jean confess to Lill when the latter spent a week-end at home before Jean's departure.

"One of us could always come back if we are needed," Lill said. "We've got a house now that is easy to look after, and no men except Da and Grandpa to feed. Edith is old enough to wipe dishes and do other little jobs to help out after school, and Jessie's spells seem to be a thing of the past. Take your chance, Jean, there may not be another."

And Jean took her chance. New or old, home lacked a certain security without her presence, but everyone was happy for her and change seemed to be the order of that year. Ernest had left us for a trial employment before returning to college. Old ways had indeed become new ways. There was plenty of opportunity now for the silence required to pursue my studies in the evenings and over week-ends.

Patsy's daily visits lightened the quiet of a limited household. Grandpa still entertained us with his songs and stories, and Edith, now twelve years old, romped and played with a new acquisition, a collie pup which was added to our household when we left the farm. For years Teve had been Al's companion in the fields and it would not have been fair to separate them. There was a family gathering at Christmas, with Jean in her old place as chief cook. Ernest came to join us and the New Year started happily.

But Al's destiny seemed to be marked with repeated tragedies. While Patsy shared with Lill the pleasures of knitting and sewing, in preparation for the birth of her first child, death came with incredible suddenness, taking both the unborn and its mother.

I had thought of death and I had written of death, but until then it had been a stranger.

I was at school the day Patsy died. When I returned from school, Jean met me at the entrance to the driveway. She was now in her second year at college and had been appointed House President by the student body. It was Thursday.

"You're home, Jean," I exclaimed. "Why?"

Jean's sober expression alarmed me.

"They sent for me," she said. "I got home at noon. It's Patsy, Jessie. The doctor has been with her all day. She's gone."

I don't remember answering Jean. She reached for my hand and we walked toward the house together.

"Mother has gone up to be with Al," she said. "Al came for Lill and she's been there all day helping. They thought at first they might be able to save the baby but they couldn't. It's awful, Jessie, but we must control our feelings for Al's sake."

My father was also with Al. The full brunt of death was then borne by the family of the deceased; there were no funeral homes. The undertakers were already at work and in the morning Patsy and her unborn child would rest in the little parlour.

My father came in shortly after Jean and I reached the house.

"I'm going back to fetch Mother home," he said. "She's not fit for this. I'll stay the night with Al. Lill will stay too and make a bit of supper, though I doubt if he'll eat. He hasn't touched food all day and he won't leave her side though he knows she's gone. It's an awful blow to the boy, but we must do what we can."

The following days are clouded in memory by the stunned nature of my reaction to my first encounter with the loss of a loved one. There was a strangeness about everything, almost as if the world had stopped turning, for as a family we were in a state of shock.

But it was for Al that our concern became acute.

"The doctor says he's on the verge of a nervous breakdown," I heard Lill telling Jean the day after the funeral. "I have two weeks before I go to my new job. I'll stay with him, but I'm so broken up myself that I'm afraid I won't be much use to him." Lill had been appointed dietitian in Military Service.

"He can't be left alone." Jean spoke firmly. "You have a job to go to. I have none and college can wait as long as it has to wait. I'm going to move up with Al, Lill."

Lill flung her arms around Jean.

"You're not," she protested sturdily. "You've never had your chance, and now that you have it you're not going to lose it. There are other jobs, and Pat was my best friend. I'm coming to look after things for her. It's the least I can do."

"Be sensible, Lill," Jean reasoned. "You are able to earn and you are qualified for the position you've been offered. I have no qualifications to worry about. You're too upset to think sensibly right now. I've been thinking ever since this happened and I know what I'm going to do."

Lill spent two weeks in the old house trying to hide her own sorrow in an effort to stabilize the emotions of a broken-hearted man, but Jean came home and in a pattern of life of her own choosing, once more she assumed the support of someone in need, while Lill returned to a career which was to lead her from height to height.

Now, the word "death" had a different meaning for me, and living, a different dimension. A stranger had become a reality.

XXIV

The Demon Reappears

The soul that feeds on books alone –
I count that soul exceeding small.

Lord Byron

For five years I had dreamed of becoming a high-school student. I was now in Second Form and attended by disillusionment. In order to absorb the knowledge which I had acquired earlier and forgotten, I worked desperately to keep pace with my companions in the classroom. "Work without play makes Jack a dull boy" proved true of me, for by the time I was a Second Form student, going to school had become a lustreless occupation. I had found it necessary to learn much which seemed unimportant to me and to lose the required time for the pursuit of creativity. Again, at frequent intervals, I felt that prodding pain which threatened to interfere with what I had set out to do. I would finish high school, I believed, and after that there would be university with a wide choice in courses of study. My father was prepared to meet the cost. This he could do without undue sacrifice and it was understood that I should be qualified for a type of work which would not require too much physical effort.

It was February 1916 when I found myself the victim of a trouble which had remained almost forgotten for more than a year. Dr. C., who had been proud of my believed recovery and interested in my progress as a high-school student, stood by my bed. He looked sorrowfully down at me. The pain had come on in early

Three sisters at twenty-three: Jeanie
Lillie Ann, Jessie Louise.

morning and he had reached our home by daylight. Morphia had been administered. I was not suffering physically now but something of the destroyed faith in a normal future must have looked from my eyes as they met his.

"Don't give up, Jessie," he said. "Don't be downhearted. You had a year and a half of respite. We will lick this thing yet and you will be back in school in no time at all."

I loved him for his encouragement but we both knew that his words were a hope, not a promise. I did return to school after three weeks and I did meet and pass the high standard in examinations required to permit taking the next two years in one year. This I had been determined to do because of the delay in my secondary education.

But when autumn came, Jean came into my bedroom carrying a birthday cake with twenty-one pink candles. I had come of age but I had not left behind me the threatening cloud which had hovered above me from early childhood.

When Jean had offered her birthday greetings and returned downstairs, I buried my face in my hands and sobbed. It was to be almost a year before I went back to school.

Before that year was out, I began to realize that my family and friends did not share my belief that I would recover sufficiently to continue my education. A relative of my mother's from a nearby town was a deeply religious woman. She felt it her duty to come frequently to share her firm convictions with me. She was a woman who dressed very well and wore petticoats of taffeta which always rustled. She had been a pretty girl but now, with greying hair which had a lifeless look about it, a skin which was grey and dry and lips which were dry and colourless, she brought with her an atmosphere of gloom. She deemed it her duty, when visiting me, to remind me by word and by deed that my life hung in the balance. After quoting rather meaningless and depressing verses of Scripture she never failed to kneel by my bedside, praying aloud in a voice of conviction and prophecy. When she rose, she bent to kiss me before leaving. She smelled of Lifebuoy soap and the touch of her lips reminded me of dried parchment. I cannot recall her exact words of farewell but always they contained a note of finality which told me that she had little hope of seeing me again. I dreaded her touch.

In contrast there was the little minister with a wrinkled face and twitching eyes who rode his bicycle from town to our door. His words were cheerful and acceptable, and a brief prayer upon departure was said while he rested a gentle hand upon my head. His touch had the touch of God's mercy in it.

I would not accept my fate as foreordained. I would get well. In preparation, I began to search the advertisements of help wanted in *The Globe*, which was our chosen newspaper. A family, living in Toronto, would spend the summer at their residence by Lake Simcoe. They had three children – ages nine, six and three. They sought a substitute for the governess in their employ. The substitute would accompany the family to their summer home and would assist in the care of the children.

Little Sister, now a good student at school, read out the words to me. I took the paper from her and pored over the advertisement. There was a box number only. What could have been better suited to my needs than a summer by the lakeside in the company of children? I would answer the advertisement without telling anyone.

That night I crept down the stairs and brought the family to the living-room by playing the loved melody of Mendelssohn's "Spring Song." This was accepted evidence that I was on the way to recovery.

Two weeks later a letter reached me from the family of Donald Ross, accepting my application but requesting an interview.

It was a challenge. Would I be permitted to meet it? There was a family conference and the doctor was consulted. His approval was granted.

Was my illness psychosomatic? Time was to prove that it was not, but the touch of the unseen was upon me and surely it can be said, for an extended period my determination to return again to the stream of life carried me back into its surge.

For this interview I was accompanied by Jennie who anxiously waited in the spacious hall of an enormous house on Walmer Road, Toronto, while the children's mother interviewed me in the drawing-room.

"Don't look as if you are examining everything when you visit another person's house," my Mother had taught me.

Obeying her was difficult in the elaborate surroundings of a room larger and more beautifully furnished than any which I had ever seen. But my attention was directed to creating the impression of a mature young woman capable of assuming the duties of a governess.

"I knew you'd got the job as soon as I set eyes on you," Jennie whispered after we had left the house and were being whisked in a modern automobile to the Union Station. Our chauffeur was uniformed. He did not speak to us and when we reached our destination he quickly got out and assisted us to alight.

"You sure got yourself into a fancy place," Jennie said as the train chugged away toward home. "I just hope you keep well, Jessie, for you'll have lots of new things to write about after two months with people like that."

At the end of two months I would return to school, but this secret belief I did not confide to anyone but Jennie.

For the first time in my life, I set off alone to occupy a position which I could only hope would not be too taxing for me physically nor mentally. I had not met the children but I was to meet them that evening, while their parents advised me, in formal dress before leaving to keep a dinner date, that except for the servants, I would be in full charge of them and alone in the "upstairs."

In quiet watchfulness the children sat with me in a private dining-room off the nursery, for our exclusive use. A maid was in attendance. Beside my foot under the table was a serving bell to summon any attention which we might require.

It was the beginning of June, a time when the strawberries in our garden land were still green. My young charges and I partook, that evening dinner hour, of a baked salmon trout, served on a platter which the maid set before me, and accompanying vegetables, and in unbelief my eyes rested upon a large cut-glass bowl which waited on a small serving table until our first course was removed. The bowl was heaped high with the largest, ripest strawberries I had ever seen. There were other delicacies, but the effect of the unusual items of the meal itself, of the elegant surroundings, of the maid service, these were lost sight of in dealing with a situation for which I was wholly unprepared.

Setting the large bowl of strawberries before me with accompanying smaller bowls and a pitcher of thick cream, the maid said, "Will that be all, Mademoiselle?"

"Yes, thank you," I all but stammered.

"Then I'll go downstairs but if you need me for anything, just ring. I think I should warn you that you may have some trouble."

She had scarcely left the room after placing the fruit before me, which I then served, when the eldest child, a boy of nine, gulping down his portion with inelegant haste, rose from the table. He began circling the room, shouting at the top of his lungs.

The other two children, Jim, aged six, and "Bunty," aged three, went quietly on eating their dessert as if nothing unusual were happening.

I looked at the wide-open windows. I thought of the neighbours who could hear, and the servants, who the maid had indicated were below stairs. I would be considered incapable for the position which I had undertaken. Across my mind flashed a picture of myself returning home, a failure.

The ailment of high blood pressure had not yet been identified as a cause for alarm. I cannot remember having heard of this trouble but I do remember the pounding in my head and the flaming of my face as I, too, left the table. I closed the windows to the accompaniment of continued shouting and then, without speaking, I directed the attention of the rebel to the door of the bedroom which was open. With an expression of fearlessness but with fear in my heart, I stood by the open door, waiting. At that moment someone turned the knob of another door leading from the nursery and a gaunt elderly woman with fiery eyes trained them full upon the shouting child. All was still.

"Master Douglas," she ordered. "Go into your room. Your father will attend to you in the morning."

As erect as a soldier, but silently, he did as he was told and closed the door.

The two other children went on eating.

"I'm the cook's helper," the woman said. "We were expecting this. He tries it on every new one that comes and in a day or two they go home. It makes him feel like a man. He's a nice boy but don't let him fright you."

She went out and I returned to the table but the waiting strawberries were not eaten by me.

I had been told that daily baths at bedtime were a requirement. The two younger children allowed themselves to be directed and when they were safely tucked into bed, Jim in his brother's room and Bunty in her dainty little girl's room, I turned to the culprit. He was lying face down, quiet, alert, not knowing what to expect. He was a child, he had struggled and lost and he was tired.

As I rubbed him down after his bath, which took place without conversation, I smiled to him and to my surprise his arms went around my neck and with his head on my shoulder he sobbed, "I don't like you. I don't like anybody but my own mother. I want her to bath me and put me to bed. I don't like you but I don't hate you."

"I know what you mean," I told him. "I want my own mother too."

I continued with my duties and it was a sorrowful little boy who permitted me to tuck him in, for the night was cool.

"Would you like me to tell you a story?" I asked, and soon all three of us were on a desert island with Robinsoe Crusoe. For authors such as Daniel Defoe, may there be a special kind of heaven.

I spent two lonely but interesting months in what was really a position halfway Downstairs, so that I was deprived of association with the six servants, interesting personalities, and at the same time rarely accepted as an equal by Upstairs. But there were the children. I had been conqueror in my first and last challenge of authority while I remained a substitute governess in the house of Ross. At the end of the second week, we removed to the spacious summer home of the children's grandparents on Lake Simcoe.

As well as the children, whom I learned to love, there was the contact with nature in a form unfamiliar to my previous experience. The great turbulent lake known for its sudden upheavals and treacherous behaviour, the surrounding woodlands with a majority of white birches, the cry of loons at night and the calling of land birds during the day. Nature was dear to me and although, like the small boy who had rebelled against my authority, I wanted my mother and the other members of my family whose presence completed the picture of home. I had tested my strength and I had not found it wanting. For two months I followed a daily routine required in the care of three children, and when the summer ended I went home more determined than ever to prove that I was not one set apart.

At the beginning of the school year, I assembled my books and returned to the Galt Collegiate Institute to take the last two years of Matriculation and Senior Normal Entrance in the period of one year.

There were frightening interruptions when I found myself in bed again, stricken by the fierce attacks of pain which, despite his determined efforts, Dr. C. had not identified. Was my illness indeed psychosomatic? I did not know. It was an accepted fact, however, that the effort of further formal education was not for me until there had been at least an interlude of rest.

In spite of my inability to participate in the extracurricular activities of school life and my lack of interest in certain subjects under study, there were memorable occasions. These occasions took place in the classroom. Love of poetry and of dignified prose was born in me, I think. Therefore, hours spent in the study of great works of literature under the able direction of Dr. Thomas Carscadden I shall always treasure. He was probably threescore years and ten, tall, spare, with a classic handsomeness of feature. Where beauty was to be found in the world of literature, he found it, and directed our attention to the theme as well as the construction. Today I know of many students advanced to Grade Thirteen who have never read the works of the mediaeval and romantic poets. In 1919 we fed upon them. After a lesson when we examined the unforgettable significance of Robert Browning's "My Last Duchess," an incident occurred which revealed the sensitivity and insensitivity of the human mind.

Dr. Carscadden had drawn with skill an image of the woman whose emotional nature and love of humanity had angered her husband as an artist tried to catch her spirit with his brush. The young wife whose self he desired to fully possess had remained capable of response to servant and master alike.

"Don't you think she may have been a shallow, fickle type?"

The question was asked by the most qualified mathematician in our classroom. The usually pallid face of a man with the title of Doctor of Literature changed colour. I had never before seen a flush on those rather hollow cheeks nor the flash of indignation in those blue eyes.

"I classify you with this husband," he snapped. "Would you have a stone image for a woman? The more we feel," he went on, "the more we give and the more we are."

Some years later, when I had dared to present my first small book of verse to a generous public, I received a letter from Dr.

208

Carscadden asking me to pay him a visit. He was then bedridden and before the year was out he was lost to the many who loved and admired him. I accepted his invitation and, sitting by his bedside, I found the courage and the inspiration to remain loyal to my own opinion of what comprised beauty in literary composition. His praise was more than I deserved but it carried me forward.

Ancient History was a second favourite subject with me, probably because the man who led us through Greek and Roman myths and legends to a true picture of man in early times was himself an exceptional critic and historian. J. G. Althouse, later honoured with a doctorate in the Classics, held my attention throughout that last year of High School without a falter of interest upon my part. There was the day set aside for the study of a man called great by the judgement of all men. We did not use our notebooks that day. We were requested to leave them closed. The teacher closed his textbook also and sitting behind his desk, fingers threaded together, he talked to us for the double period allotted to him by special permission. In that hour the man Socrates lived for us from birth to death. When I recall that occasion I remember especially the almost breathless attention of all who listened. Surely this was a great teacher in the presentation of the life and death of a great teacher.

There were other periods of inspiration and unforgettable words of encouragement from certain men and women among our instructors who recognized the effort being made by a girl in ill health to live a normal life.

XXV

Before a New Beginning

Nothing that is can pause or stay;
The moon will wax, the moon will wane,
The mist and cloud will turn to rain,
The rain to mist and cloud again,
Tomorrow be today.

H. W. Longfellow

Although I completed my high-school education successfully, receiving honours, the memory of those years is tinged with a feeling of inadequacy.

The radial car which I boarded at the Preston Junction carried boys and girls from several villages and towns within easy reach. I can still hear their chatter and their laughter as we covered the few miles from Preston to Galt. I was with them but I was not one of them. To retain my place I frequently resorted to deception. The nagging pain came and went while I told no one. The effort to accomplish two years of study in one required staying up late and getting up early. Often, as I looked from the window of the car moving through the populated stretch of semi-country between town and city, I longed to escape from the fun and laughter and to lie prone upon the soft green of the well-kept lawns which we passed by. I experienced a great weariness which was almost a sickness. That I was testing my endurance both physically and mentally, I knew well. Often, I was overcome by a depression unnatural to a normal girlhood.

Among the verses which I wrote on rare occasions when time permitted during those years, I find a positive evidence of painful experiences. I quote from a crumpled piece of paper in my Latin textbook, dated 1916:

Earth, do I lay my cheek against your breast.
I am your child, returned to you for rest.
Take me, O Mother, fold your mighty arms
Around my body stricken. With your charms,
Ancient and simple, let me soon forget
I bear a mind, a heart within me ...

There were several verses in the same vein.

But I had surprised my family and myself by showing more resistance to disease than others who were considered stronger of body than I. There had been the dread epidemic of influenza. True, I had succumbed to it, the first to do so in our family and before its serious nature was recognized.

"A bad attack of La Grippe," the doctor said.

Soon the disease passed like a demon from home to home. Al suffered seriously from it but no one else of our family except myself was affected. Grief for those bereaved saddened all. Among the victims were the wives of my doctor and our Latin teacher. Few pregnant women escaped.

"Had Patsy lived until now," Jean said, "perhaps she would have been taken too."

When further threat from the fatal germ had passed, people everywhere turned to the business of living, thankful the siege was at an end, though sorrow-filled.

A new challenge was now to be met. In 1918 World War I came to an end, but not the suffering. Thousands had lost their lives in battle but thousands more, wounded and in need of care, came home.

Lill had been ordered from her position in a civilian hospital to take up the duties of a dietitian under military command.

Ernest, a lieutenant with the American Expeditionary Force, was quartered at a barracks in the Eastern States. He had seen four of his companions carried from his tent, victims of the plague. After narrowly escaping their fate, he came to us for a brief convalescence. He left for France shortly after. It was several years before we saw him again.

211

My father had retired, but resisting the threat of idleness to an energetic nature, he had built himself on our new property a miniature greenhouse.

"The amount of fuel he burns to keep it warm," my mother commented one day, "would buy twenty times the number of plants he raises."

The seedlings raised would be planted in our own garden and to beautify the grounds.

"But I haven't the heart to remind him that he's being plain extravagant," Mother went on with a tenderness in her voice. "After he's been working with the soil he comes in with such a contented look. I want him to stay that way."

And my father stayed that way while Mother, too, fully recovered in health, enjoyed the responsibilities of two cows in the stable of the small barn and a flock of chickens in the glassed chicken-house. A touch of the past had been carried by my parents into their period of retirement.

Jean had resisted the suggestion that Al resort to engaging a housekeeper. She assumed a dual guardianship as she came and went daily with a face unclouded by resentment or frustration. Had Jean queried her own position, she might have replied, "What is life for, if not to help others to live it?"

Grandpa, hale and hearty, was still with us. Between my father and himself there was an acceptance and understanding, a relationship we often remarked upon. Mutual consideration was maintained despite the knowledge of both that one was becoming more and more financially dependent on the other. This situation was never aired.

Little Sister, growing into womanhood, protested against a secondary education. She took upon herself a share in the duties of the household, now headed by my mother, while I contributed what help I could.

There were still weeks and many days when I was confronted by the undiagnosed pain, and now, after High School graduation I had come home to possess again The Little Room, the spacious desk and the loved piano. The making of music and the attempts to write more ambitious types of poetry and prose brought me back to a way of life which had held me for five years and by which I was now recaptured.

The doctor's visits were a source of comfort to me although of continued frustration to him.

"We must keep on searching, Jessie," he said to me as he put his hypodermic needle into its case one sunny May day while I struggled to conceal the degree of pain that I still felt. The magical drug seemed to be losing its effect; or was the pain becoming more severe? What was to be the outcome?

He turned to my mother.

"We've had doctors in consultation, good doctors over a period of years," he said, "and I think it's time that we made a further investigation. There is a specialist highly praised as a diagnostician – Jessie would have to spend a ten-day period in the Toronto General Hospital while he would put her through a series of tests. She is a young woman now and we must give her every chance to enjoy a full life. As things are she cannot do so."

A new challenge to my own self-respect was met on the day I prepared to return home after a final interview with the specialist. For this interview, I was required to keep an appointment at his office.

The doctor smiled.

"You will be pleased to hear," he said, "that the number of tests which have been made with consideration for your complaint of pain have now been examined. All are negative."

It may be that my shocked expression prompted the addition of these words.

"Now, I am not stating that there is factual evidence of faking, but we must accept that what you complain about as pain is not pain, my dear, merely a figment of your imagination."

I was young and inexperienced in dealing with what I now recall as the most cruel insult to my integrity that I was ever to know. My back stiffened and I rose to face the condemnation with a rebuttal. Tears were coursing down my cheeks but my voice did not tremble as I replied:

"Doctor, you are telling me that nothing whatsoever is wrong with me. You have not discovered the cause of my pain but some day, someone will discover it."

"I believe you are right," he admitted.

Although my voice had not faltered in wording my own defence, although I believed that I was speaking the truth, I left his office suffering from an emotion which was surely similar to that of an innocent person convicted of a crime. The source of my illness might remain undiscovered but the determination to ignore its effect did not prevent its continuance. What was left to be done?

A year later, with strength of body and strength of purpose each contributing to the other, I again boarded a train for Toronto. My destination this time was to be not a hospital, but the office of a well-known publishing house. I carried with me in a home-made folder a collection of some fifty-odd poems. It was mid-afternoon before I reached Toronto and I welcomed the sight of a policeman at the corner outside the railway station. He was kind and explicit in his directions. Under his watchful eyes, I boarded a Yonge Street car.

"Be sure and ask for a transfer," he had called after me, "and go west."

A little frightened but determined, I entered a large building and was whisked by an elevator to the second floor. As I left the elevator the operator pointed to an open door.

"He's the only one of them left," he said. "You come pretty late."

A large clock in the corridor attracted my attention. It was then 4:45 p.m. I hurried.

I stopped at the open door. A stout, middle-aged man sat behind the desk. I waited.

"Come in," he said, "and what can I do for you?"

I did not sit down. I faced him over the desk. I laid the folder open before him.

"I brought this," I said, "to find out if I am a poet."

"Well, well," he commented. "Usually they know. Just give me your name and address and we'll let you hear from us."

He was about to close the folder and as he prepared to do so, my heart sank. Then he hesitated. My name and address were at the top of the cover. His thumb in the opening of the manuscript, he looked curiously at me.

"You're from out of town," he said. "From Blair? Is it a village?"

I answered, "Yes."

He reopened the manuscript.

The poem on the page which faced him was titled "The Prisoner." I watched while he read it in full; then he turned over

214

the page. He turned several pages. He looked up at me, not curiously now but respectfully.

"Sit down, my dear," he said.

My heart was beating very fast as I watched while he moved from page to page. Then, unable to control myself, I said, "Will you please tell me if I am a poet. If I am not, I don't want to think that I am."

Mr. E. H. Moore of The Ryerson Press read on.

"You are a poet," he said, "and this manuscript will be published by us. You look surprised. Trust yourself, young lady. You have the gift."

I did not return to the Union Station by streetcar at the close of the interview. My train left for the city of Galt at six o'clock. I had found not only a publisher but a friend. It was Mr. E. H. Moore who conveyed me to the railway station, who saw me safely to my train, who sent me back to my Little Room with a feeling of happiness and a confidence in myself. Less than a year later, a book of my poems appeared with the imprint of The Ryerson Press of Canada.

My career as a writer had begun.

I would leave the quiet pool and enter the open sea.

PART TWO

THE OPEN SEA

Life is a gathering of emotional experiences and art is
remembering them in tranquillity.

(Alex Tough, in private correspondence,

Dieppe, 1942)

XXVI

Setting Sail

Lured by the promise of the open sea
I ventured fearing from the sheltering cove.

The author

Nature was putting forth again in all the varied greens of spring when a call came from the city of Kitchener twelve miles away.

The head librarian of that city, Miss Mabel Dunham, was herself an author. Her attention had been drawn to my modest efforts toward that goal. She was in need of a relief assistant in the children's department who would also assume the position of story-teller on Saturday mornings. I received a request from Miss Dunham for a personal interview. The salary was fifty cents an hour.

It was in this way that I began my journey from home but still remained a resident there, going and coming with a song in my heart. After three months I was offered a full-time position in the adult department.

Thus began an experience of life in close contact with books and with people so necessary a preparation for my chosen career. The social life in that small city was ambitious for self-improvement as well as for entertainment – a church connection, membership in a literary club, participation in sports and amusements of which I had been deprived. New friendships and contacts with people in all walks of life frequently began over the circulation desk of the library. After a year came a summer

219

vacation when I joined three others on a journey into Canada's northland. I felt incredulous. Could it be that such a pleasure was rightfully mine? Wabikon Camp was a resort on Lake Temagami. There we were lulled to sleep by lapping water at the foot of our open tents, by the cry of the loon trailing her notes along the path of the moonbeams reflected from a great expanse of sky. What we did during our days was commonplace for those who had enjoyed an annual summer holiday – walking through woodland trails of the dense forest, going on canoe trips to mysterious islands and up shallow rivers, cooking fish freshly caught where the lake teemed with bass and salmon trout. Sometimes we went in parties by launch with a guide and other times two and two in canoes or rowboats. Such pleasures were usual events for my companions but for me a never-to-be-forgotten first adventure into a beautiful unspoiled part of Canada. The prodding pain was still there but when it came I clenched my teeth and temporarily absented myself from those who might suspect. Romance went with us and left us a little desolate when the holiday was over.

I spent almost two years as a library assistant in Kitchener, Ontario, enjoying week-ends at home and retaining a close tie with my family who harboured a continuing concern for me. After a period of semi-independence, I became dissatisfied. While appreciating this concern it reminded me that I was not as others who were free to plan an adventurous future with marriage as a natural accompaniment.

About this time I received an invitation from the Canadian Authors' Association to attend a meeting of the Toronto Branch. The invitation came from the famed poet, Charles G. D. Roberts (later Sir Charles). He had read my small book of poetry and believed that I should become a member of the Association. "I am interested in the quality of your work," he wrote. "I find here a craft equal to your range."

Six months later I made application for membership. Two sponsors were needed and Sir Charles was one of them, the other a staff member of the *Daily Mail and Empire*. Neither was personally known to me.

I attended the annual authors' dinner which was held at the Arts and Letters Club of Toronto. Although greeted warmly enough I felt shy and ill-at-ease. All present, except myself, were in evening attire. A display of books was arranged at the end of the banquet hall. I concentrated my attention upon them while the handsomely attired company laughed and chatted among themselves. A tall, well-built man seemed to share my affected interest. He regarded me with curiosity, finally approaching me. He asked my name.

"I'm Donald French," he said, "just a cog in the wheel of the firm McClelland and Stewart. This is your first meeting?" I said that it was. He reached for my hand and gave it a kindly pressure.

"I'm shy, too," he confided, "but don't let these people frighten you." He gave a half wave of his hand toward the gay assembly. The audible conversation was in carefully selected speech, precise and indicative of a claim to a special distinction. "Don't let these people frighten you," he repeated, "less than half of them are writers of merit. The other half are want-to-be's."

His statement brought to mind an earlier fear. To which half did I belong? Despite the reassurances of Mr. E. H. Moore, I continued to question my status as a writer. This questioning was to plague me for many years.

Before the evening ended, however, I had a feeling of kinship with those who were honestly striving toward my own goal. "The more of life you can experience, the farther you travel in learning the variety of ways in which people find and develop their own egos, the greater your skill will become." This statement by the speaker of the evening, William Arthur Deacon, sent me home to ponder.

Many changes were taking place in our family life. Lill, freed from military duties as a teaching dietitian, had set off for an extended holiday in the British Isles. There she had visited the Nesbitt home and Elizabeth, a sister of Patsy, had returned to Canada with her. The sisters were so alike that it seemed to us a magical resurrection. Elizabeth was to replace Jean in the old house, bringing Al a second happiness. Jean could now return to complete her course at Macdonald Institute.

A desire for change was affecting a post-war world. I, too, was affected. My world had been a small one. To become a writer of stature I must take the risk of separating myself from those whose solicitude continued to remind me of limitations which I was determined to prove non-existent.

Early the following summer I knelt beside an open trunk in our guest room preparing to permanently sever connections with home. A vacancy in Buffalo Public Library was reported by a visiting relative from that city. My letter of application was followed by a personal interview with Mr. Walter H. Brown, Chief Librarian.

"May I ask," Mr. Walter Brown had inquired of me, "why you, a Canadian, and without a college education, should entertain the hope that you might become a member of our staff?"

My reply was, "I want to extend my knowledge of library work and I believe that I could do so here."

My application was accepted. I would be a student librarian working part time and studying library science part time at the University of Buffalo.

"Of course your salary will be based upon your working time," he warned me. "You will receive sixty dollars a month while you are a student. After two years, if your progress is satisfactory, your salary will be increased."

The reaction of my parents to my decision to take a position in an American city was one of obvious concern, but loyal acceptance. Perhaps they understood my secret desire for full independence.

While I packed my trunk Mother appeared at the door.

"I wonder whatever has taken Da," she said. "He's off to town in the buggy without changing his clothes. It isn't like him."

While I was putting the finishing touches on packing that evening, I heard footsteps, quiet footsteps. Da, wearing slippers, was on his way to bed. He came close to me and spoke in a low voice.

"You've got good stuff in you to go off like this," he said. "We'll miss you but I'm glad you're going. You haven't had much experience with money and you'll find it will cost you a lot more than you expect. Never mind, the main thing is you'll be learning how to get along on your own. In case you need more than you can earn at first, you should have some laid by you. Your mother and I will rest easier, that way."

He placed in my hand a roll of bills amounting to one hundred dollars.

I had hidden signs of a natural heartache until that moment. I clasped my arms around my father's knees and leaned my cheek against him. I shed the first tears of parting.

He put a hand on my head and his voice was husky as he said with an attempt at cheerfulness, "Oh, you'll get along all right and

222

come home as often as you can. Buffalo isn't so far away. I guess because it's an American city we think of it as the other end of the world."

I don't remember what I said in thanking him but he went out rather quickly and for a few minutes I cried shamelessly into my roll of riches. Yes, I would come home often if it cost all my earnings, for to earn was not the important thing but to be able to earn. This opinion is still mine.

It was a sunny June morning when the trunk was loaded into the back of the democrat. Little Sister went along astride it, to add a note of cheer to my leave-taking. Mother showed her suppressed emotion at parting by a second enfolding of me in her arms. My sisters stood with her. No one had chided me but I knew that anxiety was present in their hearts. Grandpa had his word of counsel, coming close to the democrat where I sat beside my father, to say:

"Dinna be taken wi' all the finery they put on over the border. And if things go a bit hard, remember your ancestors, the Gregors. When Rob Roy was on his death bed and his enemy came to see him, he called for his sword and his coat of armour. He was in bed, ye ken, but they set him up for the occasion."

Grandpa put out his hand to touch my arm.

"We'll be seeing you soon. It's no so far."

With Grandpa's hearty words in my ears I rode beside my father the four miles to town.

The train trip was confusing for an inexperienced traveller. There were several changes, but eventually the great forks of the tracks at Black Rock appeared. I was not afraid but I was somewhat bewildered as I handed over the checks for my luggage. The redcap explained that my trunk would follow me to the Y.W.C.A. where I had written and received confirmation that a room would be reserved for me. I carried an old-fashioned suitcase which must surely have marked me as a novice.

"You'll want a cab, lady?"

I said that I would and soon I was rolling along the streets of the big city toward my destination.

The desk clerk at the Y.W.C.A. gave me disturbing information. It would be necessary for me to share a room with another girl. There were three double rooms available on the second floor. Would I like to inspect them? Murmuring assent I went along the

223

dull dreary hallways to a long stair. Three doors were opened. At the first she said:

"This girl is nice but she has a poodle that doesn't like other people. It nips their heels. She takes it to work with her in the morning and brings it home at night. It's against the rules but we do make exceptions. I don't think – " She paused.

I faltered my refusal and we went on. At the door of number two I detected a very heavy odour. Looking in I saw three bird-cages.

"Miss --- is a bird-lover," the clerk explained. "She has two love-birds, a canary, and a finch. Sometimes they all sing at once, but of course you're from the country I believe, and you wouldn't mind that."

I didn't mind that but I did mind the odour which became more pronounced as she led me into the room for its inspection. The birds fluttered about excitedly and, as she had said, they all spoke at once.

"I don't think this will do," I ventured.

I was relieved when she nodded, understandingly.

"I think the next room will suit you," she said.

She opened a door.

"The girl who lives here is a sales clerk at Adams. She comes from up state and I think you'll get along. As soon as we have a single room we'll give it to you if you want it."

I would want it but I was too exhausted to answer her. As she closed the door on me, I dropped my suitcase and threw myself on the single bed which she had indicated was mine. I sobbed. I was not sorry for my venture and it was too soon for homesickness, but I was physically exhausted and still confused. I had not expected the necessity of settling details. I was almost asleep when the door burst open. A tall thin girl with beak-like nose and very large brown eyes, dressed in a tailored suit and wearing a small sailor hat, strode nonchalantly across the room without speaking, tossed her hat on the dresser and turned her full gaze upon me. In quick rotation she said:

"Hello – who are you? – what's your name? – where'd you come from?"

I opened my mouth to answer her but she didn't wait.

"My name's Agnes," she announced. "You could call me Ag. Most of them do. I sell notions. I'm twenty-three. My boy friend's a policeman. We're going to the Policeman's Ball tonight. Am I ever tired. I picked up a sandwich on my way home. No supper for me. I'm going to take a bath and go to bed. You see, the affair doesn't begin until nine o'clock. If I'm still asleep when he comes – they'll 'phone from the desk – you wake me."

She didn't pause for any response to her directions. In a minute she was out of her clothing, into a robe, and off to take the bath.

The clerk had told me that supper would be served in the dining-room, but like Agnes, I did not eat supper that night. She was soon in bed and fast asleep, and I followed her example.

I was awakened by someone shaking me roughly by the shoulder. Agnes was standing over me, partly dressed and holding a large powder puff in her hand.

"He's here," she said. "He's here. Wake up will you, and powder my back?"

Half dazed, I obeyed while she rattled on.

"Oh, I'm so excited. He's never taken me to a Ball before. He had another girl but he gave her up when we met. He said it was my eyes."

She turned them full on me again.

"Know what I mean? Thanks. Now tell me, shall I wear one sleeve or two sleeves in this dress?"

She lifted a silky dark-green, princess-styled garment from the bed and held it up against her. It had a cream lace sleeve on the right side extending to the elbow. The left side was sleeveless. She held the left sleeve in her hand. She draped it against the arm.

"Smarter with or without?" she asked. "Come on, kid, help me to make up my mind."

How could I, until she added, "It's the new style, you know – one sleeve."

"Well, if you like to be in style," I began, but I got no further.

She nodded vehemently, tossed the loose sleeve onto the bedside table and slipped into the dress.

"Heaven knows when I'll be home," she said. "You look beat. Go back to sleep and think of me having a swell time. Boy, is he ever a snazzy guy."

I felt as someone who has been tossed from an anchored ship into the midst of a turbulent sea. Only over-fatigue brought sleep to me that night.

The dark little room, now unlighted, had one window which faced the east. A summer moon was slipping up the sky and somehow between high buildings found space to reach that window. It laid a path of light on a floor disfigured by long use. It would be shining through the windows at home. There was comfort in the thought.

It must have been past midnight when I was awakened by movement in the room. Horror-filled, I watched a figure creeping on hands and knees from the fire escape outside the window across the floor. I stopped breathing.

"Agnes?"

I breathed again. It was a woman but it was not Agnes. The figure heard me stir and crept to the side of my bed.

"Sh," said a voice. "Don't be scared. I'm Agnes's friend. I came for her old shoes. Her feet are killing her. I know where she keeps them. Don't tell on her or she'll be in trouble."

That was all. She made a stealthy trip to the clothes cupboard and, with the shoes in one hand, she waved the other to me jauntily and tiptoed to the fire escape.

I do not know when Agnes came home. She was still absent when the rising bell rang. I had had enough. That morning, after breakfast, I repeated my request for a single room and it was supplied. From my room I could see only the walls of other dingy buildings, neither tree nor sky nor the green grass of summer. Although my experience as a librarian in Buffalo was to prove an adventurous and valuable one, no sickness overtaking me in my lifetime had been harder to bear than the homesickness which I endured during my first week of complete separation from all that was familiar to me.

I joined the staff of the Buffalo Public Library aware of my handicaps. As Mr. Brown had said, I was not an American and I was not a college graduate. Among more than one hundred librarians and library assistants, I was the least qualified academically. It was explained to me that I would attend morning classes at the local university. Before taking this training, I would spend two weeks in each department and a report of my capabilities would then be examined. After that I would be placed in the department for which I had shown the most aptitude. In other words, I was an alien, on trial. The challenge before me was demanding but exciting. Somewhere in that great institution there would be a

226

niche for me. Failure I did not consider to be a possibility. I ate sparingly. I went to bed every night at seven o'clock, applying heat to an area where the nagging pain persisted. A kind of fury overtook me at the thought of recurring illness which would force me again to be set apart from others. I believe that my observation of those better qualified must have amounted to a fight against fate.

At the end of my testing period, I was summoned to the Chief Librarian's office.

"Well," he said, "all the reports are in and I think we will keep you. You will be on full-time and on a salary of one hundred dollars per month. As to the lectures at the university, shall we forget them at present? Your pace has been pretty steady. Of course, if we find a reason, we'll have to ask you to step down for more training, but I don't think that is going to happen."

It didn't happen and for two years I lived and moved and had my being as a fully-paid member of the Buffalo Public Library Staff. The second year I was promoted to First Assistant in the Children's Department of the main library, but the nagging pain persisted despite the precautions I had learned to take. However, during the winter months of night classes in editorial work under the instruction of Marc Rose, I spent two evenings a week at the university. I had not forgotten the ambition which had been mine from childhood.

Every third week-end I was granted Saturday leave that I might make a trip home. Saturday was a busy day and, in retrospect, I think gratefully of the understanding of Mr. Walter Brown. By returning to Hamilton on Sunday evening where I spent the night, I was able to catch an early morning train on Monday for Buffalo, in time to take my place with the others at 9 a.m. The ties of home were strong. As my father had predicted, the cost of living and of travelling amounted to almost the total of my earnings, but I was proud and I was happy.

XXVII

First Love

It is not always he who tills the soil who plants the seed.

The author

There is a word which I shall not use in this book. It appears so often on the printed page in story, article, and as a lure to the perusal of advertisements. It has in fact become so commonplace, while representing a very natural, respectable, desirable and enviable experience of life, that it has lost its charm and gained for itself an ugliness by its very common use. It is like the actor on stage who would steal the show to draw special attention to his own powers and destroy the purpose of the playwright who sought to create a balanced picture of life.

The great importance of the relationship which unites a man and a woman has been honoured by a word seldom included in their story today. The desire to create is in all of us if it is our privilege to grow to maturity. Even in childhood there is the wish to make mud pies out of common clay and castles out of seaside sand. By child training, by education in school and college, by technical direction in institute and shop, we stimulate the creative impulse. And by the normal association of male and female in every walk of life, each seeks to find his or her counterpart. The mating instinct is in all of us and when accompanied by love it acquires the beauty of holiness. Its consequences do not always produce a happy experience, but whether happy or sad, through its medium, life becomes a great adventure. I emphasize, I do not minimize the importance of that about which I write. Without the creative impulse we would exist only. We would not breathe. It is with earnestness that I wish this experience for everyone.

My neighbour has a beautiful lawn but she makes war upon dandelions.

"They are so common," she says, "that one thinks of them as ugly, when really a dandelion flower is a pretty thing."

It was late in August. I was enjoying my first summer vacation from my work at the Buffalo library. The longing to see the old swamp again was upon me. My father had been fortunate in his purchasing of land. There was a stretch of low-lying woodland on the east of the road and another on the west, there almost hidden from view by a hilly pasture field.

Behind the pasture, two acres had been cleared and were in cultivation for celery planting. My brother was continuing the market gardening which my father had begun. There were rows of yellow-leafed and dark green-leafed plants with generous spaces of black loam between the rows. Sometimes one could find a snowy shell left by an absent snail, a deserted house crumbling under the foot with age. But Al had not disturbed the old swamp beyond the clearing. There was still an acre of slashing rich with undergrowth – elderberries in season, wild plums, blackcaps and abundant red raspberries. It was the remembered fragrance of the place which sent me with a small tin pail to gather raspberries that day.

The sun was at full height and a dreamy stillness brought a sense of mystery. The sky was softly blue with a hint of cloud over the sun, not enough to withhold its heat but enough to make it seem higher in the heavens than it really was. In the standing trees birds concealed themselves, some panting a little, some daring to fly down where an indentation in the earth allowed the gathering of water.

The place was as I had remembered it, lovely with that quiet which is only found in undisturbed country. I was alone with nature and I felt that nature welcomed me. A frog leaped ahead of me as I stepped between two fallen logs half-covered with moss and with winter-greens growing in the powdered wood. I centred my attention upon a special clump of bushes. There would be enough berries here to more than fill my requirements. I need not move but a few steps.

All was still. That wonderful stillness. How often in the heart of a city I had longed for it. There seemed nothing there to separate me from a consciousness of God. Not a sound but the rustle of the leaves under the touch of a delicate breeze and the droning, softly, of a katydid hidden from view in the branches of a swamp willow.

Time passed and did not pass. It seemed to stand still and I with it. Scarcely consciously, I was composing poetry which would never be written. Scarcely consciously, I was overcome by a feeling of deep longing, undefined. There was a rail fence between the swamp and a neighbouring field. The sound of movement behind me made me turn. A young man had vaulted the fence and was standing motionless, looking at me.

I, too, stood motionless, looking at him.

He was tall and strongly built. His very blond hair caught the sunlight and when he blinked in its glare, I noticed that his eyebrows and eyelashes were blond too, the eyes half-closed from the sun. They were blue eyes.

I don't know who spoke first but we both said "Hello." We were too mature for shyness and yet that is what I felt as I turned from him to go on picking raspberries.

It was a matter of a yard or two which divided us. I heard him step toward me.

"This is a nice spot, isn't it?" he said.

His voice was quiet, like the place, not equal in nature with his stature.

"Yes, it is," I said, and stopped picking berries.

I turned to look at him again. He was nearer now.

"I'm visiting at Johnson's," he said. "He's my uncle. Do you live here?"

"No, not now," I replied, "but when I was a little girl."

"Ah," he said understandingly. "You must love this place."

"I do love it," I said.

He came close then, picked a few berries from the bushes beside me, ate them, muttered "Sweet, aren't they?" and went on, "I live on a farm too when I'm not working – I teach school and hate it. I'd rather work on land than on educating children."

We laughed then and he asked, very politely, "Could we sit down and talk for a while?"

He may have noticed my hesitation for he said quickly: "It must be getting close to supper time. I'll have to get along soon, but – it's very pleasant here, isn't it?"

He brushed a log clean of wood chips and dust and looked at

230

me, waiting. It was I who must take the initiative. This was a gentleman, I thought. He would not sit down and leave me standing. I took a place on the log and set my pail beside me. He was alert. He knew the reason and took his place a polite distance from the pail. Although this was a stranger, I trusted him.

"I suppose you are on holiday," he said, and I answered,

"Yes, I am – for two weeks."

"From what occupation, may I ask?"

I told him.

"And where?"

I told him.

He whistled softly and raised his eyebrows.

"Gone American, eh?"

"No," I said firmly. "Just working there. It's interesting."

"I wish I could say as much for my job," he confided.

It may have been a half hour, it may have been more. We were serious-minded. We spoke of such things as the recent war, the flu epidemic, the impending depression. But sometimes we did not talk at all for there was so much to hear – the song of a wood thrush, the twittering of little birds hiding in the leaves of the alders, the katydid, the chirping of a cricket and the intermittent music of the soft summer wind in the leaves of the trees bordering the swamp. We were impersonal and yet we were not.

"You didn't ask me where I'm from," he said.

"But I wondered," I admitted.

He gave me a slow kindly smile.

"Saskatchewan," he told me. "We're a long way from each other – usually."

I got up and lifted my pail.

"Yes we are," I answered. "And I must be getting home. I promised raspberries for supper."

He got up too.

"How far?" he said.

"About half a mile."

"I'll walk you there."

He made the statement half in question.

"Thank you," I replied, because he did not presume.

We walked very quietly through the pasture field to the roadway and from there to our gate.

"I'll have to take to my heels now," he said with a laugh, "or there won't be anything for my supper."

I stood still, watching his tall figure receding up the other fork of the road. I opened the gate and walked slowly along the driveway. The hollyhocks were in bloom and Lill had planted a row of them against the grey wall of the house. There was a slight breeze and they seemed to nod in approval as I approached.

A few days later, Mother suggested that another batch of berries would have ripened.

"I'd like to make some raspberry pies," she said.

She did not ask me to go to the swamp but I went and I listened for the creak of someone vaulting the grey rail fence. But I did not hear it.

With a half-filled pail I turned to go home. It was then I noticed two small children kneeling on the other side of the fence. They were peering between the rails at me. The girl spoke first.

"He's gone home," she said, and the boy continued:

"You ain't going to see him anymore, so there! He don't like Ontario, but we like him."

I smiled pleasantly as I left them. But the swamp seemed to have a sorrowful beauty now and I walked home thinking.

Would I ever see the stranger again?

It was gratifying to my pride (or is determination a better word), that I had spent a full year without a longer break than two or three days of illness and on only two occasions. The persistence of that illness I did not reveal to my employers. I had become established as capable of earning a living and of acquiring knowledge at the same time, which was to lead me into more advanced positions. I had done this, however, at the expense of all other freedoms with the exception of three staff occasions. Resident in a large American city, I had not once otherwise participated in its social life. There had been invitations from the friendly members of the circulation department where I had worked. I longed to accept these opportunities to share in a life still strange to me. I could not share without jeopardizing the continuance of something still more important to me – a career and, with it, proof that I was physically able to earn a living.

Following my first earned vacation at the library, I took up my new duties under the supervision of Miss Evans, head librarian of the Children's Department. I felt a glow of pride. In the adult section with others I had shared in serving a vast number of university students who required books from what we called our "closed stacks." There was an "Open room" where borrowers could choose for themselves. From the closed stacks we provided them with the material called for. Between the floor and the high ceilings were two levels of shelves. To reach the second level it was necessary to climb a flight of eight iron steps, and the lighting was artificial. On busy days we were overwhelmed by borrowers who often formed lines from the several wickets to the large main doors. A policeman was on duty. Perhaps the excessive physical effort required, added to the necessity for close concentration, helped to blur the ever-present nagging pain, at least sufficiently to keep me on duty. When others were sharing in evening and week-end entertainment, I was thankfully lying in bed in order to spare myself for the challenge of continuing at work. I was not sorry for myself. I was proud. There were the breaks, the week-ends at home where love and attending concern prepared me for the stretch of days among strangers who knew nothing of the physical challenge. I had one regret, however. Under such discipline, I had neither the time nor the energy for creative writing. But the time for that would come, was being prepared for, was as certainly my objective as it had been from childhood.

But when I returned from my first summer vacation I brought with me a feeling of unrest. The stranger who had overtaken me in the old swamp I had a serious wish to see again. As he walked me home, he had offered to carry my pail of berries. In the exchange our hands had touched and our eyes had met. I had enjoyed social life in a small Ontario city with young men and women. There had been dances and other forms of entertainment with permissible contacts. They had been pleasant contacts but no more. Now I knew that while I achieved one objective – independence – another had been awakened in me which was still beyond reach. Love was one thing, marriage another. I could never honestly enter into a relationship which required health of body as well as health of mind. I could not be a cheat. Therefore, I was still one apart. Unless, by some miracle, a cure was discovered for my undefined complaint, I would always be a reject. Then, on my twenty-sixth birthday, a cousin in California sent me *Sonnets from the Portuguese*. The introduction contained the life story of Elizabeth Barrett Browning.

"How do I love thee? Let me count the ways."

If for one, perhaps for another, the miracle.

233

XXVIII

Contact with Reality

Law is a promise which may be honourably broken.

T. R. James

It was a chilly November night. Rain was falling with a sleety coldness which reminded one that winter was around the corner. My regular hours of duty at Buffalo Public Library were from 9 a.m. until 6 p.m. with one exception. Each member of staff, in whatever department, was required to spend one evening assisting in the circulation.

I had moved from the dingy Y.W.C.A. to an attractive residence on Delaware Avenue, sponsored by the Presbyterian Church as a home for girls away from home. I cannot remember who directed me there but a pleasant-faced house mother opened the door to me and I was at once impressed by the cheerfulness of the place and the friendly atmosphere. There were rooms for one, two and three according to the amount of one's income. I longed for a room of my own but the rent was prohibitive. There was a community kitchen where breakfast and the evening meal might be prepared. At the library, a hot lunch was served at noon by a caterer.

I was to share an airy dormitory with two other girls. They were in the room when I made my choice. One was a shopgirl, the other the secretary in a social agency.

The location of the residence was within walking distance of the library building, a well-lighted area. Near the corner of Niagara Street a small restaurant displayed the sign "Best in

234

Town." Through shining windows two men in spotless white uniforms and chefs' caps could be seen pouring a mixture on hot plates of stainless steel. Whenever I passed by, every seat along the curving counter appeared to be filled. The place was famous for one menu only – scrambled eggs, toast and coffee. But what an art in cookery was here displayed. Never have I tasted more delicious simple fare. Each of the three items had a perfection indescribable. On work evenings, after nine, I became a regular customer.

On that November night a young girl, perhaps seventeen, sat on the next stool to mine. She was delicate of feature, with large dark eyes and hair twisted into a rope at her neck. As we enjoyed similar fare, I smiled at her, only to discover that the dark eyes were full of tears. I looked away but was aware that she drew a handkerchief from her purse several times.

I felt attracted to her, with an impulsive desire to be helpful. The number of people at the counter began to thin out. The two chefs were busy preparing orders for others who straggled in.

"Aren't you feeling well?" I asked.

She burst into open crying.

"I don't know what to do," she said.

Nor did I. Here was someone in trouble, someone about whom I knew nothing. It was not possible to give or receive confidences in such a place. But where? The rain ceased.

"Where do you live?" I asked her.

She was staying at the Y, she said, which was nearby.

"I live three blocks the other direction," I replied. "I work at the library and I'm on my way home. Could we walk together? To the square?"

We had both finished eating. Our bills paid, we walked out. She did not turn at the square. The stars were shining now. The wind was still keen. She pulled her coat around her as she walked on with me but she did not confide in me. Suddenly she stopped.

"Can I talk to you again?" she asked. "I'm not scared to talk to you. I know you won't tell anybody and I don't know what to do."

I would not go to the Y to talk with anyone. The very thought of its dreary interior reminded me of experiences more than a year ago. I could not ask this girl into the residence. I knew that she shrank for some reason from recognition. She worked in a factory, she said. Certain girls in the residence also worked in factories.

235

What she had to tell me was a secret. If I wanted to help her I must share in her secrecy.

"Do you ever eat at Linton's Lunch?" I asked her. "Day after tomorrow's Sunday. I could meet you there and we could talk. Not many people go there on Sunday."

Linton's Lunch was situated on Main Street. She was eager in her acceptance. It was arranged that we should meet at three o'clock on Sunday afternoon.

We met at Linton's Lunch. I did not sleep well that night, thinking of the plight of someone alone and afraid in a big city. Probably there were many thousands of such people in trouble in Buffalo, New York. I had not thought of this before. In a way I had carried my own little world with me and for the most part I was still living within its shelter. As I lay in the darkness of the dormitory with the friendly sound of two others peacefully sleeping there, I experienced a shock – my first awareness of my own selfish attitude toward life.

This girl's anxiety proved to be for another – a cousin who, she said, had fled to her from her home in Canada, on the pretence of a lengthy visit. Really to hide herself from a father of six, four of them girls. He had warned them in adolescence that if any one of them became pregnant out of wedlock, she would be turned out and forever disowned.

It had happened.

"She's the nicest of all my cousins," my companion told me, over a cup of tea and toast. "They live in the West, you see, and don't have such good times because it's a farm. There's a village but that's a mile off. Everybody goes there on Saturday night to the dance hall and that's where she met him. She's shy and doesn't dance too well but she's awful pretty. I guess that's what did it. He come from quite a ways off but he was always there she said. Maybe he was lonesome too, like she said she was. Maybe, I don't know. When she found out she told my uncle a lie. I went there last year on my holidays. She was just working at home – she told him she was coming to me for a visit. He grumbled about the money it would cost. He didn't figure though that she'd have to pay her own food and room with me. I got her a place near me until two weeks ago but I couldn't keep it up. She wants to pretend that she has a job. She wants to stay here until it's over. I took it up with a nice woman I know at work and she told me about a place for girls like that, with a matron and all that stuff."

236

"I went to see the matron. She was real kind. She took her in but she asked me what was to happen to the baby after? They take care of adoptions but they wouldn't take in a Canadian girl that way, they had too many American kids to look after. I don't know what to do. She has to stay or take the baby home with her. I mean she has to stay and work for her keep until the baby's old enough for her to get a job somewhere else and look after it. I don't know what to do," she repeated. "You don't know my uncle. He means what he says. My aunt's a nice woman and I know she would take her back quick and look after her but he's the boss."

Something very cold had gripped me around my heart as I listened. I could not eat but I sipped my tea as I asked, "The West – where in the West?"

"Oh, I didn't tell you," she apologized. "Saskatchewan. We're Italian, and when we came from Italy my father wanted to live in the United States but my uncle bought a homestead in Canada. It's swell out there, I love it, but there's not much for a girl to do once she's growed up, and I guess that's how it happened, that and Shirley being the kind of girl she is."

Shirley. It was my first clue to identification.

"Could I know your name?" I asked politely.

"It's Mary Dedetta," she said, "and I'm an American. My people came here before I was born. I'm so glad I'm an American. I won't get myself into a fix like Shirley has, I promise you that, but even if I did, you see I wouldn't be in a fix. I'm an American," she repeated proudly.

My mind was divided between anguish for the girl and apprehension – Saskatchewan.

"What," I asked, without wanting to ask it, "did the man, I mean Shirley's – you know what I mean, what did he look like?"

"Oh, she's got a picture of him," Mary assured me. "She could get after him for it but she won't. I guess she loves the guy. You want to know what he looks like? He's great big and not dark like us – a Swede I think, blue eyes and all that."

My heart was beating rapidly and I scarcely recognized my own voice, it was so faint as I asked another question.

"Is he a teacher?"

Mary laughed.

"Teacher," she said scornfully. "Now why would you think that? He can't even talk our language right, I mean English. He's a digger or something on the railroads and when he's not working, he hangs around the town hotel."

Mary mentioned the name of a place unknown to me.

I was now the one with tears in my eyes. They were tears of relief. Why had I doubted?

"I think I can help you," I said. "There is a girl, really my room-mate, who works for a social agency. She has told me about the way they try to help people like your cousin. May I talk to her? I don't know what can be done but I'm sure something can."

Mary, with Latin impulsiveness, raised herself and kissed me across the table. There were very few people in the restaurant and we sat in a booth concealed from everyone. Her beautiful brown eyes showed such relief that I came willingly out of my safe little world.

I took the social worker into my confidence. That night, under cover of darkness and in secrecy, I went with Mary to interview the matron of a home for unwed mothers.

"It's the only way to learn the exact regulations," my room-mate had advised me. "It may be different in different Homes, you see. If I knew the name of the Home, I could speak for you," she offered. "But it would be much better, since you know the girl's case, if you took up the matter yourself. You won't be involved, I can assure you, and you may be able to unravel the puzzle for them. I know a clergyman who supervises adoptions for people. He has authority too. When you find out all you can, I'll speak to him."

That night I found out all I could. The matron of the Home which we entered after passing through a dimly lit ghetto, was a pleasant-faced woman. We were ushered into a sitting-room for visitors where Mary would wait to see her cousin.

"Your sister is at prayers right now," the matron told Mary, and I realized then that to protect Shirley, Mary had lied about their relationship, that she was willing to go all the way. I was becoming willing too, for in a room, doubtless a chapel, some distance from the sitting-room there was the sound of singing – young voices raised in an appeal to the Creator who had endowed them with the desire to create. With the singing there was the sound of a girl sobbing.

"That's Shirley," Mary whispered. "That's Shirley."

It was all I needed to send me resolutely into action. After prayers, while Mary visited with her cousin in a small room

238

provided for such a purpose, I asked for an interview with the matron.

After an explanation upon my part of Shirley's plight as explained to me by Mary, I asked for an outline of the regulations which might interfere with a safe solution to her involved situation.

There was comfort in the kindly solicitude displayed by the matron as she explained to me the firm laws of the Department of Immigration.

"I'm sorry," she admitted. "I'm truly sorry. This is an unusually pathetic case. But an attempt was made to enter this girl under a fictitious name and as an American. That was a poor beginning. Lies lead to more lies and who can guess the truth?"

"But laws are made to help the people, not to harm them," I argued. "There must be times of exception."

The matron looked at me thoughtfully.

"There should be times of exception," she said. "Perhaps there are. Would you like to talk to someone in control? We have had questions raised before and answered honestly by him. He's very decided in approving law-making, not law-breaking. But I think I would like you to have a talk with him since you are not personally a part of this affair, only, as I see it, a social worker without the name." She smiled at me.

She did not win my affection by the smile nor did she raise my hopes. It was a pleasant way to dispose of an unpleasant responsibility, I thought. But I asked if I might have the name of this person in authority.

She wrote quickly on a slip of paper and handed it to me.

"I'll tell him you're coming," she said.

That was fifty years ago and I remember neither the name of the official of immigration nor his address.

Mary reappeared wiping her eyes, crying quietly. We went out together.

"I don't know what I can do," I said as we walked home through the murky atmosphere of an ugly part of the city. "I may not be able to do anything, but I am going to try."

When she left me at the square for her drab little room at the Y, she flung her arms around me impulsively again in a gesture of thanks.

When I prayed that night I thanked God that Shirley's lover was not a school teacher, while I prayed for wisdom to help her in her plight. But selfishly, after that prayer, I allowed myself to relive a summer day in an old swamp.

Although I patronized the "Best in Town" two evenings that week, hoping to find Mary, she did not come. That was my week-end to go home but I did not go. Early on Sunday morning I left the residence for a part of the city through which I had passed with Mary and its atmosphere had frightened me. But it was a bright Sunday morning and after changing streetcars three times I found myself beyond the ghetto in a suburb consisting of modern and attractive houses with well-kept grounds. Many of the houses in the inner city were built of clapboard. These were bricked and stuccoed. They were clean, situated far enough from the industrial area to escape most of the smog. It was 9 a.m. when I pressed the electric button on the frame of a front door. A woman answered my ring. She wore a flowered dressing-gown and her hair was still in curlers. If there were children I did not hear their voices. I handed to the woman the slip of paper given me by the matron. I asked if I might see the person whose name it bore. She stared at me.

"My dear," she said, "you are early. Step in and I'll deliver your message." From her words I realized that I was expected.

She showed me into an attractive living-room and told me to sit down. In a matter of minutes a man in shirt sleeves, middle-aged and greying, appeared in the doorway. He looked at me with curious but not unfriendly eyes.

I told him Shirley's story. I told him of the unrelenting, unforgiving father.

In turn, he told me firmly the rules and regulations governing the Department of Immigration of the United States of America. I was prepared for this and I had prepared myself to meet his arguments with the rebuttal which, during sleepless hours, I had delivered in imagination.

"Would you be kind enough," I said, "to allow me the privilege of expressing my point of view by an illustration from a very old story?"

"Go ahead," he said.

"And will you permit me to relate this illustration without any interruption?"

His expression hardened.

"You come ready, don't you?" he frightened me a little by saying.

"Only because I am familiar with the story," I answered. "And I am afraid that if I do not tell it properly, I may not make

240

my point clear."

"Go ahead," he said again.

"When I think of law-making," I reflected, "I think of making promises. Really a law is a promise, isn't it? It is a man-made regulation in directing man's affairs. Thousands of years ago a promise was made by a King to a woman who pleased him. He promised that he would give to her whatever she asked of him. Because of the hate of another she was requested to ask for the head of an innocent man. Because the King had made a promise and although he knew the man to be good and innocent, he kept his promise. John the Baptist's head was delivered to Salome in a charger. My father told me this story," I said, "one winter night when I sat on his knee by the coal fire in a house in Canada. He made one comment after the telling which I shall never forget. He said, 'Promises, like laws, are man-made and sometimes should be broken.'"

I had composed my brief appeal with repeated recitation to myself during the night before that memorable Sunday morning.

Surely I was compelled by a power stronger than my own will.

The immigration officer of the United States of America did not speak for a full minute nor did he take his eyes from my face. When he did speak I could not answer him.

"You tell a good story," he said. "Your father taught you the truth. The girl will stay in this city until she is ready to go home and her child will be entered for adoption. A law is a law but I am sure that the United States of America will not be harmed by this exception."

I could not thank him but he was thanked, I believe, by the tears which I could not restrain.

That afternoon I met Mary in Linton's Lunch. We rejoiced together. But there was still a hurdle to be surmounted. Mary brought the troublous fact to me. The matron was now willing to keep Shirley. The adoption board had agreed to place the child but not until it had been nourished on mother's milk for a stated number of weeks. Counting the time before the child would be delivered, Mary rejoiced that her cousin would be home in time for Christmas, but informed of the unshakable decision of the Board of Management in the Home that all babies must be breast fed for at least six weeks before adoption, she knew that a return to Canada could not be arranged in time for the final deception. There was one way out, the matron had said – mother's milk could be provided from another source for as long as it was required if paid for by someone. The price was high. Mary counted her savings. There was not enough and there would not be enough in time to settle the account.

I had not deposited the roll of riches given to me more than a year before by a father whose concern for me could never be altered by any act of mine. Wrapped in a fine handkerchief and suspended by two strong safety-pins, I had carried it between my breasts day after day, cherishing its touch as evidence of other treasure. That afternoon, before Mary and I went our separate ways, the roll changed hands. Shirley would be home for Christmas.

It was the end of February and a retarded January thaw was turning the blanket of snow recently fallen to an ugly grey. I was at my desk in the Children's Department when I was approached by a small grey-haired man in clerical dress who spoke my name. He then identified himself. It was early afternoon and only a few children were examining the shelves. The Second Assistant would take care of them as I led my visitor to a quiet place in an alcove of the magazine room on the same floor. He explained to me that he was in charge of the funds used for special expenses incurred by those who took shelter in the Home for Unwed Mothers from which Shirley had departed before Christmas. He had talked with and counselled the cousins before the young mother left for Canada. Mary had told him of the exchange which had taken place that Sunday afternoon in early December. He drew a billfold from his pocket and handed me an envelope.

"It is not fair," he said, "that a young girl like yourself should be required to do what you have done. The amount on the cheque enclosed will be added by me to the general expenses of a department which is really an effort by our church to perform the work for which we stand." He added words of approval which I felt were undeserved by me.

As I watched him enter the elevator which would take him to the first floor I did not seem to be where I was. The sun was warm and the raspberries were at their fullest yield. Small birds in the alders twittered happily and a delicate breeze played in the standing trees. I heard the creaking of a rail in the fence.

I went back to my duties at the desk in the Children's Department.

XXIX

The Crisis

The ever-whirling wheele
Of Change, the which all mortall things
doth sway.

Edmund Spenser

I did not enjoy life in the city of Buffalo, New York, but I am glad that I went to Buffalo and that I remained for more than two years. I had come from a smaller city. My world had been a little one, a place of security and filial love set in beautiful countryside, where nature could be claimed as a parent by those who accepted that they were a part of her. The people might be counted in thousands but one saw familiar faces every day. No words needed to be spoken to ascertain that these were friends. The criminal, the immoral, the cheat, the abhorrent hypocrite, they were there, but the all-encompassing influence was one of orderliness, civility and the presence of God. This Presence was revealed in the flowery paths of spring, in the songs of summer, in the transformed colours which appeared with the dying of the year. Death became a thing triumphant followed by the resting period of winter and the promise of resurrection in spring. One did not talk about this feeling which accompanied the sense of being alive, but it was there, created by the country setting in which the city stood.

In Buffalo, the tramp of human feet hurrying to and from places of employment, sweatshops, deafening foundries which moulded steel and decomposed man, the certainty that evil walked

as surely as virtue wherever the streets carried the multitudes –
fear; this was the bigger city.

Yet there was something warm and assuring like the touch of
a woollen blanket around one's shoulders on a cold day. There was
the awareness of being a part of everyone, alone but never alone,
sharing perhaps unwillingly but nevertheless sharing in the evil
and the good. How can I describe the feeling? "We are all going
the same way," was the thought as we went our many ways, and
somehow thinking thus brought comfort.

It was not a clean city. It was old and scarred. Much of that
which took place there was hidden from the eyes of the respectable
or from those who, in identifying themselves, claimed the title of
respectability. From a total stranger I slowly became a participant
of life as lived around me. Faced by one enigma of behaviour after
another I doubted the reliability of my own convictions. I began to
turn them over and over, finding flaws and attempting to repair
them or to replace them by honest reasoning.

In the residence where I lived, a social worker rubbed
shoulders with a prostitute. The latter was a sweet kindly girl who
won my liking before I learned of her occasional illicit occupation.
When I discovered this I became very unsure of my first
impressions of everyone I met, and more seriously, I looked upon
her occupation with new eyes.

In the murky darkness of city streets there prowled disillusionment which crept through the unlocked doors and windows of the
mind.

I had hoped to enjoy my course in editorial work at the
university but I learned quickly that I was not a newspaper woman
and never would be. When the course neared an end and my final
assignment was "The Collapse of Italy after 1918," as an editorial
of 1500 words, I anticipated failure. There would be no credits for
me, I was sure. I knew very little about Italy and World War I was a
horrible memory. My way of examining a subject had been
through the lives of people, not through laws and regulations, facts
and figures. Now as I prepared to research the subject of my
assignment, I lost interest because of its magnitude. I ended by
choosing to discuss the plight of the Italian poor in contrast with
the excessive riches of many in high places. I became heatedly
indignant as I depicted the trials and tribulations of the lower
classes and the indifference of those in authority over them.

I received a D rating and the comment, "You have turned this into a moral issue instead of analysing a national crisis."

I had never entertained the ambition of becoming a newspaper woman but my failure to impress our instructor in editorial work affected unfavourably my opinion of myself as a writer. The challenge which every day brought to meet the physical and mental requirements of my occupation as a librarian left little strength and little inspiration for creative writing. Pursuing me daily was that undiagnosed demon, and during my second year I more frequently followed a practice of retiring at 7 p.m. with a comforting application of heat to my upper abdomen. To this method of survival was added the now regular practice of a nightly dose of aromatic spirits of ammonia prescribed as a "relaxer" for nerves.

Fortunately no one seemed to guess the necessity for my peculiar behaviour. My room-mates eyed me a little uncertainly at times. Might I be a drug addict or at least a potential? Then came the revelation.

It was the month of June and two weeks before a much desired vacation. The caterer at the main library where most of the staff ate their noonday meal had prepared a hot meat loaf with gravy and a tossed salad. The meat loaf contained generous pieces of red and green pepper. It was delicious and I ate every morsel of my serving. I have never eaten green pepper since, for within an hour I was draped over a basin in the washroom suffering the most severe pain that I had ever experienced. A head librarian from the circulation, Miss Fox, found me there. A doctor was called. The truth was out. I was accompanied home to my room after an injection of morphia. Miss Fox drove me there herself. The doctor had so required. He promised to see me again that evening.

"Have you ever had this pain before?" Miss Fox asked me as she helped me to disrobe.

Confession was necessary. Her face was grave.

"You should have told us this long ago," she said. "We would have given you more consideration. You work hard."

"Please," I begged, "I don't want consideration. I am quite well, really I am, but I shouldn't eat green peppers."

We both laughed then.

"You won't tell the others that I've been sick a lot, will you?" I asked of her.

"I won't," she said. "I see why you feel like this. You haven't missed more than a day or two at work since you came. It's not necessary to tell everybody everything, but you must promise me that you'll keep in touch with the doctor and do what he says."

Impulsively she bent and kissed me. Only then did I shed the tears which were choking me. I so desperately wanted to be like others. I would be like others. I was like others. I preferred to believe that the complaint was a figment of my imagination.

But the doctor who called to see me that evening was of a different opinion. When he discovered that I was a stranger in Buffalo and from Canada, he had advice to offer after a positive diagnosis.

"You should enter the hospital and have an X-ray," he said. "I am prepared to wager that you have a gall-stone. Has this condition been of long standing?"

I had to admit that it had been.

"A very wealthy patient of mine," he went on then, "left me a legacy in her will – the use of a private room in our hospital for the care of anyone whom I considered deserved immediate and expensive attention. I think she would have said that you qualify." He paused a minute. He cast a glance around the humble dormitory. Three beds. He looked at me thoughtfully. "If you need an operation," he continued, "which I suspect you do, hospitalization would be necessary for several weeks. You would have private room care and every attention. The cost to you would be nil except of course the surgeon's fee, should he be required. That might be two hundred dollars."

In recollection the offer sounds to me like a fairy tale but when it was made I could think only of my distance from home and that immediate treatment of such a nature would create an inferior status for me in my place of employment. Again I would be a reject. I would not be a reject.

I did not commit myself and the doctor considered me a little coldly as I thanked him. I reached for my purse which lay on a table beside my bed and asked his fee. His expression softened.

"Put that away," he said. "Let's pretend that this is Christmas Eve. I waive all fees at Christmas time. My father was a doctor before me and he set me this example. Good luck to you, but think my advice over carefully," he cautioned. "You're going to need help, of that I am certain."

Two days later I returned to my desk in the Children's Department of the public library. I was completely free of pain now except for that occasional prodding which I had learned to expect.

On the thirtieth of June I journeyed home for a two weeks' vacation. I looked on my parents with new eyes. They seemed older, more frail, although I had spent a week-end with them only a month before. My own attack of sickness had made me supersensitive to the physical condition of others.

In October of that year something happened which brought the end for me of a fight against the inevitable. Little Sister had become a young woman of charm. It was expected that she would marry early and on her twenty-second birthday she became engaged to a country lad. The wedding was set for the following summer. My older sisters had embarked on a business venture which included the operation of two tea-rooms and a lodge. When Edith married, my parents would be alone. This could not be. In the spring I resigned my position at Buffalo Public Library and, like someone released from the self-imposed treading of an endless belt, I went home with a song in my heart. I went home to be with those I loved and to rediscover the self which I had sublimated to prove the existence of a physical tolerance which I did not have and was never to achieve. I returned to the piano and the small room, to the desk where I had stored the partly written novel in the lower drawer, and to a way of life where rules and regulations were self-made. I would do common tasks and sing of freedom.

My grandfather was now approaching his one hundredth birthday. When I went home for a week-end two months before, he took me aside.

"Lassie," he confided, "when Little Edie is married, something tells me I'll no be here. But Cissy and your father need company. They're getting on too and I'm thankful that you're coming to be wi' them."

I could not sleep that night. My parents were growing older but Grandpa was failing in spite of his retained faculties of sight and hearing and of his alert mind. It was coming.

"It was my will," he had once confided, "to live a hundred years and I believe the Almighty will respect my wish but sometimes I doubt it."

Grandpa's wish was respected but the next summer, before Little Sister's wedding day, he slipped easily away from us. He had been a member of our household for so long that when I came home to assume the responsibilities of guardian to my parents, I often heard his step and the sound of his voice.

Now, like Jo March, when Amy burned her fairy tales, I was to suffer a personal loss. The partly written manuscript of a novel which I had stored carefully in the lower drawer of the big desk was missing. I stared at the vacant place which it had occupied with incredulous eyes. The mystery of its disappearance was never solved. I could remember too little of its content to rebuild the story half-told. After days of searching I resolved to attempt shorter works while I entertained the conviction that it would be found. Perhaps this was a wiser approach to reclaiming my right to achieve the long-cherished dream of a writing career.

However, after a few months of life at home in happy association with those most dear to me, the attack which I had suffered that day in Buffalo Public Library was repeated with even more severity. The duties which I had assumed at home were handed over to Jennie while I faced an emergency operation in Hamilton General Hospital. The deception was at an end and from my hospital bed, five days after the removal of a gall-stone, I wrote a letter to the specialist who had found no physical basis for my pains.

I would live on with a new faith in my own integrity. I would have a confidence which I had never known.

And so it was to be.

Eight weeks after I was released from hospital, the head librarian in the nearby town of Preston accepted a position elsewhere. I was offered the vacancy.

"You're pretty wobbly yet to take any kind of work," commented Dr. J. K. MacGregor of Hamilton.

Yes, I was wobbly but the position was less than two miles from Willow Bank. I would live at home.

My work would entail minor physical effort. I would have an assistant to serve at the desk while I engaged in the choosing and examining of the books purchased. I accepted the offer. But again I put a newly begun book manuscript in the lower drawer of the old desk.

XXX

My Parents

There falls no shadow where there shines no sun.

Hilaire Belloc

The reason for laying aside the few chapters of the novel which I had begun was the serious illness of my father. For two years with failing sight, he had continued to join us with few words of complaint but we could see that his strength was ebbing fast. My mother seldom laughed now and there was a look of fear in her eyes when they rested upon him. She was never far from his side while she sewed on the garments for poor families in the district or knitted diligently on infants' wear for the Red Cross.

Jean had sold her share of the tea-room business to come home again as a support for us all. We tried to maintain a cheerful attitude but the handwriting was on the wall and it was difficult to ignore it. Whether he was resting on the couch in the living-room, or, in summer weather, on the lounging chair under the maple tree, Mother was somewhere near. Then came the hour of certainty when he was confined to bed for nine months with nurses in attendance.

Grief dwelt in our house as an invisible presence. While we refused to admit that a parting must come, this refusal was cruel. It interfered with an easing of my father's departure. The use of drugs was limited more than it should have been because of a dread that such drugs might shorten his days with us in a state of full consciousness. Especially my mother could not seem to release him, and that I did not assert my conviction that our love for him had become a form of cruelty has been the deepest regret of my life. There were others to decide, but that did not absolve me from stating an opinion.

My father accepted his situation calmly. Sometimes he spoke frankly to me.

"Don't fret over me, my girl," he said when signs of concern were difficult to hide. "I've had a good life. When I lie here without talking I am really enjoying myself. What time of day is it?"

"It's almost supper time," I answered him.

"Is the sun shining?" It was early September.

"Yes, but it will soon be setting," I replied.

He smiled.

"I thought so," he said. "It was a day like this the year after your mother and I bought the farm," he mused. "There wasn't much land cleared but I took out the oxen to do a bit of fall plowing. I got so taken up with what I was doing that I forgot the time. The sun was behind the trees on the pinnacle when I realized how late it was. I looked at my furrows. They were a kind of rosy brown from the last rays of the sun. I was proud of those furrows and what it meant to us to have cleared land. But I quickly unhitched the oxen and hurried them down the road to home. I could see your mother standing watching for me in the door of the house with the two little boys beside her and I waved my hat in the air. Those were good days. I was so happy that I tried to whistle. You know, I never could whistle." He gave a low laugh. He looked at me with unseeing eyes. He reached for my hand. "Yes, I've had a good life," he repeated.

I was glad that conditions in my own life had brought me home and had kept me there for the last two years he spent with us.

The first springtime, although he worked more by touch than by sight, he sowed seeds in the small greenhouse and removed the delicate plants to their place in the garden. The rows were not straight, but the plants took root and many a morning he could be seen bending low to measure the overnight growth with his fingers. Once I followed him and apologetically he stood up at the sound of my coming and explained.

The end of the next winter he went away – the last day of

250

March. The first robin sang in the elm tree by the porch. But for the robin there was a silence over everything, a hush before rebirth.

I am not a spiritualist and I cannot explain a happening on that morning. It was shortly after dawn when the nurse summoned us. As we gathered about his bed where he had lain unconscious for several days, he opened his eyes and great joy was audible in the words which he said. Great joy and astonishment. His voice was strong. He spoke the names of two brothers and a parent whom he had all but worshipped. "Murray – Will – Father." They had gone before him but even as he spoke he, too, was gone.

It seems to me in recall that I began to question the fundamentals of organized religion from adolescence. My scepticism did not doubt the existence of God but avoided full encounter with what I could not understand. I continued to attend church and to pray but in the verses which became my vehicle of intimate thoughts, questions were raised and frequently they were not answered. I accepted death as an inevitable part of life but when I was confronted by it I did not seem to grasp its full significance. I claimed to believe in a future life and an all-loving Providence. But after the death of my father I stood confronted before an almost total atheism. My perspective became a confusion of unrelated images. After surviving many challenges to faith during years of illness I had met the supreme challenge. I was without belief in a merciful Creator who could limit mortal suffering if all-powerful. I lost the power to create except in words of fatalism. I wrote:

My faith I lost when the first darkness fell –
She left me stricken on Grief's lonely hill;
I called her through the deepening hush of hell,
But all was still.

Some months later, a friend of the family, C. R. Tibb, once a magazine editor in Toronto, came to spend a few days with us. We had not been in touch for years. On our living-room table lay my two small books of poetry. Leafing them over he turned to me and asked, "Have you ever tried prose?"

I answered in the affirmative.

"A novel?"

I told him that I had begun a novel two years before but I could not finish it. He asked me the reason for this and I answered honestly.

"How much have you written?" he inquired.

"Two chapters and an outline."

"May I see them?"

With some misgivings and a sense of betraying someone or something, I agreed to show him what I had begun. I could not analyse this feeling. It was as if I believed irrationally that the world should stop turning because my father had died.

Our visitor took the manuscript with him to sit under the shade of the large maple where my father had so often sat.

"No one will ever cut down this tree with my permission," he once told me, "not for any sum of money they might offer."

Through the window I looked at the tree and suffered such a sense of guilt and disloyalty that I went to my room to conceal an outburst of weeping.

But the tears which I shed that morning were like the blood-letting from a poisoned wound. The healing began.

That evening Mr. Tibb returned the manuscript to me.

"This is strong stuff," he said, "worth finishing."

I had not put into blunt words the condition of my spiritual health before that morning but now it was necessary.

"I don't believe in God," I said.

Mr. Tibb smiled at me with reassurance.

"I advise that you shut yourself up for a year and finish this novel. If you do so I predict that you will find God."

In order that I might remain at home and assist in the duties of nursing, I had acquired a part-time occupation. A new family had come to take over a pioneer estate on the other side of the mill pond. There were four children in ages from six to eighteen. Their great-grandfather was Sir William Johnson, whose second wife was Molly Brant, and they were the grandchildren of Sir William Dickson, co-founder with Absalom Shade of the city of Galt. Their parents sought a tutor for them and I was consulted. I was not a graduate teacher and was therefore, I believed, unqualified, but a request for an interview with me was received from Dr. V. K. Greer, Chief Inspector of Public Schools for Ontario. I was granted a permit to conduct a private school.

My father had rejoiced when this offer came to me, "Now you won't be going away."

I did not go away for four and a half years. The Little Room became a schoolroom with second-hand desks and from nine o'clock until three every school day I presided there. Not only was I given permission to teach but a free hand in the planning of a course of study. It was the time of change in Ontario's public school system. Upon a second visit to Dr. Greer, I was presented with the new plan to be adopted shortly after as "The New Curriculum."

"Try this out," he instructed me, "of course, with variations. Make it as original as you think advisable and at the end of a year report back to me. You won't be interfered with."

I was not interfered with and in the spare hours after school and on week-ends, following Mr. Tibb's advice, I went into seclusion with my unfinished novel.

Meanwhile I experienced a new excitement as my little school grew.

I entered the classroom each day with a sense of challenge and a kind of happiness which I had not believed would ever be mine again. The novel was progressing too, and with it the experience of teaching children by a wayside stream or in the heart of a woods. For as soon as the warmth of May touched the countryside, lessons were held outdoors and wherever the children willed to hold them. The informality and the possibility to study nature while studying reading, writing and arithmetic made school days, writes one former pupil, "forever memorable and the happiest days of my life."

Talent which might have been undiscovered in a regular classroom was revealed through frustration. I set my own examinations and in four and a half years I did not receive an inspector's visit, but I made frequent reports to Dr. Greer. He was delighted to find that none of the formal subjects of elementary education required to be neglected in order to allow the informality which encouraged creativity.

As an example, there was the child of nine who, from the first day of school, at six, decorated the pages of her scribblers with pictures. But when the number of questions in an arithmetic examination was ten, her usual submission was five. If requested to measure the perimeter of a field, there would be a well-travelled roadway around the field and, inside, animals and children in various poses.

"Why didn't you finish your paper?" I would ask, and she would answer:

"Jessie, I didn't have time."

Ten years later she graduated with honours from a well-known college of art.

"How can I ever thank you," she wrote, "for not stifling the side of me which has meant so much in my life?"

Today her work includes the designing of fashions for a prominent advertising firm.

There was the boy who failed in Upper School English because he could not bear to "pull beautiful quotations to pieces." He successfully tried entrance examinations to an American university. There was the girl, crippled and unable to attend regular school, who "hated poetry" and became the author of several books including two of verse. There was the small lad whose shyness made reading and oral spelling almost impossible to him at nine years. During World War II he became a Flight Lieutenant with the R.C.A.F.

A year and a half after my father's death I completed the book which I had believed I could never finish. I made an appointment with The Macmillan Company of Canada and delivered the manuscript in person to Mr. Hugh Eayrs, publisher.

In the meantime another threat to our security as a family was evident to all of us except to the one threatened – my mother.

My mother said very little about the absence of my father from our family circle but her silences were more alarming to us than words would have been. We watched her slip out alone to sit, with hands folded, in her chair under the tree beside the chair no longer occupied. When it seemed wise to do so, one of us would join her, but the silence was difficult to break because of the brevity of her answers, polite but not interested, and a far-away look in her very blue and sad eyes. She had never been talkative when, as a family, we enjoyed discussing subjects from politics and religion to community affairs. My brothers were frequent visitors at our table. Al and Elizabeth were only a five-minute walk away. The old house had been remodelled by them. When I looked through the window and along the curving road to where it stood on the hill it seemed to me like a loved friend determined to impersonate some respected stranger by wearing unfamiliar dress. For the clapboard was now covered by a popular stucco and the two-sided veranda had been removed to make way for a walled-in porch.

Mother had not visited the house since its renovation but every Sunday evening we shared Sunday supper with my brother and his wife. It was Al now who sat in the captain's chair at the head of the long table and who said Grace, but in words unfamiliar to me. As he said them I could hear my father's voice:

Gracious God, look down upon us in mercy at this time,
Pardon all our shortcomings and make us obedient to Thy
  will.
We ask for continuing favour from Thee,
For Christ's sake, Amen.

His voice had been thoughtful and reverent but never pious.

Will and Oma, with their three children, were frequently there. Our table was well filled but Mother's hand had become unsteady. She gave over her place to Jean, who now poured the tea. My mother did not share in the pleasant chatter, and her stature and frame had shrunk. Dr. C. visited her, ostensibly as a sympathizing friend but really to assess her condition. He spoke confidentially with us.

"Part of her has gone," he said, "and it won't come back. Sixty years, you say, and an unfaltering love for each other. Love takes its toll. We pay according to worth. Try to interest her in something new. Change the house. She may object, may even be hurt at first, but as I see it, it's the only way." He looked with significance toward the vacant reclining chair under the maple tree. "It may seem cruel and unkind to suggest it," he said very low, "but get that out of sight."

We understood his meaning.

After Mother had retired that evening we discussed plans.

"We'll change the whole house around," said Lill in a sweeping suggestion which proved to be an effective one.

The Little Room was left untouched but every other part of the interior was altered.

One day when Jean was discussing new drapes for the living-room, Mother voiced her first interest.

"Plan something that won't shut out the view."

But it was two years before she regained her will to live.

XXXI

A Playwright and a Novelist

For he that naught n'assaieth, naught n'acheveth.

Chaucer

Our small village nestled on a gentle curve of land beside the Grand River. The population had only slightly varied for almost fifty years – about one hundred people. When I returned from Buffalo to reside with my parents at Willow Bank, I was awakened to a sense of responsibility which I had never felt before.

"You don't live here, do you?" asked a child one day.

I was making my way from the village store up what we called the "school hill" toward home. She was sleigh-riding on the hill.

"Why yes, I live here," I said. "Don't you know who I am?"

She nodded.

"I know you stay here," she persisted, "but you don't really live here, do you?"

I walked on thoughtfully. There had been a fresh fall of snow, and a soft whisper of wind was shaking it down from the bare branches of the trees which lined both sides of the road where I crossed the mill pond. Except for a small semi-circle of blue water the pond was covered by ice and a thin white blanket. On the left just before crossing, I noticed several sleighs drawn up beside the mill. Farmers were laying in a supply of chopped grain for their livestock with the onset of January, often the snowiest month of the year. Roads might soon be drifted as much as six feet high when wheelways were shovelled out. I turned in our driveway with a

Act I of "The Four-Leafed Clover."
There were twenty-two in the cast, all
under sixteen years of age. It was their
first play and none missed a rehearsal.

feeling of unhappiness about myself which I had not experienced before. I approached our comfortable home. True, it was across the pond from the village but it was part of the village and according to the reasoning of my questioner I did not live there.

"What do the young people have in the way of entertainment?" I asked that evening when a neighbour came in for a chat with my father.

He laughed a little scornfully.

"What can they do?" he asked me. "There's nothing here for them. Some skate of course in the winter and go to house dances in the summer but there's really nothing else for them to do together, if that's what you mean."

That was what I meant. No clubs, no societies, no organized activities for twenty-two boys and girls, men and women, ranging in ages from eleven to twenty-four.

I lay awake thinking until long after midnight. The next day I sent out twenty-two invitations. A week later, on a clear night with a temperature below zero, twenty-two young people came to my home.

It was midnight before they left, after a display of enthusiasm which I had not expected. A drama club had been organized and I would write a play to include all of them.

It would not be the first play I had written. "The Visitor," a simple drama in three acts, had been performed by six boys and girls of my own age for our Sunday School entertainment, the Christmas of 1911. There had been the melodrama based upon a poem, "The Highwayman" by Alfred Noyes, presented in Kitchener, Ontario, and an operetta, "The Call of the Caravan" in blank verse, set to music. All had been directed by me. The musical had received high praise from the press.

I examined these earlier attempts at play-writing. To expand them for a larger cast would be to ruin them. I must create a drama suitable to the material at hand.

Thus came into being "The Four Leafed Clover," an Irish play with a production length of two hours. At least three-quarters of the actors had never taken part in so much as a dialogue before.

It was one of the coldest winters on record. Our rehearsals took place in the small village schoolhouse where the fires were allowed to die down at four o'clock. Only one member of that cast missed a rehearsal. She was confined to the house for a week with tonsilitis.

258

We met bi-weekly and at the end of March a billboard in the village store announced the date and location of the production.

No obstacle was insurmountable, no amount of work too challenging. What could not be collected in props from our homes was made. A fireplace was essential. It was built of old grey boards marked into the pattern of stones by white chalk, as effective and deceptive as any piece of amateur artistry I have seen. The artist was an extremely shy young man of seventeen, a farm boy who took his part in the play as an aged man, with such excellent imitation that no one in the audience realized who he was.

The settings were simple and limited. A point emphasized was that a good actor or actress could produce an effective play without props if necessary – for example, William Shakespeare.

As director, I marvelled at the professionalism of boys and girls without training. The facial expressions, the timing, the ability to be someone else, these were accomplishments learned in three months of preparation.

The village came alive. We were invited to reproduce the play in several other communities. The handicaps to be overcome in so doing were many. The limited props were not difficult to transport, but in one case when we had been promised a suitable size of stage, and wall coverings for ugly blackboards, we arrived at 5:30 p.m. to find carpenters still at work on the platform extension and the walls as ugly as walls in an old schoolroom can be. A girl of nineteen in the cast had been loaned the family car. Swiftly, she turned it around and made for a paper factory. Four large rolls of grey cardboard were purchased just as the factory doors were about to close. Next door to the schoolhouse a woman was repapering her living-room. The paperhangers had miscalculated. There were single rolls left over. The pattern was a floral pink. What could be better? Soon three walls in alternating panels of pale grey and flowered pink delighted our eyes. At 7:55 the money-changer was at his post, the curtains were hung and carefully closed, the two small curtain-girls stood ready at attention. There were scores of people waiting outside. Excited talking as to prospects of failure were gleefully heard by us. Promptly at 8:00 p.m. the doors were opened.

News of the play's production had travelled far. A photographer arrived from Toronto. Would we leave the stage intact and the additional properties available until the following day

259

(Saturday)? Would the actors and actresses oblige him by being present at two o'clock? Would I accompany them?

I wrote a story about the production of that play with its problems and its triumphs. The story appeared with illustrations from pictures taken by the photographer. With the money collected from four such productions we opened a small library in our little village. It was "my" little village now.

After the death of my father and the completion and delivery of the novel manuscript to Macmillan Company of Canada, I received two offers of positions in Toronto – one with the Department of Agriculture for Ontario as a teacher of drama under the auspices of the Women's Institutes; the other as a director of cultural recreation with the Community Welfare Council of Ontario. The latter offered a six weeks' preliminary course by Melville Keay, director of Hart House Theatre, before the beginning of a lecture tour of the province. In each community visited, I would be required to give five hour-length lectures covering the history, the direction and the production of plays. This production was divided into acting, stage settings and the art of make-up. The lectures were to be followed by the presentation of a one-act play before leaving the community.

We were in the midst of a depression and incredibly these two offers reached me within one day of each other. The first offered a more easy routine but the second presented the greater challenge. The difference in the salaries was negligible.

I had never given a lecture in my lifetime and the thought of holding the attention of an audience for periods of one hour sent me to bed each night trembling with the knowledge of my own inadequacies. I told no one of my fears. I wrote a letter of acceptance to the executive director of the Community Welfare Council. My duties would not begin until September. It was the middle of May. With regret, which was outbalanced by excitement, I prepared to close my little school and to cast myself adrift on a new venture. Leaving home was never easy for me, but two crises had come and passed. In one we had been the conquerors. My mother was alive and well. My older sisters now resided with her. I could leave with a clear conscience.

While I made practical preparations to remove to Toronto I received a letter from Mr. Hugh Eayrs. He did not mention the manuscript which I had submitted to him. The letter contained the name and address of someone unknown to me – Lady Willison, the wife of Sir John Willison, editor of *Saturday Night*. Mr. Eayrs wrote, "She desires your company to tea." A date was given.

Bewildered and not a little overwhelmed, I replied to Mr. Eayrs' letter accepting the invitation. The address given was of a street in Rosedale.

"You'll never find your way in that part of the city," Lill said. "You'd better take a cab from the railway station. It will be expensive but it's the only thing to do, and see that you get there on time. There's something behind this." Surely there could be no explanation but one. The interest of Mr. Hugh Eayrs and of the Lady must be in my manuscript and not in me.

With a feeling of grandeur but trembling a little, I rolled up in a gaudy taxi-cab to the given address.

The person who opened the door to me was a slight, quiet-spoken woman in black, of obvious gentility. She ushered me into a drawing-room as modestly furnished as she was modestly dressed. Almost immediately she brought in a tea tray. There was a bird cage on a stand by the window.

The canary was duly fed a morsel of cake before tea was poured.

Polite conversation included respectful questions regarding my education, my interests and my ambitions; but the book manuscript was not mentioned.

When the teacups had been drained I rose to leave with a sense of disappointment. This seemed the polite thing to do. As I went from the drawing-room into the hall, Lady Willison asked:

"My dear, how old are you?"

I told her.

Her expression was that of disappointment, I thought.

"My child," she counselled, "don't tell Mr. Eayrs. He thinks you're much younger. He permitted me to read your manuscript and I believe he intends to publish it."

I went home in a state of mind difficult to describe. One week later I received a letter of acceptance from The Macmillan Company of Canada. The letter contained this comment:

"We believe that this book should be published and with our imprint."

A contract for my signature accompanied the letter and a

261

report as written by Lady Willison of her opinion of the manuscript. With unbelief I read, "There is here a resemblance to Charlotte Brontë."

An ambition which I had entertained from my earliest recollection was to be realized. I was already established as Director of Cultural Recreation with the Community Welfare Council of Ontario when my first novel was released by the publisher.

Those who know the length of time required for the issuance of a book will understand why the date of publication fell late, a year after my appointment to the Council.

It was the date of our annual meeting in the College Street dining-room of the T. Eaton Company. Two glassed-in windows formed pillars between the doors. Both windows had been dressed by an artistic arrangement of a book showing, on its jacket, the picture of a little girl sitting beside her father on a wagon seat as two horses carried them at sunset up a winding road to an old house.

My first summer with the Community Welfare Council had given me six weeks of training in the art of the theatre. I discovered that I had followed the rules of that art in the production of my own plays. I had followed in a blundering sort of way. Now I had the opportunity to learn many of the short cuts to success in play producing.

The photographs of "The Four-Leafed Clover" taken for magazine reproduction were purchased by the Council. A set of coloured slides showing preparation for and scenes from the play had been made from photographs and were shown at the Canadian National Exhibition. When autumn approached and I had finished the course, I was appointed to take charge of a drama booth there. Amateur playwrights and theatrical societies came to discuss subjects, from the choice of plays to the art of presentation. Each day I was costumed by Hart House Theatre as the leading lady in a Shakespearean drama. The intense heat of late summer all but wilted my enthusiasm as I impersonated such over-dressed characters as Catherine of Aragon (in hoops and red velvet), Hero in *Much Ado About Nothing*, Titania in *A Midsummer Night's Dream*, Juliet in *Romeo and Juliet*, and Ophelia in *Hamlet*. Such characters were supplemented by "A Georgian Lady" in bustled

262

and basqued pink taffeta with blue velvet bows and "A Victorian Princess" in a low-cut bodice and mauve tulle over hoops.

Standing at rest one afternoon, motionless from the excessive fatigue caused by the heat, I turned my head and beheld a young man with wide eyes stumbling backward from the curtained rail which outlined the booth.

"Oh Miss," he muttered, "you frightened the life out of me. I thought you was a statue."

I dared to be flattered, but in an hour as I was whisked away in the front seat of a Ford coupé with my hoops out of control and resting on the shoulder of the driver, I lost my vanity. I was being transported in haste for a fifteen-minute broadcast on "The Cultural Use of Leisure." The broadcast, one of six given during a ten-day period, was offered from a local radio station. When it was over I was whisked as quickly back to my duties at the C.N.E.

Publishing houses with their headquarters in Toronto had heard of the new venture. They sent to me many current publications on play producing. These books were suitably arranged in the booth.

When the Exhibition ended I heaved a sigh of relief as I settled into my comfortable office on Bloor Street West. But I was not to remain there for long. Letters began to pour in from all parts of the province asking for help in the nature of a week-long visit to communities. The interest in drama had been stimulated.

So began my journeyings which brought me a wealth of experiences inimitable and treasured.

Meanwhile, my first novel was gaining attention and in the midst of a crowded program of lecturing and of answering an increasing amount of correspondence I received a letter from the publishers asking for a sequel.

1935. The author as Catherine of
Aragon at the Canadian National
Exhibition. Costumes provided by Hart
House Theatre for ten appearances.

XXXII

The New Recreation

> The great law of culture is: Let each become all that he
> was created capable of being.
>
> Thomas Carlyle

While favourable reviews of *Hill-Top* came tumbling in from
across Canada, I went on with my work as Director of Cultural
Recreation with the Community Welfare Council of Ontario.

The work which I had undertaken required my full attention
for at least another year. When that had passed, I planned to ask
for a leave of absence in order to extend the story of the Ross
Family.

I was now involved in an activity which took all my time and
tested my physical endurance.

It seemed that for many years interest in the cultural welfare
of country people had been overlooked while the nation went on
concentrating its efforts on extended education in cities. Ambitious
young people were leaving the land. If a country boy or girl did not
show some desire to "go out in the world" he or she was considered
to be without "push." Even today, young people who remain on
the land to support their parents in agricultural pursuits are seldom
pointed to with pride. But if William goes to town and sells socks
for a living, he may return to his community a step higher on the
social scale than his brother who grows the finest wheat in the
country and lives close to the heart of the great outdoors.

Such was the condition of affairs in the early nineteen thirties.

265

The Council's intention was to give assistance in the development of cultural activities not only to rural areas but to small towns and villages.

The approach was to be either through existing organizations or through an independent club or society. The press referred to the new program enthusiastically and helped to publicize a work which was to take me to all parts of the province.

My own experience of life was enriched during those years of almost breathless activity. As well as the evening lectures, there were visits to schools for story-telling and to special groups who assembled for instruction in community leadership. Also, time had to be found for the rehearsals of the one-act plays which climaxed each visit.

I was a frightened though outwardly composed young woman when I mounted the platform steps of a community hall to face two hundred and fifty assembled and interested young people. Although the population of that small town was less than two thousand, the attendance mounted nightly until it reached three hundred and fifty. It was my first venture. I was saved from stage fright by the sight of a four-year-old in bouffant dress carrying a bouquet of roses almost as large as herself. Near to tears, I descended the steps when she reached them to accept the bouquet. Had someone realized my timidity? Their gesture gave me the confidence which I had lacked. I was never overcome by stage fright again. In two years I addressed hundreds of audiences with comfortable confidence.

My problem was to find the time and a place to conduct the play rehearsals. The English comedy *Alicia Proposes* required a tall young man to take the part of a snobbish English officer. I chose the village barber. He was twenty-three, the proper height and with a natural dignity. Since he could not leave his shop without closing it, we went there. There was not room for the props but there was room for substitutes of them. For instance, the stage setting required a piano; a board across an armchair sufficed. As director, I sat in the barber's chair facing an imaginary stage in an extension of the room where each prop was represented so that there might be no confusion later. When a customer appeared the rehearsal stopped and the director gave her place to the customer. When he was properly "shaven and shorn" he vacated the chair and the director reclaimed it. The cast had a keen sense of humour and our difficulties added to our pleasure.

Of the many productions given during my years with the Council, no single actor gave a more perfect rendition of his part, without a falter or a sign of nervousness, than did the owner of that barber shop. As an example of the ardour with which many young people participated, I repeat the confidence given to me by his mother.

"Believe me, my dear," she said, "the boy didn't eat a bit for two days but he drank plenty of milk, so I didn't worry. I never saw him so happy about anything."

The cultural pursuits that had been withdrawn by necessity from the lives of the pioneers were now offered to their offspring. Drama seemed to be the most suitable medium because so many branches of artistic expression were available through it.

Usually I was billeted and became, through this medium, not an outsider but a partner. Special needs, which might not have become known, were discovered. I arrived back at my office on Saturday mornings to answer letters requesting help. The demand was far beyond the supply which could be offered by one worker. It was necessary to be selective.

Our meeting place might be a country school, a village hall, or a church basement where the furnace smoked and our heads almost touched the ceiling. As well as a discourse on drama the evening included folk dancing and folk singing followed by refreshments. In true country style, meetings often extended almost to midnight. In summer moonlight or, later, along snowy roadways I staggered home to my billet accompanied by the family of whom I was a guest. Usually there were others who wished to prolong the discussion of what could be done. Delightful and valuable as this interest was, it left me too short a time to recover from growing fatigue which was to interfere with the progress of my work during the second year.

We were well into a depression. Although the Council's work was financed principally by voluntary contributions, these contributions increased rather than diminished during that period of financial crisis in Canada.

Laying a cheque for $8,000.00 on my desk one day, the gift of an individual to support the program of which I was director, my manager said to me, "Now, how do you feel about that?"

My answer was, "It makes me feel very humble and inadequate."

The funds expended upon the new work were no doubt justified, but in view of the poverty which had overtaken many at that time – people who suffered privation, both physical and cultural – I sometimes wondered!

However, one of the encouraging features of this work was the eagerness with which plans were accepted for improving community life. There was almost a pathetic willingness to be led rather than a confidence to accept leadership themselves. The time of waiting had taken its toll. In one community where dancing was the only recreation within easy reach, there was an attendance of only fourteen souls on the first evening while more than a hundred tripped to the strains of "Nellie Gray" a stone's throw away.

After a talk had been given and the purpose of our work explained, we went to the dance. The next evening our attendance was seventy-five, and later in that district a progressive community club flourished which provided an outside speaker each month as well as developing talent within the community itself.

It was in a settlement born of a determination to fight the humiliations of a depression that I found my greatest challenge. This consisted of forty families who had left the city to escape the indignities of accepting relief. They preferred to suffer the uprooting necessary to take advantage of an alternative. This alternative, provided by the Government of Ontario, was a tenancy of one and a half acres of land containing a dwelling, the temporary possession of which was to provide an independent means of livelihood. From this strange settlement, perhaps sarcastically called Happy Valley and situated about forty miles north of Toronto, there came an appeal for help which could not be denied. This letter of appeal stated that although the settlement contained a village and was encircled by a number of prosperous farms it might as well have stood in the middle of a desert. There was no communication between the pioneer residents and the unwelcome newcomers.

It was a chilly day in November when I set out for Happy Valley. After a long ride by bus, I was met by an older man with a car of uncertain age which roared and rattled with us over a rough and lightly snow-covered road. I soon learned the impossibility of communication. I made several polite comments about the

268

countryside but they were ignored. He was all but completely deaf. As night fell and we continued driving through an area with no sign of buildings except rough huts in the middle of fields, he stopped the car and sat staring first to one side and then to the other.

"What is the matter?" I wanted to know. I repeated my question several times; then, with my lips near his ear, I made a shout of it, adding, "Are we lost?"

He took a worn cap from his head and scratched his sparse grey hair vigorously. He had heard me.

"Well now," he said, "well now, I believe we are."

But for a wagon approaching from the opposite direction, which he hailed, we might have still been sitting there. The exchange of words was in an unfamiliar language but after this happened the wagon rolled cheerily on and the motor of the car gave a snort of either indignation or satisfaction and we moved forward at a quicker speed than I had thought possible in such a vehicle. We arrived at dusk at a small clapboard house sitting squat only a few yards from the wheelways. There was a shed nearby and a pink-skinned pig was rooting through the freshly fallen snow into a rut of what must have been part of a garden. My arrival was attended by a feeling of uneasiness but this was quickly dispelled. As I got down from the car the door of the house opened and a middle-aged couple in neat attire and with smiling friendly faces came forward to welcome me.

James Ware and Mina, his wife, were charming and interesting people. He was a wiry man with reddish hair and a long moustache. She was taller, plump and blond. They were Scottish. There were two children, ages nine and thirteen, Jeanie and James Jr.

I soon forgot my trying journey as I warmed myself beside a Quebec heater stuffed to capacity with dried sticks of pine which exploded merrily in welcome.

Mina's art of cookery had Scottish excellence which made every meal in that humble home satisfying.

The house was without a foundation. I affected to be warm but my feet were half-frozen. The house had four rooms and was heated by only the Quebec heater and an inadequate kitchen range. It was lit by oil lamps and there were no toilet facilities inside. One passed through a shed to a little building on an outer wall with the usual tilted roof.

I crawled into bed that night without undressing and in my fur coat. When I climbed between icy sheets intended to honour me, I found a heated water jug wrapped in a woollen shawl at my feet.

I did not sleep that night but how could I complain, for just outside my open door to ensure that I did not freeze to death lay my host on a narrow couch, fully dressed. He kept the fire replenished regularly. Yes, how could I complain when my breakfast of oatmeal porridge, hot toast and excellent tea consisted also of fried slices of the sweetest pork I have ever tasted.

I learned later that a companion to the rooting pig had been slain on the previous day to provide the best they had to offer.

I have never seen such poverty and refinement hand in hand. The small barn contained the pig, a horse and a cow. There were chickens in an outer pen. The barn and the pen had been built from discarded boards salvaged from a nearby wooden shell left after a recent fire. The only pets which the children had were a half dozen sparrows with whom they had made friends, in the barn. Mina saved crumbs for them from her home-made loaves.

The only building available to accommodate the planned activities was a shabby school, set down in the corner of a field a mile away, which the children of the new settlers attended. It had neither trees nor a charted playground. The first request for permission to use it as a meeting place had met with a firm refusal. A number of the families were from foreign lands and it was a period when Russia's five-year plan had aroused fear that Communism might spread like some horrible disease into Canada.

The word Community in the name of our Council had aroused suspicion. The school trustees had subsequently granted use of the building but had refused to provide heat or light.

That night as I walked to the schoolhouse accompanied by the Ware family I witnessed a sight which stirred in me both determination and sympathy. I would help these people who were coming from all directions across snowy fields, lanterns swinging at their sides and bearing armfuls of wood from their own private supplies. It had stopped snowing. Overhead smiled the stars. In my heart was a revolt against unproven suspicions which dared to deprive those eager for the opportunity to help themselves.

An advance company of two young men opened the doors to

270

us. By the light of a single lantern they had started the fires in the low iron stoves. Soon a dozen lanterns were strung on wires reaching from wall to wall. A woman took an oil lamp from under her cape and in no time it was casting a bright glow on the teacher's desk which was to be my podium.

The school had no musical instrument, but from somewhere an organ had been brought for use during the period of my visit.

The chill of the room gave way to a pleasant warmth and a sense of challenge stimulated me as I explained the purpose of my presence.

A stern-looking, middle-aged man sat apart from the others, partially hidden by the pipes from one of the stoves. He did not speak to anyone, nor did anyone approach him. After I had finished speaking and the meeting was dismissed, he came to me and apologized.

"I am chairman of the Board of Trustees," he said. "I came expecting to cancel this whole program. Perhaps you don't know it but the man who asked you to come here is a Russian. Oh, I'm not saying he's a Red, but we need to keep an eye on these people. I admit a mistake in our judgement this time, though. There'll be heat and light for you as long as your work continues. I came to find out what was going on. I may come again but not for the same reason. If you want any assistance in getting things going, just call on me."

I didn't need any assistance. Those who had need themselves attended to that.

I spent four cold nights and five eventful days in that community. The handful of people who came to hear me that first evening increased to a sizable number by the end of my visit. Three months later I was invited back to Happy Valley. On my first visit a drama club was formed with six members. When I returned, the membership had swelled to sixty-three. Someone had sold the club a discarded piano for twenty-five dollars. A community library of fifty books had been purchased. A program had been prepared in my honour, and as I looked and listened to the accomplished performers I realized that the name of the valley was a suitable one.

But the prejudice and suspicion were still there, for on the morning of my leave-taking, James Ware, a loyal Canadian, opened his door to find it decorated with a hammer and sickle. Suspicion dies hard.

A few months later I was invited to another community, made up totally of native Canadians. There I found a different kind of poverty. Sitting across the table from an intelligent-looking English boy employed as a farm hand, I asked him if he were interested in reading.

His reply was grimly spoken: "I am when I have something to read."

The farmer's wife laughed a little scornfully.

"You should see what he reads," she said, "dime novels and stuff like that. He gets them from a fellow at the blacksmith's shop."

The young man flushed, and when he spoke his voice was sharp.

"I read whatever I can get to read," he admitted. "There's nothing else."

The wife of his employer laughed again.

"No, we don't have books around here," she said, "only the Bible and the dictionary."

When I returned to Toronto I related this incident to a friend who was an editor. He sent Sidney Chambers a box of books among which were works of Charles Dickens (Sidney's favourite author, he had confided to me). Yes, at that time, young men and women in the outlying communities of Ontario needed the services of the Community Welfare Council.

After almost three years with the Council, prodded by encouragement from Mr. Hugh Eayrs, I went home to write *Three Measures*, a second book about the Ross family.

In the fall of 1937, the novel was accepted for publication and I turned again to a field of endeavour related to that which I had previously pursued.

XXXIII

Behind Locked Doors

. . . to renounce when that shall be necessary
. . . and not to be embittered . . .

Robert Louis Stevenson

There was nothing to indicate that the Ontario Training School for Girls at Galt was other than a boarding school – there were no fences, no bars, but I was to find that the work required of me was to be done behind locked doors. I have said there were no bars. This statement I must qualify. In the major behaviour cottage where I was to become House Mother, there was one small room with a grating inside the window. It contained a single cot and a chair. There were toilet facilities. A girl might be confined there at the discretion of the superintendent for behaviour believed to demand solitary treatment. There was also a "detention wing." It was not barred, but the door of the entrance to it was kept locked. Confinement was only necessitated because a newcomer, desperately disturbed and frightened, was a potential run-away.

The Training School for Girls had been recently opened in the city of Galt, and I was offered a position as House Mother. Now I found myself a full-time social worker.

Although I was to be provided with excellent accommodation, a row of numbered electric bells connected with the girls' rooms was concealed in the wall above the head of my bed. After "Lights out," if a door was opened, a bell rang. It took me many months to become accustomed to interrupted sleep. Often I found myself out of bed and ready to investigate before I was really awake. This alarm system was to prove the most difficult feature of my supervisory position.

Before I assumed my duties as House Mother, there was a waiting period of almost six weeks. During that period, I wrote feverishly. When I moved into my new home, I had completed an assignment of six feature articles for a magazine and submitted for consideration several short stories. I knew well that the position which I was undertaking would leave me no time for creative writing. But what a wealth of new experiences lay before me!

Some awareness of the impending challenge came on the day I took over my duties. As I crossed the campus to announce my arrival to the superintendent, a small girl walking in the opposite direction said:

"You're Staff, aren't you? I don't like Staff."

Yes, I was Staff. An hour after, the superintendent handed me a bunch of keys.

"These are yours," she said. "Never lay them down and never entrust them to anyone."

She accompanied me to Coronation Cottage and spoke seriously of the responsibilities to be mine there. She unlocked the door and relocked it. She sat down with me in my attractive sitting-room, probably noticing a timidity which I could not hide.

"If you are in doubt about what to do," she said, "just call me at anytime. Don't hesitate. There are always problems and uncertainties in a place like this. We need each other."

I stood in the door of my sitting-room and watched her leave the building, locking the outside door carefully behind her. To the left and right of me stretched long clean corridors with doors on either side.

At one end of the corridor was a cheery dining-room with many tables for four and a long Staff table facing them. At the other end, I looked into the attractive Common Room. There were curtains of gay chintz and matching cushions on the chesterfields and chairs. There were bookshelves, a ping-pong table and a piano. The lighting was excellent. There was a pleasant disorder, giving a homey atmosphere.

I climbed the stairs to the second floor and found another corridor and many more doors. An obstructing wall cut off "Detention Wing." The sobbing came from in there and I found the key that fitted the heavy door and let myself in. Before I could reach the weeping girl, a second key had to be used. I was unprepared for the volley of obscenities and the look of hate which sharpened the features of a pale young face.

The fact that my own face was not recognized as "Staff" and that my expression was, no doubt, one of shock may have saved the situation for me.

We stood looking at each other. I put out my hand to her, but I made no attempt to take hers. The difference worked. The vicious expression of the face changed to that of a bewildered child and in a minute, Laura was in the circle of my arms.

My first encounter with Laura set the pattern for our later relationship. As she came with me to my sitting-room, we passed by the room which was reserved for emergencies. Laura whispered to me, "You won't put me in The Cage, will you?"

"Of course not," I said.

We walked together down the stairs and soon, in the privacy of my room, I was listening to a confession which must surely have been burdening and distorting a young mind.

While I listened to Laura's story, I wanted to cry. I had been warned against emotionalism, but she may have seen tears in my eyes. Many fictional stories were invented for sympathy by the girls, but Laura's story was true.

My new work commenced with a triumph, for on that day, Laura's reform began.

I was to learn the disadvantages of using physical restraint in the treatment of juvenile delinquency. Locked doors may have been necessary, but they were not effective in controlling the appetite for what lay beyond them.

I was to discover that the girls who lived behind them were not "different" from others, only less fortunate. When discipline was required, it was of little use if administered without compassion.

I began with Laura's story because that is where my experience in a girls' training school began.

When you feed an animal that is lost and hungry, it attaches itself to you with a loyalty that is lifelong. When you place a child behind locked doors, it never forgets the shape of the hand that turns the key. Until you can prove that the act was done in love, you will remain an enemy and will anyone listen to an enemy's counsel?

275

Our superintendent was a great woman. She not only believed in, she practised treatment by love. But we were of many minds. We said, "Yes, Miss Wark," and "No, Miss Wark," as the girls said to us. We tried to impress her with our willingness to follow her lead. Some of us were as deceitful as any inmate. We sat in conference with her, outwardly attentive, co-operative. Often we left her and returned to our posts in classroom, kitchen, laundry and cottage, unchanged in our opinions. And the less we knew about human behaviour, the more self-opinionated we were.

She was a wonderful teacher, but certain of us were indifferent pupils. Others thought they knew more than she.

She told us that Roberta hated adults because she had been handed from one to another since childhood, in orphanages, detention homes, and training schools, without finding anybody who really wanted her. She wasn't pretty. She wasn't appealing in any way, and, even when they tried to deceive her, she knew they didn't like her. Nobody liked her. She had been tolerated. She didn't want to get into serious trouble – she had had long institutional experience – she knew how to keep out of it and yet get even with us for rejecting her. She plagued us to death.

During my first year at the school, I came in contact with Roberta only occasionally. She did not reside in Coronation Cottage. She was not a major behaviour problem and she was not a potential run-away. By staff members, she was known as "The Pest." She attended elementary school on the grounds. In residence, she was under the supervision of a capable social worker as House Mother. They early developed a distaste for each other.

After a year in Coronation Cottage, I was transferred to Honour Cottage and it was at this time that the superintendent spoke to me about Roberta's case. There were no locked doors here. The day charts were fairly free of crosses. Privileges were common. After trial periods under relaxed discipline, the girls went from Honour Cottage to take jobs or to be placed with a family as a foster child. Some went home. Everyone in Honour Cottage was eager to prove worthy of liberty.

"Roberta isn't ready for placement, as you know," the superintendent said, "but what are we to do with her? She's deserving of more freedom than she is having and that may be one reason for her naughtiness. She's got half the staff ready to give notice. One even suggested the Mercer (a women's reformatory in

276

Toronto). But the poor child hasn't actually done anything beyond making life miserable for everybody. Will you take her?"

I didn't want Roberta. She was then in "The Cage." She had been there for six days, after a violent clash with her House Mother. She hadn't broken windows, nor destroyed furniture, nor struck a staff member, nor tried to run away. She hadn't actually refused to obey. She hadn't used profane or obscene language nor been caught in an objectionable act. She had simply wriggled when told to walk properly, she had strolled when told to hurry, she had laughed out when told to be silent during church and prayers, she had dropped her cutlery on the floor, had rattled her dishes at table, had spilled her milk, giggled, stuck out her tongue, dawdled over her lessons in the classroom, turned, twisted, whispered, and in the cottage during "free" hours, she had followed the distraught staff about asking inane questions, small unwanted favours, which yet had to be granted or the reason for refusal explained – in short, had one object in life, that of annoying persons who could not or did not hide their feelings of disgust and dislike for this unwanted, unlovely child. Until, finally, she had been "chucked in The Cage" (words used by a staff member to describe the incident). They were not literally true. Roberta had been sent for by the all-patient superintendent; she had been questioned and counselled; she had been warned. She had entered the despised room without resistance. She had remained there quiet and uncomplaining. To be separated from the ill-concealed dislike of those in authority over her may have been a relief.

I didn't want Roberta, as I said, but neither did anyone else. And, after all, incorrigibility, even when it took the form of wiggles and giggles, could condemn her to a period of detention which might end in the disintegration of a decent little character.

Before she became a resident under my supervision, I was privately interviewed by the psychiatrist, Dr. Brillinger of Hamilton, who visited the school monthly to chair a Round Table with staff members. In Roberta's case, he suspected a possible unbalance and I was required to give him a written report of her progress each month.

After a period of a few months, Dr. Brillinger agreed with me that Roberta was a normal little girl, bent upon getting attention at whatever cost.

But when the twenty-odd girls in Honour Cottage heard that

Roberta was to join us, they groaned, for she was disliked as heartily by them as she was by long-suffering staff members. Most of the Honour girls were progressing toward adulthood while Roberta, at thirteen, remained a troublesome child. They regarded her admission as an insult to them.

Among them was a girl of twenty whose emotional instability had kept her with us longer than her behaviour warranted. She was of superior intelligence, high-strung, artistic and unrecovered from an experience which came by way of a High School party, following a game. When an attempt was made to learn the name of the participant, she refused to reveal it. She was, she said, as guilty as he. She had refused also to give up her child for adoption. She lived for the day when she could support herself and the small son who had been placed in a foster home meanwhile. In an effort to live two lives, she was under constant nervous tension. When placement came, it was possible to bring about a co-ordinating of interests; Rose became a salesgirl in the Baby's Wear Department of a large store.

But before placement, Rose proved a help in the adjustment of Roberta.

"Poor kid," Rose said to me. "Nobody wants her and it's going to be the same here."

"No, Rose," I said, "it's not going to be the same here. We want Roberta, don't we – you and I? Because we know how unhappy she is. Whatever she does, however tired of her we may feel, we'll still want her, because she needs us."

A few times Rose came to me in desperation and tears.

"I don't think I can stand it, really I don't, Mother," she sobbed. "She tags me like a stray kitten and she's so *oily*. When she touches me, I feel sticky and dirty and ready to scream."

"She is a stray kitten," I said. "She's been starved for the milk of human kindness. There are two of us in this thing, but she is alone."

Rose stood by me.

Roberta had been in Honour Cottage six weeks when she came to my sitting-room one Saturday afternoon, tapped on the door, and said, "Mother?"

"Come in, Roberta. What can I do for you?"

She sidled in and stood very still beside me. She grinned. She said in a small, frightened voice, "Have you begun to hate me yet?"

I laid my hands on her shoulders and looked honestly and clearly into her large, hungry eyes.

"Hate you?" I said. "Why, Roberta, what a strange question to ask me. Whatever gave you the idea that I could hate you?"

She wiggled under my touch. She hung her head. She swallowed a sob.

"Oh, I just thought it was about time," she replied. "Everybody that starts off liking me does it. You started off liking me, didn't you?"

"Of course I started off liking you, dear," I answered as firmly as I could, "and I am going to keep on that way. Why, Roberta, how could I begin to hate you, *when I love you?*"

She raised her head and tried to see into my soul.

"You wouldn't tell a lie, would you, Miss?" she cornered.

"I wouldn't. What about you?"

We met under the same scrutiny and became friends.

"I wouldn't," she said, "I love you, too."

Rose did more than I did. She stood by me and she acted on every cue. She discovered that Roberta could compose music. Rose wrote poetry. In the Common Room, given to them to share as a "privilege" while the other girls were occupied elsewhere, they met at the piano and collaborated in pretty little songs. Later, an interested "friend" gave Rose singing lessons and Roberta instruction in piano.

Three months passed. On other parts of the campus, Roberta still met and gave back the old dislike. But there was always "home" to come to. With two allies, she was tolerated.

It was my custom, permitted by the superintendent, to invite a family on Sunday night to take supper and spend an evening with the girls. The occasion never failed to delight. There was music, sometimes provided by the guests, but always with participation by the girls.

It was bedtime and I was making the rounds of each room to say good-night, before turning on the "buzzers."

Roberta was sitting up in bed when I opened her door. Her arms reached for me. There were no tears on her cheeks, but in her eyes, the tragedy of tragedies – hopelessness.

"Oh, Mother," she burst out, "why can't I have a home and

parents? Why can't I? I know I'm not pretty and I'm not smart. My hair's straight and my nose is short and pudgy. I make a mess of things when I do them, like spilling ink in school and like cutting the wrong way to make a skirt. And everybody is tired of me being a pest to them and I know that I am a pest to them. But, oh, Mother, if only I could live in a real home and have a real family, I would just die to please them. I would just stay still and not talk and I would sing in my heart all the time instead of out loud. I would be as nice as those children were tonight. They were so dear and so sweet. But do you know what made them like that? I know. They belong to somebody. Oh, please will you ask Miss Wark to ask Miss Murray to find me a home somewhere? Please, will they try me, just once. If they try me, I will be able to prove that I am telling the truth when I say that I will never be a pest again."

I promised.

We did not kiss the girls good-night, but when I left Roberta, after tucking her into bed, I kissed her.

My love for Roberta was not a duty now. She was dearer to me than any child in my care. You would have felt the same as I.

Roberta went to a foster home. She stayed six months. She came back to us for a little while, but when she went out the second time, she didn't come back. She had learned to like and to be liked.

Five years later, I stepped into a modern elevator in a large department store in Toronto. The operator turned to ask:

"Which floor, Madame?"

Her fair hair was prettily curled, her skin clear, her make-up just right. She stood well. The great hazel eyes which had expressed the loneliness of rejection were bright with happiness.

"Mother!" she exclaimed.

We were alone.

"Come back, won't you, in half an hour," she begged. "It's my coffee break. I do want to tell you everything."

We had a cup of coffee together. A job – a boy friend – a ring – a wedding date.

"And he knows everything about me," she said. "I told him because I couldn't keep from telling him. He said it didn't matter at all. He said it and he meant it. Oh, I am so happy."

In every institution designed for the treatment and care of behaviour-problem children, there must be keys, there must be bells, there must be discipline and regimentation. There will be girls and boys who affect the efficiency of the staff and there will be staff who interfere with the recovery of the girls and boys.

"I'll be good so she'll give me what I want," the child says.

"Yes, I know this was my week-end off, but I told the boss I would work because we're short-staffed. One of these days, I'm going to ask for a raise ... " This from a staff member.

Within an institution of correction, a hapless incident, a misinterpreted remark, discipline administered in excess of the misdemeanour, a privilege withdrawn unfairly, so judged by "the girls," may produce a riot. The hand that casts the stone must be free from stain.

There was no reason to suspect the loss of virginity in one who used a certain type of sanitary equipment. But when, on a picnic, the purse of a staff member fell open revealing a box of this popular equipment, more than a hundred young women decided within the hour that "she" was a harlot. Before bedtime that night, a dozen "leaders" refused to accept orders from her and brought about a sit-down strike.

The innocent offender met their accusation in an effective way. She called them together and offered to resign. She went beyond that – she refused to stay unless there was a unanimous vote of confidence in her virtue. In this way, she regained their respect and her influence. Had she resented their suspicions, she could not have remained.

Those who worked behind locked doors, as those who are confined behind them, know the strain this environment places on the nervous system, the need for alertness, for quickness of decision, for the most exact fairness and the most thoughtful judgement.

The constant tension for almost three years brought migraines, mental fatigue and a threatened nervous breakdown. There had been wonderful satisfactions – a play based upon *Little Women* written and produced, a library opened, a creative writing class for seniors organized, and positive proof that miracles can be performed when "charity suffereth long, and is kind."

Perhaps one of the factors affecting a depression of mind was the advent of World War II. It was 1939. A few weeks before I went home to recuperate, I met our solemn-faced psychologist on my way to the Administration Building.

"This is the end of the world as we know it," she said.

XXXIV

A Turning Point

A series of little ships bear me across the sea of change.

A. R. Williams

After leaving the Training School I realized that a period of readjustment was necessary, and during that time I could not be idle. I had extended my experiences but I was not ready to record a changed set of values in the written word. I felt unsettled.

On a visit to married friends with whom I had retained contact since my first library experience in Kitchener, I learned the reason for my unrest. After a pleasant evening, I turned to wave good-bye. They were standing in a lighted doorway with a child between them. As I reached the corner toward town, the door closed and I walked on alone in the semi-darkness. My soul was in revolt. In happy pursuit of a career and in concentration upon a work which challenged my full attention, I had brushed aside a need which was now overpowering. Had I sold my birthright for a mess of pottage?

I accepted an invitation from a cousin in British Columbia, who lived by the sea. Ever since a sojourn with Jean in Atlantic City, the sea had retained a lure for me. A letter from my publisher reminded me that a convention of authors would be held in Victoria that summer. He emphasized his belief that I should come to the convention and thereby renew my interest in novel writing. I had promised another novel. When did I intend to write it?

I recognized that his letter was a carefully worded effort to stir me into action and I decided to follow his advice.

At the convention, I met Franklin McDowell, author of *The Champlain Road*, who had previously written me a letter of congratulations when my first novel was published. He now spoke of *Three Measures* and his faith in my ability as a novelist. It seemed to me that he was speaking of books written by another. I answered him, "Thank you, but I don't really feel that I wrote them. They don't belong to me, somehow." His reply was, "You aren't being honest with yourself. They are as much a part of you as anything you will ever write. You're going through a transitory phase of some sort. What has happened to you?"

He had sensed the turbulence within me. Our hands met in a warm clasp. "This happened once before," I said, "when my father died – but in a different way. Then I didn't believe in God; now I don't believe in myself." He kept my hand in his while he answered gently, "You will, Jessie – you will."

We did not speak again during those convention days until the close of the last session. As I was leaving the Empress Hotel, he was waiting for someone in the foyer. He came to me. "Keep on looking," he said. "You'll find your way."

I was charmed by the beauty of the Pacific Coast. A cousin was Professor of Zoology at the University of British Columbia. Another was head of the French department of New Westminster High School. They persuaded me to stay in Vancouver and to accept a position on the Public Library Staff. Was I going backward or forward? I did not know. But very soon I knew that working with books lacked the challenge of working with human beings. Perhaps I would return to the latter when something within me was healed and something else satisfied. The position at the library provided a sense of security and left me time for another pursuit. I began to write again.

World War II was approaching a critical stage. Often on the street corner, in a restaurant, or over the circulation counter of the Public Library, I listened to comments which revealed to me the conflicting opinions about the war. I was shocked to find a lack of patriotism among English-speaking Canadians. A woman of refinement sat across the table from me in a select coffee shop. I had been startled that day by news of fresh Allied losses which had made headlines in the morning paper. I mentioned regretfully this fact in conversation. Her reply was, "Oh, really? I have stopped reading the paper. We showed ignorance in getting into this war and we won't be intelligent until we find a way out of it."

On a busy street corner, two men in khaki waited for the light to change. "One of these days, I'm going AWOL," said the younger, "and if I can find a way out, I'm not coming back unless they catch me."

Two officers turned their backs to me outside a book shop where both had stopped to make a purchase. "Nice to be away from home," one said and laughed suggestively.

"Not for me," his companion answered him. "I love my wife and kids."

"So what?" was the reply.

The following afternoon was my time off from the library. I went to see a staff member of the *Vancouver Province*. I did not have an appointment, but he received me graciously. "People are talking to themselves and others, but not out loud," I said.

That is how I received an assignment. I called my column, "I Listen In." Now there was an incentive to examine ways of thinking among a cosmopolitan population infiltrated by all branches of the armed services. An old enthusiasm returned. I began wishing for more hours of freedom in which to write. I began searching in special places for different viewpoints. My world became lit with purpose once again. I would work among people, but with a changed outlook. I would not listen critically, but to learn.

Vancouver offered opportunities which were seldom found in Canadian cities. With Canada at war, there was a battalion stationed only twelve miles away. The harbour was crowded with ships. There was a Sailors' Home seeking volunteers to provide comforts and friendships for those away from home.

I was soon to find that there were more stories to write than could be written by one with my limited experience. I took on several branches of voluntary service with zeal.

Captain and Mrs. Johnston supervised the Sailors' Home. I was introduced to them by a fellow librarian. There were planned programs of entertainment for those temporarily on land.

I heard stories of adventure and tragedy. I began to write far into the night.

I became friends with the Johnstons and a frequent guest in their home. I was in the parlour of the old house again when I sat at

284

their organ, losing myself in remembered melodies. But I had made an enemy. Polly was the largest parrot I have ever seen. Chained to her perch, at sight of me she showed her inheritance of a vulture-like disposition. What she had against me, I do not know. No human voice could be heard above her violent denunciations as she strained the chain to reach me, wings spread out and beak open, ready for attack. After one or two such demonstrations of hate, she was confined in her cage before my visits and covered by a black cloth, that she might not catch sight of me. Even so, she uttered unintelligible words of derision.

After I had completed a half dozen columns for "I Listen In," I set out for the offices of the *Vancouver Province*. It was my morning off at the library, a rainy morning, and I was early. I would never learn that being early was a waste of time. The newspaper office was not far from the wharf, with its comfortable waiting room. I closed my umbrella and went in. I settled myself on an empty seat, which stood back to back with another. I drew my manuscript from its brown manilla envelope and began to re-read what I had written.

My concentration was interfered with by voices behind me. Two men were discussing a problem of war. They had just returned from leave. They seemed to have come from an area of the interior. One complained that certain of his garden tools were missing, the other that thieves had entered his stables and made off with one of his horses and a valuable saddle. The impression was that while men were absent from home in defence of their country, others, unwilling to make the sacrifice, were taking liberties with their possessions.

They talked on and on. The voice of one was mature and had an English accent. Without turning my head, I knew that there was considerable difference in their ages. A new column was forming. When I got up to go, I told them. The older man drew a wallet from his pocket and produced several fascinating pictures of the hill country.

"This is very interesting," I said, "but I must go ... I have an appointment."

"We must go too," he said. A ship's whistle sounded.

"But I wish we could talk longer," he took time to add. "Do you live in Vancouver?"

I told him that I was a librarian there.

"If I come through this way again," he said, "may I look you up? If you are interested in a story, I have one to tell you." He touched his officer's cap and was gone.

I felt, without knowing why, that the past, the present and the future had suddenly become united.

I was preparing to leave the library at closing time, three weeks later, when he stood smiling in my path. It was the beginning of an interesting friendship, but there was to be an interruption.

It was the fourth day of December, 1941, when I was stricken with an attack of pleurisy. I found myself confined to bed by doctor's orders, with a nurse in attendance.

On the morning of December the seventh, a Sunday morning, my nurse came in with my breakfast tray. As she set down the tray, she said, "Well, prepare yourself for a shock. The Japanese have bombed Pearl Harbor. America will declare war on Japan and, of course, we're in it too. This place is lousy with Japanese, you know, and all our troops have been confined to barracks."

By nightfall, men were hanging blackout curtains over windows. All lights were forbidden. Even the fireplace in my room was reduced to a faint glow. The nurse uttered an oath as she fell over a coal scuttle in the darkness. Before midnight, a watchman sat on the veranda outside my window. There were no street lights and motor cars crept slowly in fear of collision. If a match flickered anywhere among passers-by, there was an instant shouted order from the watchman.

I was not afraid. I have never been able to understand my lack of fear. Not only was I bedridden, but thousands of miles from those I loved. I felt calm in the face of probable disaster. Already, rumours were flying that several squadrons of Japanese planes had been sighted off the north-west coast and that warships from Japan were putting out for Canadian shores.

In looking back, it seems to me that I had lived within the protection of my own little world until that hour. Now, inescapably, I had become one of millions, never again to be counted alone, and I experienced a strange sense of freedom from long imprisonment.

The private hotel in which I resided had a pleasant dining-room with tables which could accommodate five. The hostess brought people together who she believed would be congenial. I shared a table with Morris Epstein from Montreal (a nephew of the famous sculptor), an Italian musician associated with the Vancouver Symphony Orchestra, a German engineer from Powell River and a graduate nurse on holiday from Saskatchewan. It was she who took charge of me during my illness.

A table nearby was reserved for a retired British naval officer and his charming lady, the daughter of a university professor. They had met in Tokyo twenty-five years before and it had been love at first sight. She was admired by all of us, especially when, for Sunday evening dinner and on holidays, she wore kimono, pausing at the entrance to the dining room to bow in true Oriental fashion. They were both British subjects.

The German engineer and the Italian musician were not naturalized Canadians. Italy and Germany were at that time our enemies at war, but the way of these young men had not been interfered with.

After December the seventh, the retired British naval officer sat alone at his table. The beautiful Japanese woman was confined to their suite, some said at the request of the management. For whatever reason, we never saw her again although her husband was appointed a night guard in the city. When the Japanese-Canadians were evacuated from their homes along the coast and taken to places of internment a hundred miles inland, we were told that she was one of them. None was exempt from suspicion, although many had been born in Canada of Canadian-born parents.

When I emerged from my room to resume my place with those at my table, gone was the atmosphere of friendliness. The British officer sitting alone was a symbol of the unjustified suspicions which turned the eyes of the world upon our unforgivable behaviour as a nation.

After I resumed my work at the library, I did not see a Japanese, child or adult, making use of its facilities. In places of entertainment, in restaurants and cafés, I saw none. This was true even before evacuation procedures came into effect. Without being proved guilty, all were to live under a cloud of suspicion and to endure restrictions unfairly imposed.

On main thoroughfares, we now met more men in uniform than in civilian dress, for Vancouver had become the focal point from which forces were assigned coastal duties.

I was walking along Georgia Street on my way home from the

library. It was the middle of December and a cold rain was falling. Its penetrating effect was augmented by a wind from the east. I held my umbrella at an angle to reduce the storm's impact. I stepped aside as a tall figure in army uniform and beret swung into my path, from the opposite direction. With a muttered apology, he strode on. That voice, where had I heard it before? Temporarily closing my umbrella, to avoid its being caught by the wind, I turned to look after him. His back was toward me. There was no identifying feature. The hair was hidden under the beret, but I knew that blue eyes looked out through a fringe of sunny-fair lashes. I stood undecided for a half minute. My impulse was to run after him, to call out. But what would I say? I had never heard his name and I could be wrong. No, I could not be wrong. At this point, I watched as he took to his heels in an effort to escape an increasing downpour. What was it he had said on that summer afternoon when handing me the pail of berries at our gate? "I must run or I'll be late for supper." I opened my umbrella and continued on my way. Shortly after, the tragic raid on Dieppe occurred. Western regiments were involved. Was he one of the casualties?

A telegram, received the following day, informed me of the serious anxiety of my mother and asked that I return to the East.

XXXV

I Become a Fortune-Teller

Dame Fortune is a fickle gipsy . . .

Winthrop Mackworth Praed

Relieved of anxiety by my return from the war-threatened West Coast, my mother recovered her health. I would go on writing but I must also find a more remunerative occupation. The offer of a position as caseworker with the Big Sister Association of Toronto provided the answer. It included the opportunity to attend a special one-year course in Social Work at the University of Toronto, set up to relieve the scarcity of trained workers at that time.

Until I thus became preoccupied with the problems of others, I was thrust by the continuing devastation of war into a state of unnatural pessimism. I felt that all effort was useless. What I wrote was tinged with despair. I quote:

> Throw you the pen away, the brush, the moistened clay.
> War has returned to-day.
> Cease then to love, to dream, at last to live –
> What use is life
> Which ends in bitter strife?
>
> Sonnet so musical,
> Canvas still wet,
> Statue of chiselled snow,
> Into the dust you go!

Now, plunged into the problems of families where an

outsider's compassionate but emotionally unstrained viewpoint could help, I found much to restore my faith in life and effort. Whole chapters could be written about the parental devotion, the courage, the humour and the talents discovered during my three years with the Big Sisters.

Even more important in lifting the mood of despair was the friendship which had begun on a rainy day on Vancouver's wharf, a friendship that was to develop by correspondence into a deeper relationship. Because of the continuance of the war, the waiting period for its culmination in marriage was longer than had been planned.

In the spring of 1943, David came east on furlough. After a quiet church wedding, he returned for a temporary period to military duty while I continued my casework in Toronto.

My husband was forty-nine years old and anticipated an early retirement. This came within a few months of our marriage and was followed by the offer of a desirable government position. I resigned my own position with the Big Sister Association and joined him in Vancouver for a waiting period of almost two months. I found him restless and highly nervous about the impending return to civilian responsibilities. He had been a Westerner for many years and preferred British Columbia to Ontario, but he expected that Ontario would be his location.

Substantial credits due to him from his army service were slow in arriving. We had sufficient means to carry on comfortably, but he was a generous man by nature and fretful when forced to economize. We took a modest apartment overlooking English Bay. He was in daily pursuit of some temporary work to add to our resources which did not allow for careless spending.

I had applied for the position of Assistant Reference Librarian at the University. At that time I was unaware that we might be leaving British Columbia. My services were not required until September. It was now the month of May.

David had mineral holdings in the interior. He had placed these holdings for sale with a real-estate company. It would be easier to discuss offers in person than by correspondence. With a potential purchaser he agreed to accompany the agent to their location, four hundred miles from the city of Vancouver, in the Cariboo country. "That means leaving you for a few days," David said. "I don't like it, but I've got to do it."

Rain was a common part of weather in Vancouver but on the day David left me for the Cariboo, the Little Red Hen would have said the sky was falling. All night rain had dashed against the windows and fallen upon the roof with torrential force.

I did not sleep. At five o'clock it gave way to a fog which crept up from the sea and down from the mountains, enveloping the entire city. The streets along the waterfront were completely blotted out. They remained impassable until noon, except for pedestrians. Fog horns were blowing in a chorus of angry competition, but ships were starting out determinedly despite the blanket of grey concealing their courses for half a mile into the ocean. David rose and took one look from the window. He came back to me. "It's not easy to tell you this," he said, "but I've got to go today. I didn't tell you last night because I thought you might worry. Thank goodness the downpour has stopped and, as to the fog, the ships know their way." He sat down on the bedside and took one of my hands. "Don't worry," he said, "the sooner it's over the better."

"The ships?" my voice faltered.

"Yes," he explained, "we go by boat a short distance up the coast and from there by train – an old-fashioned line that goes into the interior. Rest easy. Don't attempt to come to the boat with me in this devilish weather. Stay inside. Have you enough money until I come back?"

I told him that I had but he gave me twenty-five dollars more. "In case of any emergency," he said. When we had eaten breakfast and he had gone, I too looked from the window. I, too, was restless and despite his caution to stay inside, I would go out. A feeling of foreboding hung over me. It was many years before I learned the reason.

We shared a bathroom with another tenant. It stood between our small apartments and could be reached only from the hallway.

I would have a tub bath, then I would dress and find relief by shopping without buying, an idle woman's pastime for which I had no respect. I opened the door into the hallway and closed it behind me. I locked it carefully and forgot to remove the key. When I returned after a soothing bath, I discovered my carelessness. I unlocked the door and inserted the key inside, turned it and went about dressing myself for the street. I strolled down Davy Street toward Granville. The fog pinched my nostrils. I slipped into a small coffee shop around the corner. The air was dry and warm, the aroma of coffee comforting. I sat in a cosy booth and sipped the beverage leisurely. At the counter gulping down a second cup was a policeman conversing in friendly fashion with the attractive young waitress. Covering his beat had not been a pleasant occupation that morning. He loitered.

I, too, loitered. At last, I approached the counter to pay for the refreshing drink. The waitress had been kind. She had offered me a second cup and I had accepted it.

I would tip her. I opened my purse. It contained a powder compact, a lipstick and a handkerchief. It contained also the key to my apartment, but nothing else.

For a moment I could not speak. I looked at her and she looked at me. She must have suspected what was coming for her smile disappeared. The policeman sitting on the stool suspected also.

"I'm sorry," I said, "I can't pay you. Someone has taken everything." I held the purse open for her to examine it. The policeman moved from his stool to the one beside the cash register and looked too.

"My husband is away," I said and my voice sounded guilty, "but when he comes home I will come back and pay you." The policeman reached into his pocket and pulled out notebook and pencil. He gave the girl a knowing wink. "What is your name and address?" he asked me.

I was not a stranger to that little coffee shop. Perhaps the waitress saw tears gathering in my eyes, for they were gathering. She looked at the officer and shook her head. "I know this lady," she told him, "and I'll look after it." She reached under the counter, pulled out her own purse, opened it and dropped two dimes into the cash register. The officer slipped his notebook and pencil back into his pocket.

I don't remember thanking her, but my relief was evident. Out on the street, I re-opened my purse and took out my handkerchief. I had need of it.

What was the solution to my problem? David had not left an address where I could reach him. "There are no post offices nor telephones where we are going," he had said. "The nearest that I know about would be seventeen miles away. When we reach the end of the railroad, we can take a stagecoach, but for the rest of the journey, likely we'll have to foot it."

I had a relative in New Westminster and another in Powell River. A professor at the university was my cousin. I would not starve. There was food in the apartment to last, with sparing use, for several days. I resisted making an appeal for additional funds from anyone, although there might be other needs to be met. Who could say? I was newly married and I had the reputation of a husband to preserve. My story of being robbed might be accepted, but, even to me, it seemed questionable. Why not search for adventure by seeking work back-stage as I had been tempted to do many times during my pursuance of a journalistic career?

David's sudden decision to go into an area of country strange to me filled me with foreboding. He had not confided in me about his possession of mining property during our long courtship. His departure had contained an element of mystery. What if he were attacked in the unfamiliar territory, still a wilderness, never to return? Fear after fear chased through my brain, but I could do nothing better than try to meet my immediate needs.

As I walked along Granville Street, it had a strangeness about it. I came to a triple-glassed show window advertising a fine new restaurant located on the second floor, and caught sight of a sign in the centre window. It read, "Teacup reader wanted."

I climbed the stairs. Almost the first question was, "Have you had experience?" My answer was, "Oh, yes," for had I not been telling fortunes at charitable functions for many years? My prospective employer was a dignified, ladylike woman. Her second question frightened me a little. I hoped to remain unknown. "Your name?" she asked. I could tell the truth and yet not reveal my identity. "Madame Louise," I replied. She inquired if I could begin work at once and I joyfully answered that I could.

"Today?"

"Yes, today, but, of course, I am not in costume."

"You have costume?" I thought of my red evening dress and my red and black bandanna. I was a collector of beads and earrings.

"I often wear gipsy costume," I suggested. "Would that be satisfactory?"

Her eyes brightened. "That would be perfect," she responded enthusiastically. "And, as to payment, you will not be paid at the tables. Our patrons will leave whatever they choose to leave with the cashier for you. We have a select clientele. They will be generous. I think you will appeal to them. Your hours will be from two until five, but you will come in early enough to have lunch and will stay for dinner as part payment."

I felt as one accepting a blind date.

"Could I dress here?" I wanted to know.

"Certainly," she said. "We have a large washroom for the waitresses. Afternoon tea is popular with Britishers, you know, and we have plenty of them in this city." She glanced at her watch. "You'd better stay as you are for today," she told me. "Just hang your coat and hat in the girls' washroom, then sit down and enjoy a good hot lunch."

In spite of my modest attire, I was commended at the end of the afternoon, provided with an excellent dinner and given $5.50. I had read only ten teacups. I was earnestly encouraged to return on the following day.

"Have you any advertising materials?" she questioned as I was leaving.

"I have none with me," I admitted, "but I can provide some." I passed an art supply shop on my way home. After I had made four purchases – a two-foot square of glossy white mounting board, a bottle of red ink, a vial of gold paint and a small paintbrush – I paid my debt at the coffee shop and hurried home. It was 10:30 p.m. when I finished my poster. I had traced the outline of my hand in red ink and then filled it in with gold paint. In clear, large lettering circling the portrait, I invited: HAVE MADAME LOUISE REVEAL YOUR CHARACTER.

The fortune-telling developed into palmistry as well as teacup reading and, in gipsy style, with dark glasses to avoid recognition by University personnel who patronized the place, I added fifteen more customers to my following. When I collected twelve dollars before leaving, the second day, my employer told me that my hours would be from two to four only, "because," she said, "the waitresses complain that tipping is falling off for them." This would limit my time to tea hours, but I would remain as before to enjoy a dinner myself.

After a fourth most successful afternoon, I lay jubilantly resting from my labours, so easy and so fascinating (for the attitude of seriousness with which both men and women considered my

294

remarks was revealing). Dusk was creeping in when I heard a familiar voice in the hall outside our apartment where the building superintendent was polishing the brass hardware of the front door. The voice was excited and anxious. "Is my wife at home?" David inquired.

We did not sleep that night for we had so much to tell each other. He laughed hysterically as I related my experiences, but wept at the same time.

"I knew there was something wrong," he said. "I knew and I couldn't reach you. It was hell. I left the other fellow to make his way home by train and I hitched a ride with a trucker coming through. That way, I got here a day earlier. The train broke down and would not be leaving for another twenty-four hours. The land agent told me he would contact me at once if the deal goes through. We're going East, my girl. This city is no place to leave a woman alone and goodness knows where I might be located if we stay here. Back there, you have your family if I'm not around." In spite of his Government appointment, there was indecision as to his location.

When he went with me the next morning to view my handiwork in the restaurant window on Granville Street, we climbed the stairs together. I gave my notice. I told my employer the true reason for my adventure in the paid business of fortune-telling.

XXXVI

Gathering Material Backstage

I lift the curtain and I witness how
Others must work with sweat upon their brow.

                                        The author

It was almost certain now that we would return to the East, owing to the failing health of my mother and to David's confirmed decision to enter the civil service field in Ontario. A contact there with a World War I army officer, with influence in government circles, might prove valuable.

"Don't take on anything permanent," David warned me.

I would not take on anything permanent, but for a writer free-lancing or engaged in authorship of any sort, the city of Vancouver was a gold mine of the unusual.

My next approach was by way of an employment office, but here I met with the stumbling-block of my own previous serious occupations, namely as librarian, teacher and social worker. Already committed on the first count, I concealed this fact and was confronted by the astonishing information that there were vacancies in both the teaching and the social work fields. My interviewer was adamant. As a social worker and a teacher, I must enter one of these fields or tell the reason for my refusal. That I would be leaving Vancouver shortly proved an unsatisfactory explanation. Why then take a job at all, even as a waitress or a domestic or a cook's helper? Why show an interest in "Attendant Wanted" in a dry-cleaning establishment? Bluntly, I was refused employment and I left the office feeling like one suspected of a questionable way of life. But I left behind me a filled-in application for work, temporary work in what was called menial occupations. I placed my telephone number on the line assigned for that purpose.

I went listlessly down the street. After my brush with the police in the coffee shop, I avoided one as he stood erect at the first street corner. But I went again to the same little coffee shop where a smiling young girl would serve me and to whom, that day, I was able to offer a tip.

While I considered my unfortunate status, I sipped coffee and watched the flow of people passing by. Granville Street was a busy thoroughfare. It was there that I found my chance to be a fortune-teller. It was not raining now. The sunshine invited me to loiter. After leaving the coffee shop, I strolled up one side of the street and down the other, my eyes in search of Help Wanted signs, and there was a stirring excitement in my heart. I would go personally to apply for employment wherever a vacancy could be found.

It was Friday morning. A shoeshine parlour, a steam bath establishment and a shoe repair shop occupied the basement of a half block near Georgia Street. Could it be possible? Yes, it was. In the window of the steam bath there was a sign – "Nursing Attendant Wanted." A spectacled man in a spotless white coat and with the appearance of refinement stood looking up at me from the window. He seemed to invite me and I went down the steps.

The doctor (self-styled) was an impressive male. Was I a trained nurse, or had I nursing experience? The latter I laid claim to. He showed me through a very clean and respectable bathing area. Only two patrons were being served that morning. I had never seen the equipment of a steam bath before. The rectangular metal boxes resembling two enormous enamelled caskets stood on end in the half-light of the place. From the upper opening of one bulged the heavy moon-shaped head of a man whose very fat cheeks lay exposed, flushed and streaming with perspiration. The sight was frightening, although his expression was calm and his eyes closed as if he were half asleep. How different the other patient, whose shrivelled face denied the need for steam bathing, the eyes wide open with a child-like terrified expression.

"Your hours would be from 10 a.m. until 5 p.m." the doctor was saying, "and the salary comparable with that of nursing assistants at the hospital." He named the amount. "I will always be here to attend to any unusual circumstances, but I require someone to give gentle reassurance to my patients. They sometimes need it, as you can see. I would like you to commence work on Monday. I usually ask for recommendations, but I feel you will be satisfactory."

He did not wait for me to say that I would take the position and I did not wait to tell him that I would not.

How good it was to be safely above those steps on the street again. I lifted my head for a look at the sunny sky and I drew a deep breath of relief.

But I was not easily discouraged by David's hearty laughter when I confessed my venture and my fears. He was busy himself looking for something temporary to do while he waited for the confirmed sale of his mineral holdings. That night, devising a humorous approach, I wrote the story of my search for work, and before the month was out I cashed a cheque for fifty-five dollars.

I no longer hoped for a call from the office of the Employment Service. I examined the columns of Help Wanted in the local newspapers. It would appear that there were many vacancies, but regarding their nature the advertisements were sometimes misleading.

A modest appeal caught my eye: "Wanted. Someone to answer the telephone five days a week in an apartment. Business calls for absent employer." The location was a favourable one.

Despite David's protests, I made off the next morning to investigate. "This sounds like an easy one," I said, "and who knows, I may have time to write a story while I work."

"Easy and fishy," said David grimly.

We were both right. The woman who interviewed me explained that her husband's business was dependent largely upon telephone calls for service. What service, she did not explain. It was necessary for him to travel to all parts of the city. This left her tied to the house all day, which she bitterly resented. She was a raw-boned young woman with long reddish hair and heavily freckled. She had inscrutable grey-green eyes. She wore mannish clothes. I was soon ensconced behind the telephone. She remained at home on my first day, observant yet friendly. A coffee pot stood on the stove, over a flame turned low. Every hour that day she filled two mugs with coffee and offered one to me. There was something pitiful about her eagerness for companionship.

298

"You have wanted to talk and you have been afraid," thought the social worker in me. And time proved that I was right.

After the first day, during which the telephone remained silent, she left me alone for brief intervals with no explanation, coming and going frequently and unexpectedly.

How could I refrain from being curious? Surely there was a story, here, but what sort of a story?

She grew more and more friendly. On the third day, the telephone rang twice and each time a man's voice asked for my employer by name. Given telephone numbers were recorded by me, but no messages were confided. Mr. --- had left the apartment each day before my arrival and had come home just as I was leaving. He wore rough clothing and, beyond a curt nod, did not greet me.

When I realized the time I was wasting, I asked permission of Mrs. --- to bring my writing materials. I frankly admitted to her that I was a journalist. I did not dignify myself with the title of author. She willingly agreed that I should use my spare time for writing. I did not write of my new environment. Rather, I experimented with fairy tales.

While with the Big Sister Association in Toronto, prior to my marriage, I had been given for use in my literary work, five thousand sheets of record paper because it had been misprinted. The reverse side was equal to the best quality of typewriter Bond. In a small briefcase I brought a dozen sheets with me to my place of employment.

The telephone stood on a flat-topped desk before which I sat most of the time. What could have been more convenient?

It was on the fourth night that I forgot to return the paper to its case. I left the sheets on the top of the desk.

The following morning, a steely-eyed unsmiling woman met me at the door.

"You're fired," she said, in a voice as cold as ice. She handed me ten dollars. "Here's your pay."

My heart rolled over. I watched her looks soften. "Thank you," I said very politely, "but may I please have my papers?"

I had not noticed that she held them in her other hand which was behind her back. She thrust them at me.

I thanked her again as I took them from her. "I'm sorry that I was not satisfactory," I said, "and according to our agreement, you have paid me too much."

Her eyelids flickered and I saw tears in her eyes. "Take it," she said. "You're nice and I'll miss you. It's lonesome, but my husband won't have you around the place. He thinks you're a detective. Is that true?" She pointed a freckled finger at the papers which I held. "It's them," she added, with less venom. "How did you come by stuff like that?"

"I'm not a detective," I replied quietly, "but I can see why you might think so."

On the printed side of the folded papers which I held were the standard questions of a case history. Among them were such queries as:

Name of Father
Name of Mother
Married
Common Law
Children
Ages of Children
Are any illegitimate?
Do any members of the family have a prison record?
If so – for what cause?
Should there be an investigation?
Has either parent been in court?

The listed questions will suffice to explain the cause for alarm.

I was able to relieve the mind of the frightened young woman who, fortunately, believed me.

"Come in," she said, "and we'll have a coffee before you go. I wish you didn't have to go. I hate being by myself, but he's scared. Why, I can't tell you. He's plenty scared and I suppose I ought to be too, but I'm not. I think you're on the level."

We sat at the table together and had our coffee. Yes, there were tears in her eyes and when leaving, in mine. Walking home with the papers which had condemned me, I too was sorry that I would no longer pose as the answering service for a telephone which seldom rang.

Less than two weeks later, David drew my attention to a news item in the *Vancouver Sun*. A bootlegging ring, long under suspicion, had been broken open by a police raid at a given

300

address. The telephone answering service would be no more, and thinking of the lonely red-haired young woman, in the words of R.K. Ardis, "Taught by that Power who pities me, I learned to pity."

Two unusual experiences had whetted my appetite for more. True, I had earned very little as yet in hard cash, but I had been backstage and I wanted to go again. However, there was a real need to consider the material benefits from any employment which I might undertake. The time of indecision as to our eventual location was prolonged by unexplained uncertainties. Alternately, David was determined to go East and to remain in the West. Meanwhile, the date for assuming my duties in the University library was drawing very near. A sense of obligation would shortly demand that I make good the acceptance of this most desirable position.

There was time for yet one more venture while our future was unsettled. Again I looked in the columns of Help Wanted. I had been intrigued by the degree of difference as to style and reputation of the many centrally-located restaurants, cafés, cabaret and burger hang-outs in respectable downtown Vancouver. What went on behind those enclosing walls with swinging doors between dining areas and food kitchens? A special kind of person seemed drawn to seek employment in places where people of all nationalities and classes gathered to enjoy the business of eating. As a fortune-teller, my observations had stirred a variety of emotions. At times I was amused by what I saw and at other times, deeply moved to concern and to compassion. There seemed to be so many adrift in that city with no one to care that they did not know where they were going nor why. I spoke of this to David.

His reply was, "You don't know what this world is like, my girl, and I won't tell you. It would be like uprooting a gentle little flower. Oh, yes, I know you've been a social worker and that you have dealt with problems of all sorts affecting other people. But while you were doing it, while you went into ghettos and slums and worked in corrective institutions, you went about in a cellophane bag."

I lay awake a long time that night. According to the comment made, I was still a reject, still not one in the stream of life; no longer a reject physically, but while equipped to save others from drowning, I had never felt the overwhelming effect of being underneath the surface and unable to breathe. I could only imagine, I had never been there. This was still to come.

I answered an advertisement for kitchen help in a restaurant of disrepute on Hastings Street. To apply, I went in person, wearing the least attractive outfit which I possessed, wearing excessive make-up and, unsuitable for day wear, large cheap crystal earrings. In horror, David watched me leave.

"You are mad," he told me, "absolutely mad. But don't expect to escape trouble. If you get the job and you have to start right away, telephone me and I'll pick you up when you're through. It will likely be late and I'm not having you come home without protection. You don't know what you are getting into. You're asking for trouble."

I gave him my promise.

"I'm not asking for trouble," I said, "I'm only trying to get rid of that cellophane bag."

I secured the position of kitchen helper in what I shall call "The Red Lion Diner." It was a large restaurant on the main floor, a long block from the Interurban terminal. It was outwardly clean and, so far as I could see, a respectable eating place for working people. There were two small private dining-rooms for special parties. It did not have a liquor licence, but patrons were allowed to partake of their own alcoholic beverages.

The manageress was a woman of refinement. She took me on a tour of the interior. The kitchen was large, but inadequately ventilated. It was crowded with equipment and under the supervision of a florid middle-aged woman who tipped the scales at two hundred pounds, she said proudly. She was the chief cook and I was turned over to her after viewing the basement, rough-cut and uncemented except for the floor. One or two drop lights without shades relieved the darkness for limited spaces. There were all manner of sinks and tubs on one side and a pile of bagged vegetables on the other. Under one light stood an empty washtub and a chair. On both sides of the chair leaned over-filled bushels of potatoes. The cook pointed to the chair.

"There's a washroom upstairs," she said, "and pegs for coats and things. When you've hung up your stuff, you can go down and start right in to peel potatoes. We use a lot of potatoes, french fries mostly, especially at lunch-time. So get going as soon as you can."

All that day, except for a half-hour break for lunch, I sat under a drop light, peeling potatoes which I then immersed in pails of cold water. When they were filled, the kitchen porter carried the pails upstairs and replaced them with others.

No one spoke to me except the cook when she descended the stairs to stand against a wooden support at the bottom while she smoked a cigarette. She told me that smoking in the kitchen was forbidden, that she had to have an occasional fag "or drop dead." Once, she said, when I had begun to peel the second bushel and there was a cessation of pounding feet overhead, "Gettin' tired, kid? You'll soon be finished. It's two o'clock and you go at six. Kind of gloomy down here but nice and cool."

She drew a heavy breath.

"That kitchen kills me, especially in the summer. Against the law, you know, no fan nor nothing. But who's going to cry out? Not me. I need a job too bad. A drunk for a husband, and four kids."

A fire alarm sounded. She crushed out her cigarette and all but flew upstairs, despite her weight.

"Come on," she shouted and I followed.

The kitchen was full of smoke, and flames were shooting upward from a pot of grease which had boiled over, unwatched. As I escaped into the dining-room, the firemen arrived, then the policemen, then investigators. I was completely forgotten as I took shelter behind a large cooling cabinet in a niche at the front of the restaurant which was now deserted by the terrified patrons.

In an hour it was all over except for the stifling heat and the acrid smell of smoke. The cook came to find me.

"Got a scare, did you?" she said. "Well, not much harm done except to me. I got hell from the manager. Maybe I'll lose my job but damned if I care. The heat is half killing me anyway. You'd better go back to your work on the potatoes. You're lucky – it's cool down there, if it is kind of stuffy."

I went back to my chair under the light but my hands trembled a little as I picked up the paring knife which I had dropped when leaving. Shortly after, the cook's voice shouted from the top of the stairs.

"Come up, will you," she said, "this floor needs a mop."

I had never used a pail mop before. As the clock neared six, I put away the cleaning materials in their cupboard. I did not wait to ask for my wages. I had had enough. I might be in a cellophane bag but I had spent my first and last day as an employee on Hastings

Street. I would announce by telephone my abrupt intention to leave.

The manageress smiled a pleasant good-night as I passed the counter by the door where she acted as cashier.

"See you in the morning," she said and yawned. The day had been a hard one for her, too.

I replied to her good-night, but as to seeing her in the morning –

There were only a few at the tables, but someone rose to go as I opened the door. I didn't look back. I was only a few steps forward when a man's voice called, "Hi dearie," and I heard steps behind me.

He was a thin man about my own height, fair, with fallen-in cheeks and glassy small eyes.

He was beside me now. "How about a drink?" his voice had a fumble to it.

Before I could answer, I heard rather than saw a figure move out from a doorway. A skilled blow in the centre back and the thin man stumbled to the pavement.

David's firm hand took my arm. "Don't look behind you," he ordered in a low voice, "and keep going. He isn't hurt. There's a cop at the next corner. You're safe, but if you ever come to this district alone again, my woman, I'll either beat you or divorce you."

I would obey, but I lamented the loss of my earnings – four dollars a day.

David agreed to return with me the next morning for an honourable discharge.

The manageress was kind but regretful as she paid me. She gave David a chilly look as she said, "We never had nobody before who could peel so many potatoes in one day."

As she had said, french fries were their specialty.

That afternoon, David secured temporary employment in the offices of a lumber company, which lasted until we returned to the East a month later. I was ordered to stop asking for trouble and to settle down. I cancelled my appointment at the University. We travelled first to Ottawa for a brief visit with David's friend, Colonel MacDonald, and then to my home. Everyone was happy, especially when David announced that his promised appointment would be in the nearby city of Hamilton, Ontario.

304

XXXVII

The Pattern Changes

What grief to know the end will be
Far off from that I dreamed
When childhood was . . .

The author

I had dreamed of a life reduced in pressures and with sufficient freedom for a neglected career. I had been free-lancing with reasonable success even during my course of study at the university, but my longing was to apply myself seriously to the writing of several books, the subjects of which had been developing consistently in my mind for a long time.

My husband was intellectual and widely read. He was keenly interested in my chosen career. Our compatibility was unquestionable. I had believed that our love was mutual and deeply rooted in trust. For ten years this belief was sustained.

The occupation of being a homemaker was more demanding than I had expected. Distractions were many and I had dedicated myself to this as my first responsibility. After nine years, I found myself still free-lancing and attempting to contribute my share of effort to the financial requirements of everyday living by private tutoring.

During those years, two major sorrows had taken from my new-found happiness. In 1946, my mother had died after a brief illness and Jean had been stricken by an incurable disease. She turned to painting as a pastime and discovered that she was an artist of unusual talent. When I returned to the writing of books, reproductions of her paintings appeared as illustrations.

I was becoming aware of a threat to what I had believed to be an unshakable marital relationship. I had been an idealist, now I must become a realist. In an attempt to achieve this transition, I was to suffer both physically and mentally. Lacking courage to face the future as it must be lived, I turned to the past for comfort.

I experienced an embolism which required several weeks of bed rest. During this period, on a sunny April day, I mounted a white cloud floating by my hospital window and travelled back to the home of my childhood. I asked the nurse for paper and pencil.

"You're not fit for writing," she said. My reply was:

"If I don't write, I'll die."

I began a book of recollections. When I left the hospital, I had completed thirteen chapters, shakily written, but legible. By this form of therapy, I recovered temporarily, but a final disillusionment was to terminate my marriage two years later.

During the years between, I had undertaken a piece of journalism which extended into book length. My writing time was restricted to hours alone. I was commissioned by the Ryerson Press to collaborate with a boy of nineteen in relating his adventures during a trip around the world on the brigantine *Yankee*, under the command of Captain Irving Johnson, the famous American explorer. Donald Green was the only son of a Hamilton family and the only Canadian on board. I travelled with Donald, in imagination, for seven months. Again I was escaping from reality. *White Wings Around the World* was published in the fall of 1953.

Encouraged by this successful venture I re-examined the thirteen pencilled chapters accomplished two years before. I submitted this unfinished manuscript to Mr. John Gray of the Macmillan Company and was asked to expand it to book length.

It was August 26 when I delivered *Along the Road* to the Macmillan Company. Mr. Gray was in England, but I was assured by the acting editor that a contract would be sent for my signature.

On August 27, my world collapsed around me and I was taken to hospital after suffering a coronary thrombosis. I was to remain there for seven weeks. Never in my life had I experienced bitterness until that hour, when, still in an oxygen tent, my precarious condition was made known to me. The pressures under which I had lived for some time were taking their toll.

Determinedly, I began to struggle with this menace to spiritual survival by recalling memorized passages from the writings of others who had succeeded in their battle against this enemy. By such means I drove out the forerunners of hate which had challenged my will to forgive. Before I was able to leave the hospital, I had met that challenge. I could say truthfully and with a new kind of hope, "Tout comprendre, c'est tout pardonner."

Although it was now almost two months since I had submitted my manuscript, no contract had been received by me. It was yet several more weeks before I learned that the editor who had interviewed me at the Macmillan Company in Mr. Gray's absence had been taken critically ill himself, the day after my visit. Ignorant of this fact and believing that my book had been rejected, I sent a carbon copy to the Ryerson Press. I received an immediate acceptance and, four days later, an explanatory letter from Mr. Gray, with *his* acceptance.

I had already signed and returned the contract sent to me by Ryerson Press. In this way, and without malice, I changed publishers in mid-stream, by mutual agreement.

A long and satisfactory relationship followed with Dr. Lorne Pierce and his editorial staff. However, owing to personal problems, almost two years elapsed before I took up my pen again. A letter was received from Dr. Pierce warning me: "You can't afford to waste time. What about a biography? Do you know someone who has walked with nobility all the way, not counting the cost? If so, please come to Toronto and let us talk about it."

I re-read the letter several times. I had never written a biography, and to plunge into a new field at this time seemed an impossible undertaking. Later I realized that with a wish to help me, my new publisher had offered me a way of escape from pondering my own situation by writing the life story of another.

So came into being the biography of John Christie Holland, Hamilton's Man of the Year, 1953.

I had never met John Christie Holland, who died shortly after this honour was conferred upon him, but his life story took possession of me in my search for an answer to my publisher's query.

The book was published in 1956. I had accomplished the writing of three books in four years. It was going to happen – the fulfilment of a purpose born of a dream in childhood. I had become a full-time author of books.

I now occupied a ground-floor apartment overlooking the well-kept garden lands which stretched from the Waterdown hills to the shore of Lake Ontario. In the sunlit quiet of a south room, well suited to my needs, I had met with John Holland as surely as if he had been with me in the flesh. I was convinced of his unseen presence there as I wrote. Although the book was referred to proudly by Canadians as proof of our racial tolerance, this feeling was only partially justified.

I met Mrs. Rachel Holland, John Holland's widow, for lunch at a well-known restaurant. It was the noon hour. We were forced to wait in line. Two white men stood behind us. Mrs. Holland faced the desk. I was unobserved. When a table was available, the proprietor ignored her and led those next in line to the vacancy. When at last we were seated, I left Mrs. Holland on the excuse of speaking to an acquaintance. I was known to the proprietor. I asked him if he knew with whom I was taking lunch. His face flamed as he assured me that his act was not one of discrimination, but to please regular clientele.

A week later, as I walked along Main Street West, I noticed a man of colour walking before me. I recognized him. He was a city employee of some years. Coming towards us was a young woman wheeling a crying baby boy in a stroller. Before she reached me, I heard her threaten the crying child in a loud voice:

"If you don't stop, my boy," she said, "I'll tell that black man to get you."

The black man heard and turned to smile at me. I hurried.

"I'm sorry," I said.

He laughed, but a little cynically.

"Oh, don't let that worry you," he apologized to me as if he were the aggressor. "We've had a long time to get used to it."

In honour of the book's publication and in my honour, the Holland family gave a buffet dinner. There were twenty-seven present. From the oldest to the youngest, they were the kind of people one enjoys knowing. I had a speaking engagement and it was necessary to leave them early in the evening. I have said that the Reverend John Holland was with me in spirit while I wrote the book. My belief was confirmed when I received a telephone message the following day from a member of his family.

"After you left last night," she said, "we all agreed that when you were here, we forgot you weren't one of us."

While doing research for my work on John Holland, I found in the *Ontario Historical Review* a fact which stirred me to the writing of *Black Moses*.

In 1830, an escaped Negro slave had been making his way to The Forks (now London, Ontario), in Canada West. Attempting to board a coach at Brantford en route to The Forks, Josiah Henson, thinly clad on a winter's day, had been whipped by the driver to prevent his entering the vehicle. The brief record stated that the slave was invited by the driver of a covered wagon following the coach to ride beside him. The driver was Benjamin Cronyn, later the first Bishop of Huron. During that ride, while six Irish setters in the back of the wagon howled and snarled, a lasting friendship was formed. The black man who had been refused transportation in the coach was later to be entertained by Queen Victoria. He had established an ex-slave colony in Canada.

As I read of our early treatment of an escapee from slavery, I was lured to investigate further the story of Henson. In a microfilm of a small pamphlet issued in 1849 by the Anti-Slavery Society of Boston, I found an account of conditions in the southern states dictated by him. The story of Josiah Henson from childhood to old age must be written. A friend with insight suggested the title.

Black Moses was published in the autumn of 1957.

The manuscript was six weeks late in completion. It had been my intention to visit the area where Josiah Henson had lived. Did the Henson home at Dresden, Ontario, face north, south, east or west? Were relatives still residing in the area? By what direction would Harriet Beecher Stowe have driven there to visit her aging friend? I did not know. I believed in detailed research at the source, but illness prevented such a journey. My sister's life hung by a thread. To absent myself was impossible.

It was midsummer when I received the galleys. Before returning them I made my delayed visit. If the worst were found to be true, I could still alter the text.

I had said that the house faced south. I had written of stretching verdant fields. I had located the road. Now I stood looking south from the doorway of Josiah's dwelling. All was as I had described it. I sat in the old rocking-chair in which he had sat. I saw the arrival of the fringed carriage. I saw the dainty lady, Harriet Beecher Stowe, descend and stand in the doorway while Henson knelt to kiss her hand. A miracle?

Without intention, but not by chance, I had become the defender of the underprivileged. The book was reprinted in paperback as a study book for two of the largest church bodies in Canada. I was now in constant demand as a speaker. I was not new to the public platform. Two years as a lecturer with the Community Welfare Council had given me the confidence which made my new work a pleasure. There was also the feeling that I was continuing in another field, that of social service.

Although I was thought to be a successful author, the income from my chosen pursuit was not sufficient. There were continuing medical expenses and I accepted a part-time position on the staff of a school for the retarded, where I used my knowledge of music and drama in a new and challenging field. I wrote a play in pantomime for eighty-one children, ranging in age from six to twenty-two. I called my production "In the Deep Green Woods." It was made up of dramatized myths and fairy tales, linked together by a narration in verse. The narrator would be a staff member behind stage since many of the pupils lacked the power of speech. But all of them enjoyed participation in simple play-making and rhythmic inventions. Hearing of my venture, the Players' Guild of Hamilton offered the use of their theatre for the presentation. There followed three months of detailed and exacting direction in which the several teachers on the staff participated with a hidden expectancy of failure. Instead, the play unfolded with incredible smoothness until the final act. Now, the Prince, age twenty-two, in elegant wine-red velvet with plumed hat, on his way to awaken the Sleeping Beauty who reclined on a flower-bedecked couch, stepped from behind the curtains and stood still. Stage fright had been expected, but not from our hero, who possessed, we thought, every faculty except that of speech.

The Princess slept on while, unseen, the curtains were slowly drawn. Despite this one failure, the performance was given full-page publicity in our city paper and many parents of children who had never known the happiness of pretending, declared an improvement in their general health. One lad of eleven, cast as Puck, because of his natural ability to accompany, on a flute, softly played piano music, gave positive proof of the value of drama in the training of handicapped children. Epileptic seizures had been an almost daily occurrence, but Puck was unaffected from the day of our first rehearsal until three months later, following the final presentation of our play. During that time, he had temporarily cast aside himself and become another.

Difficult years were to follow, and for a time, it was necessary for me to lay aside all work in order to preserve my health.

XXXVIII

A Golden Day

Differences leave their traces in the sand
but friendships are carved in ivory.

Author unknown

It was a late October day when a slight, middle-aged man rang the
bell of my apartment. I had been unable to work for almost two
months. A letter had preceded him and I knew who he was, but I
did not know for what reason he had come.

"Have you been out?" asked Dr. Lorne Pierce. "It's a golden
day."

Hamilton is a city of trees and they had passed from the
stronger hues of autumn dress to shades of gold. From the top of
the mountain area, the streets of the city lined by maples and elms
appeared more beautiful than at any other time of the year.
Beyond the city lay the blue waters of Lake Ontario. My location
was close to the edge of the mountain. My guest had come, he said,
at the request of an organization about which, strangely enough, I
had never heard – the Canadian Writers' Foundation.

This foundation, I learned, had been organized by the late Dr.
Pelham Edgar of Toronto. His action had been stimulated by the
suicide of a gifted Canadian author. The author had been in ill
health, incapable of working and without funds. Dr. Pelham Edgar
had said at that time, "With God's help, this will never happen
again in Canada." And so, the foundation came into being. The
gifts of the foundation were not provided at the request of the

311

recipients, but proffered as an assistance when a need was discovered.

I learned from my visitor that there was a Board of Directors and an associated committee.

"Certain information provided by members of our foundation has brought me here today. We want you to go on writing books which Canada needs to have written," he said.

The surprise, the incredible knowledge that people whom I scarcely knew had such concern for my welfare, was too much for my emotional equilibrium, and for a time I was unable to converse. My visitor went on in further explanation. What was offered, he said, was not charity, but the appreciation of a grateful country. A Canada Council grant had been applied for also. Only with my permission would the plan be put into effect. It was everyone's hope that all documents required would be provided promptly – letters from doctors in attendance and a character reference.

Two weeks later, I was notified that the grant had been made and that there had been unanimous approval. A future which I had believed would contain unfulfilled ambition was to give me a freedom which had long been denied me. I resigned my teaching position and prepared to devote myself to the business of authorship. That occupation provides a fluctuating source of income and authors are not pensionable. The existence of a body of men and women watchful of conditions affecting the productivity of Canadian writers was surely of national importance.

With a partial return to health, I began to write a book which was to become of greater influence in affecting public opinion than any which I had written before. When I had completed an outline, I submitted it to my publisher. A reply contained this warning:

"We cannot promise you publication if you write on this subject. Many books have been written about the Canadian Indian and they do not sell."

The theme of the book had been inspired by attendance at a banquet given in memory of Pauline Johnson.

For the first time in my life I talked with Indian people. In the foyer of Hotel Kirby, I met Dr. Gilbert Monture, O.B.E., whose eloquence had charmed me. I met the humble and the great and I came away with a strong determination to do something for the Indian people of Canada.

312

I wrote a reply to my publisher. Even without the assurance of a market, I would write this book. The answer was encouraging: "Your enthusiasm is contagious. Proceed with the work and we shall see what we can do with it. A publisher should not look over an author's shoulder."

News had spread that the book was being written. The reservation of the Six Nations on the Grand River was the focus of my attention. A few weeks after I began to write, a revolt between two factions, the Elected Council and the People of the Longhouse, took place.

One Saturday morning my apartment was used for a meeting place between the Minister of Indian Affairs, the Honourable Ellen Fairclough, and a committee of Six Nations' representatives, a Chief, a matriarch, two clan mothers and an interpreter. After the Chief placed a string of white wampum in the hand of the Minister indicating a truce, a discussion took place which began and concluded with a friendliness on both sides that promised hope for the future.

Seldom has a writer been given such an opportunity for research at the source. Mr. Walter Rutherford, the manager of the Board of Trade in Brantford and a friend of the Indian people, acted as chauffeur to me on a number of my visits to the Six Nations reservation. It was a July day and the sun was beating down from an unclouded sky. The whistle of a factory in the city indicated that it was midday.

"Do you know what the Indian calls noontime?" queried and explained my companion. "The split in the sky. Their belief is that the deeds done for man's welfare are accomplished in the morning of the day. After the split in the sky, evil enters in."

"You have given me the title for my book," I said.

After eighteen months of research and eighteen months of writing, the story about the Canadian Indian found a market in Canada.

In the meantime, with my publisher's blessing, I began a lecture tour. Audiences were large and small. When I met with the Indians themselves on the Grand River reservation, it was in the oldest log building. The night was starlit and a whippoorwill was calling from the trees. I felt as much one of them as if I had been born in a wigwam.

In 1961, a year later, I was commissioned by the United

Church of Canada to write a book of sociological studies in fiction to be used as a study book. In this way *Hasten the Day*, a collection of ten short stories, came into being. The writing entailed much research, journeys to remote areas and a condensation of material. The extent of its market brought about further interest in previous books written by the author.

XXXIX

We Travel On

We cast our line
And as it sinks below
we trust.

The author

A change of location, from Ontario to British Columbia, brought me in contact with the problems of another minority group in Canada.

In 1941, the Caucasian population of Vancouver, except for social workers and church officials, was generally unaware of the treatment of Japanese residents. Not until I wrote "Chrysanthemum Transplanted" (in *Hasten the Day*) did I realize fully the injustices done to Japanese in Canada during World War II. Serious pondering resulted in *Strength for the Bridge*. It took me three years to research and write the novel. My first writing was in the third person. After careful examination, I rewrote the entire book in the first person.

After publication, there followed a reception at the Japanese Cultural Centre in Toronto. The guests were addressed by the Vice-Consul of Japan and the occasion was coloured by the presence of Japanese ladies in elegant kimono.

From the reviews, I believe that by opening a sore only partially healed, a second and fuller healing took place.

A few months later I received a plain postcard, handwritten, from Tokyo. Professor Yozo Onishi was a translator. He asked for

315

an interview. Might the book be used as a university textbook in Japan?

Six months later I was able to place on my bookshelf a Japanese compressed edition of my novel. Was it by accident or intent that the photograph of myself inside showed a slant to the eyes?

I was asked to present the awards in oral competitions held by the Buddhist Societies of Eastern Canada. The winners ranged in age from ten to twenty-nine years. The prize for each class of competitors was one and the same. How can I describe my pleasure when I learned that *Strength for the Bridge* had been the choice of the judges? The conference had been conducted in Japanese. I knew that I was understood at least by the younger generation when a ten-year-old boy, accepting his prize from me, said in English:

"Miss Beattie, I am proud to receive this book."

I put a question to one of the judges – why had my book been chosen?

"Because," he replied, "you avoided the stumbling block of many Caucasian writers. You did not make Christianity the only respectable religion."

I had been entertained at the Nipponia Home for Aging Japanese in Beamsville, Ontario. While we drank tea and ate watermelon I mentioned to a guest from Montreal that I had failed to find anyone who had been a passenger on a certain vessel – a cattle boat – bringing immigrants from Japan to Canada in 1908. It was on this boat that my hero, Keiichi, at seventeen, had made a crossing.

The visitor spoke English well. "I was with Keiichi Wakao in the hold of that cattle boat," he said.

Was this a predestined encounter?

The need for the Nipponia Home was explained by Mr. Y. Yamaga, then superintendent. An aged Japanese woman had been placed in a Canadian Rest Home. She could neither speak nor understand English. Remembering the evacuation, and in a strange environment, she believed herself a second time our prisoner. She became mentally unbalanced, and her case was reported to an understanding individual. Arrangements were made at once for her transfer to the Nipponia Home. Security there restored her to mental health.

Unknown to representatives of my publishers and to my publisher himself, there was an element of sadness for me in the accomplishment of my next book. I had reached Chapter Twelve. One morning when I approached the mirror in my room, my face in it was not visible to me. Before many days I was to learn that I must go through the rest of my life in partial blindness. I would finish the book, by what means I did not know. If I confided my disability, would my future as a writer be unfavourably affected? I would use a temporary deception. I managed to finish the book by dictation.

A Season Past was published in 1968, a companion book to *Along the Road*.

I had promised another book. The research had been done in 1933 and the yellowed pages of records made at that time had been preserved.

A lusty tale of the sea about Captain Charles C. Dixon had earlier been written in England by John Herries McCulloch, but much remained to be told, for the captain had been a student of life in and on the deep.

In 1936, I was contacted by W. R. Stark, who had designed the jacket of my first novel, regarding the Captain. The manuscript was purchased by an English publisher in 1939 and lost in the blitz. I had not kept a carbon copy.

Shortly after the war ended, the life of the Captain ended also. But there remained the notes, yellow with age. I did not attempt the rewriting until 1970. Events in my own life demanded my full attention. Would I ever be able to piece the scraps of information together? I was not sure, and I pushed aside the undertaking, but a sense of guilt and unfairness forced me into action.

I had passed through a period of shock after the sudden loss of the ability to read and to write. The time of bluffing was ended. I now admitted and accepted reality: as an author I was permanently handicapped. But a wonderful thing happened. Through the concern of the Canadian Institute for the Blind I was provided with a faithful volunteer who did not fail me, until loss of her own sight required the cessation of her services. By then *The Log-Line* was wholly written.

There was John Milton, you know.

After I began to rewrite *The Log-Line*, Charles C. Dixon came to me in a dream. It was midnight. In my dream, my doorbell rang

317

and I pulled on a dressing-gown. I approached the top of the stairs. I was in the house where we had collaborated. The door at the bottom of the stairs had a large panel of glass. A man stood outside. In my dream, my sister joined me.

"Don't worry," she consoled me. "The door is locked. Whoever it is, he can't get in."

With that, the knob of the door was turned from the outside. The door was pushed open and Captain Dixon stood at the foot of the stairs, dressed as I had seen him dressed before. He was looking up at me.

His keen, stern blue eyes met mine. There was a challenge in them. They said as certainly as words: "I dare you to write anything that I have not told you. This is a book of fact and not of fiction."

I woke. I felt his presence in my house although I did not see him there in reality. *The Log-Line* is a book of fact and not of fiction.

About this time, the Hamilton Public Library offered to purchase my diaries, other papers and manuscripts for their archives. This required a process of selection which I was unqualified to perform alone. Again volunteers came to my aid. After several months of sorting and cataloguing, a collection covering forty years of a writing career changed hands. This event brought in its wake a series of heartening surprises, including the publication of two manuscripts which I had not expected would appear in book form.

We had found more than six hundred published poems. A choice of two hundred resulted in the book *Winter Night*. And there was also an unmarketed historical biography, read into tape for me, from the diary and letters of Captain Francis J. Brown of Galt, Ontario. He was the first to successfully pilot a paddle-steamer across the Atlantic to Africa. The date was 1878. He planted the first Canadian flag on African soil. Such an adventure could not remain untold. By dictation it formed the book *A Rope in the Hand*.

In a quotation from James Montgomery (*The Press*):

> All that reflective memory stores,
> Or rich imagination pours;
> All that the wit of man conceives,
> All that he wishes, hopes, believes . . . "

Our world is not measured by the distance from horizon to horizon but by the extent of our understanding.

XL

Finis

Coming silently as the rose
Gone as dew on the petal goes,
Tide that flows.

The author

It will be more difficult to write an ending for this book than it was to write a beginning. To remember is to relive and the past thereby becomes the present.

I have omitted in these memoirs certain poignant events and challenging experiences which would have enriched the book but which could embarrass the living and might be unjust to the dead.

Each year of my life has emphasized that good and evil may be interchangeable, that what we seem to be is not really what we are, and what we are is rarely what we could have been. I do not believe in free will. No man is free. We are all shackled at birth by our inheritance or given a graduated measure of freedom through it. What is right for me is often what would be wrong for you. There is no good and bad but only the inevitable. I am as much to blame for what I am as society is to blame for what it has made me. Tragedy is more often brought on by the inability to control forces which are beyond our control than by refusing to be controlled.

A poet wrote, "Oh world as God has made it." There is no such world and there never will be. The truth contained in the rules and regulations which man has imposed upon his own kind has been accepted to be a truth, but is it a truth without foundation?

319

So we see the splinters flying and society, as we have allowed it to fetter man, disintegrating. Many of our castles created by idealism are uninhabitable in our present state. We were not intended to be gods and in trying to so become, we have destroyed the beauty of man as a human being.

The reversion of twentieth-century youth to primitive ways is not a desire for the primitive but a casting-off of the pretensions of a previous generation.

The savagery of uncivilized man is not less because he wears civilized clothing nor is man less civilized because he chooses unconventional attire.

The starving multitudes who are forgotten by those who feast destroy the right of the feaster to a belief in immortality.

As family life disintegrates, I here recall the happy experience of living in a period when it was an indispensable part of a great adventure.

I stand again on the well-kept lawn of a house now occupied by others. Although the beauty of its surroundings and the name Willow Bank have been retained, a fork of highway leads across the adjacent meadow. The small greenhouse where my father had busied himself in retirement has been removed and replaced by an outgoing addition to the semi-circular driveway. The three elms on the eastern point which had sheltered a hill path to the road are no more, the ancient willows remain although their elegance has gone. But the giant maple which had formed a shelter for those who loved it has sturdily withstood the passing of years. It is autumn "with all its glory spread." A falling leaf touches my cheek gently. I think of lines written many years before when I foresaw that I would stand alone:

Will you be found in the grey of the garden
Drooping and colourless – no one to see
When, from the shadow a sickle comes sweeping;
Not a farewell, nor a murmur of weeping . . .